The Science of Seers

FATIH GUNICEN

ISBN: 9781089910503

Special thanks to Nesrine Chkioua for her excellent editorial helps,

and

to Elif Erdogdu for her wise linguistic advisory.

INDEX

In the name of God, the Most Compassionate, the Most Merciful

1. Read in the name of your Lord who created –
2. Created man from an attached embryo.
3. Read, and your Lord is the most Generous –
4. Who taught by the pen –
5. Taught man what he did not know.
6. No! Indeed man transgresses
7. Because he sees himself self-sufficient.
8. Indeed, to your Lord is the return.[1] (Koran/Chapter 96)

---

[1] The first revealed verses of the Holy Koran

INTRODUCTION

Carlos Castaneda is one of the most widely read authors in history. And the twelve books he has written tell us about his unique experiences with don Juan Matus, an Indian shaman sage he once apprenticed.

However, the extraordinarily profound subjects described by Castaneda have not to this day been fully understood, and they still stand as a raw material. So, the sole purpose of this book is to process this raw material and reveal the true meaning of what Castaneda speaks of in his books.

On the other hand, this is not only a book of "What did Castaneda actually mean?" It analyzes what he has written in a simple and understandable manner, as it has never before been done, even moving to an upper level to reveal it is actually a sort of "science".

Therefore, just like the "science of matter", it is also a kind of science. And considering the importance of the creation of all things in this universe as polar twins by God Almighty, this science also claims its place in this universe as the opposite twin of modern science, forming the other side of the coin.

God Almighty allows the flourishing of the "Science of Seers" in an isolated place such as Central America, far away from the "Known World". Then, by sending an anthropologist there such as Castaneda, He enables all this information to make an appearance on the stage of history. This information becoming known through Castaneda, also makes it possible for us to carry out a cross-check of the science of matter.

Denial of religion by both sciences:

Although the science of matter and the science of seers are poles apart, there is a common ground where they meet: to reject the religion and God Almighty as its Owner. Even though their backgrounds are completely different from each other, these two sciences deny the religion. But at the same time, they also refuse to acknowledge each other, and both claim to be "the only truth".

On the other hand, don Juan states, "Our minds can only be a witness to this universe, having nothing to say about it."[2] Therefore, each of these two sciences actually takes the stand as a witness to this universe. And the Almighty God, "who taught man what he did not know,"[3] manifests to us the true nature of the things they bear witness to.

Thus, while explaining the collection of knowledge revealed by the "seers"[4], this book also places it safely on a cornerstone and explains it in the light of the Koran. Because the Koran not only clarifies many arguments used by the seers, but also displays that God Almighty is their real Owner.

On the other hand, just like the scientists, the seers also suggest that their knowledge is the one and only, which is not the case. Because God Almighty reveals their knowledge and much more to us in the Holy Koran.

Therefore, this book also contains information about Islam, and in fact, shows us that it is something very different from what is described on televisions and newspapers. Moreover, it speaks of the Prophets as Jesus and Moses mentioned in the Koran while making references to the seers.

The emergence of the Knowledge of the Seers by Castaneda:

"You, Genaro and I are stuck together by a purpose that is not our decision," says don Juan to Castaneda.[5] Thus, when don Juan and his friends found Castaneda, they thought they'd found the right person, only to realize that Castaneda's energy was not exactly what they were

---

[2] CASTANEDA, Tales of Power, Washington Square Press, The Bubble of Perception

[3] Please see the first revealed verses of the Holy Koran at page #4

[4] That's what don Juan -the teacher of Castaneda- calls the members of his knowledge.

[5] CASTANEDA, Tales of Power, Washington Square Press, The Secret of The Luminous Beings

looking for. However, they were also well aware that this was not a mistake, because Castaneda was brought to don Juan and it was said to him, "This is your apprentice":

- I didn't decide to choose you, and I didn't decide that you would be the way you are. Since I couldn't choose to whom I would impart my knowledge, I had to accept whomever the Spirit was offering me. And that person was you, and you are energetically capable only of ending, not of continuing. [6]

In another quotation, don Juan said that the man who introduced him to Castaneda had one foot in the grave. Indeed, this man passed away shortly after they had met.

Although don Juan could not make anything out of this that day, he understood it after many years and said that the death of the man actually foreshadowed the end of his own lineage.

- The Spirit was signaling to me that something was coming to an end. I thought it was my life that was coming to an end, and I accepted it as gracefully as I could. It dawned on me much, much later that it wasn't my life that was coming to an end, but my entire lineage.[7]

Consequently, God Almighty, whom the seers term as the Spirit, sent Castaneda to don Juan. Thus, the most appropriate person was assigned to reveal the accumulation of the knowledge of the seers. And don Juan's lineage no longer existed, because longstanding had achieved its goal.

According to the Koran, Muhammad is the last of the prophets. Accordingly, starting from Adam and continuing with Abraham, Moses and Jesus, this lineage ends with him. And God Almighty documents the life stories of all these prophets in the Koran, offering them for the benefit of humanity.

---

[6] CASTANEDA, Magical Passes, HarperCollins Publishers Inc., Introduction

[7] CASTANEDA, The Active Side of Infinity, HarperCollins Publishers Inc., The Unavoidable Appointment

Therefore, we have two lineages and their memories, passed on to us by God's will. This book compares these two legacies and shows us that the way God Almighty taught us through His prophets is the right way, and that the path of the seers is a man-made doctrine as opposed to its maturity.

The origin of the wisdom of the seers is actually shamanism, and my ancestors, ancient Turks, were also the believers of shamanism before their conversion. And they were easily converted because of the closeness of the teachings of shamanism to Islam and the full compliance of it with human nature. Consequently, they left the wisdom of the seers and chose the path of the Prophets.

Negligence of the Knowledge of the Seers:

Castaneda imparts the ignorance of the science of the seers by the Western World as follows:

- The perceptual claims of sorcerers, when examined in terms of the linear concepts of our Western World, make no sense whatsoever. Western civilization has been in contact with the shamans of the New World for five hundred years, and there has never been a genuine attempt on the part of scholars to formulate a serious philosophical discourse based on statements made by those shamans. [8]

Despite Castaneda's allegations, it is the science of matter itself, not the Western World, that turns a blind eye to the wisdom of seers. And the same condition is valid for anthropology, a branch of the science of matter. Although Castaneda is a loyal member of it, anthropology has not to this day considered Castaneda's writings seriously.

In fact, this is a consistent behavior for them, because the methods of these two sciences are totally different. Therefore, they do not have any intersection sets at first and they have nothing in common. But, as a result of the unity of existence, both sciences finally arrive in the same place and unite in "energy".

---

[8] CASTANEDA, Magical Passes, HarperCollins Publishers Inc., The Third Series > The Second Group

By the emergence of the science of seers, Castaneda notes that he ended up in a field that was no man's land. In his point of view, it was not the subject of anthropology, or sociology, or philosophy, or religion, for that matter.[9] But we show that this is not the case and disclose what he claims to be outside the domain of religion in the light of the Koran.

Not being fully compatible with human nature:

Don Juan says to Castaneda at some point, "The mood of a warrior is not so far-fetched from yours or anybody's world. You need it in order to cut through all the guff."[10] So, the seers live a much more enthusiastic life than an ordinary person does thanks to their teachings. Castaneda himself has been struck by this energetic life of don Juan, too. And he says he needs it more than air.

The seers have a zealous life because they discover the human nature created by God on His people and try to live accordingly. However, the methods they find do not give the optimum results at every time because they are man-made doctrines, and sometimes they make mistakes. Personally, I have to highlight that, even though I have a great respect for their maturity, the conclusions they have drawn from what they have discovered cannot hit the nail on the head at some points. And in this book, we describe both the positive and negative aspects of their teachings.

---

[9] CASTANEDA, The Teachings of Don Juan, Washington Square Press, Author's Commentaries on the Occasion of the Thirtieth Year of Publication

[10] CASTANEDA, Journey to Ixtlan, Washington Square Press, The Mood of a Warrior

1- Sorcery

SORCERY

Sorcery as being a reality:

101. We had certainly given Moses nine evident signs, so ask the Children of Israel about. When he came to them, Pharaoh said to him, "Indeed I think, O Moses, that you are affected by magic."
102. Moses said, "You have already known that none has sent down these signs except the Lord of the heavens and the earth as evidence, and indeed I think, O Pharaoh, that you are destroyed." (Koran/Chapter 17) [11]

Sorcery is a universal reality found in almost all societies on earth. Even though today's materialist societies seem to have distanced themselves from it, it still exists and people show an increasing interest in it. What's more, it is still possible to see its effects in games, movies and many other places.

Historically, sorcery reaches its peak in ancient Egypt and Central America, where it is practiced as a science. As a result, both cultures built the same pyramids thousands of kilometers from each other and achieved similar results in their knowledge.

Although this culture has completely disappeared over time in Egypt, it has been maintained in small groups in Central America by the "new

[11] All Koran translations in this book are based on Abul-Qasim Publishing House, 1997 Al-Muntada Al-Islami, 2004 Saheeh International translation.

seers" and has so far survived. And we have learned this science firsthand through Castaneda's books.

Developmental progress:

The knowledge of the seers is based on shamanism. However, their knowledge has become increasingly specific over thousands of years. Hence don Juan warns Castaneda particularly not to name his knowledge "shamanism".

The first way in which the seers begin their journey in the path of knowledge is by using the "power plants"[12]. In other words, their first starting point is physical. And then, they learn to "see" after dealing with power plants for centuries.

Don Juan calls these first seers as "old sorcerers" and talks about them as follows:

- My knowledge is that the old sorcerers ruled for four thousand years, from seven thousand to three thousand years ago. Three thousand years ago, they went to nothing. And from then on, sorcerers have been regrouping, restructuring what was left of the old ones. [13]

Don Juan thinks these ancient seers are like modern-day philosophers. He says that even though they built monumental edifices of abstractions proper to them and their time, they were not at all in control of their concatenations and eventually collapsed.[14] The new seers, on the other hand, imbued with practicality, evaluated the collection of information that the ancients put forward, in terms of their practical benefits.

---

[12] These are some psychotropic plants like peyote and jimson weed that are used by seers to change the apprentices' world view.

[13] CASTANEDA, The Art of Dreaming, HarperCollins Publishers Inc., The Fixation of The Assemblage Point

[14] CASTANEDA, The Fire From Within, Washington Square Press, The Eagle's Emanations

Hence, almost everything the seers know were found by the old seers, and left to the new ones as a "raw material". The new ones retreat when the ancients reach a dead end and re-evaluate the situation and form a new paradigm. And the first thing they do is to pay attention to disciplined actions and reduce the use of power plants.

After that, God Almighty sends the Spanish to the new seers. Thus, a difficult process begins for them to achieve impeccability:

- Warriors died like flies at the beginning of the Conquest. Their ranks were decimated. The petty tyrants could put anyone to death, simply acting on a whim. Under that kind of pressure seers reached sublime states. That was the time when the surviving seers had to exert themselves to the limit to find new ways. [15]

It may seem implicitly negative but the centuries under the yoke provide the ideal conditions for the new seers to perfect their skills. And under these challenging conditions, the new seers reach the summit of their maturity.

<u>The old seers being as sorcerers</u>:

While trying to describe the information don Juan taught him, Castaneda would like to name it as shamanism, but don Juan opposes this idea. On the other hand, he cannot make a clear definition of it and uses different expressions of his knowledge over time:

- At various times don Juan attempted to name his knowledge for my benefit. He felt that the most appropriate name was nagualism, but that the term was too obscure. Calling it simply "knowledge" made it too vague, and to call it "witchcraft" was debasing. "The mastery of intent" was too abstract, and "the search for total freedom" too long and metaphorical. Finally, because he was unable to find a more appropriate name, he called it "sorcery," although he admitted it was not really accurate. [16]

---

[15] CASTANEDA, The Fire From Within, Washington Square Press, Petty Tyrants

[16] CASTANEDA, The Power of Silence, Washington Square Press, Introduction

Don Juan is forced to call his knowledge "sorcery" because he cannot find a more appropriate name, and this name is used in most of Castaneda's books.

However, when Castaneda asked him, "Well, do you consider yourself as a sorcerer?" Don Juan replies:

- No, I don't. I am a warrior who "sees". In fact, all of us are the new seers. The old seers were the sorcerers. [17]

So, don Juan names his lineage as "new seers" and claims that they no longer engage in sorcery. However, this does not mean he is not a sorcerer. Because the new seers don Juan speaks of are people who discard the bad habits of the old ones and take the sorcery a step further, being intrinsically sorcerers.

Thus, don Juan feels himself obliged to appreciate the old ones while at the same time criticizing them. He confesses that their achievements were unique and says, "They were the first to find out everything we know and do today".[18]

The new seers:

Don Juan describes people who are sorcerers as a "person who could command an ally and could thus manipulate an ally's power to his advantage".[19]

Accordingly, the sorcerers first learn to dominate the "inorganic beings"[20] they call allies. Then, they influence other people through them and make them do whatever they wish. Therefore, don Juan calls sorcery "an attempt to influence other people".

---

[17] CASTANEDA, The Fire From Within, Washington Square Press, The New Seers

[18] CASTANEDA, The Art of Dreaming, HarperCollins Publishers Inc., Sorcerers of Antiquity: An Introduction

[19] CASTANEDA, A Separate Reality, Washington Square Press, Chapter 11

[20] Inorganic beings are the counterparts of human-beings in our system of realms. The seers learn most of their knowledge from them, so they call them allies and Koran calls them jinn.

The new seers abandon this vicious side of sorcery and take "seeing the energy as it flows in the universe" to the center of their teachings:

- To be a sorcerer is a terrible burden. And it is much better to learn to "see". A man who "sees" is everything; in comparison, the sorcerer is a sad fellow. [21]
- A man may learn certain techniques in order to command an ally and thus become a sorcerer, and yet he may never learn to "see". Besides, "seeing" is contrary to sorcery. "Seeing" makes one realize the unimportance of it all. [22]

But sorcerers fail to do so, and don Juan describes them as self-indulgent and capricious people who cannot go beyond self-regarding.

Therefore the new seers, even though their knowledge is built on the knowledge of the ancients, start a new era and call themselves the "seer", not the sorcerer.

<u>The sorcerers who challenged Prophet Moses</u>:

78. They said, "Have you come to us to turn us away from that upon which we found our fathers and so that you two may have grandeur in the land? And we are not believers in you."
79. And Pharaoh said, "Bring to me every learned magician."
80. So when the magicians came, Moses said to them, "Throw down whatever you will throw."
81. And when they had thrown, Moses said, "What you have brought is only magic. Indeed, God will expose its worthlessness. Indeed, God does not amend the work of corrupters.
82. And God will establish the truth by His words, even if the criminals dislike it." (Koran/Chapter 10)

Sorcery is also included in the Koran as a universal truth created by God Almighty and is extensively recounted in the stories of Prophet Moses.

---

[21] CASTANEDA, A Separate Reality, Washington Square Press, Chapter 13

[22] CASTANEDA, A Separate Reality, Washington Square Press, Chapter 11

Accordingly, when the Pharaoh was challenged by Prophet Moses, the former said to the latter, "You are not a messenger, but a sorcerer" and caused him to race with his own sorcerers. But when Prophet Moses overcame them by God's will, the sorcerers immediately believed and fell down in prostration:

103. Then We sent after them Moses with Our signs to Pharaoh and his establishment, but they were unjust toward them. So see how the end of the corrupters was.
104. And Moses said, "O Pharaoh, I am a messenger from the Lord of the Worlds
105. Who is obligated not to say about God except the truth. I have come to you with clear evidence from your Lord, so send with me the Children of Israel."
106. Pharaoh said, "If you have come with a sign, then bring it forth, if you should be of the truthful."
107. So Moses threw his staff, and suddenly it was a serpent manifest.
108. And he drew out his hand; thereupon it was white with radiance for the observers.
109. Said the eminent among the people of Pharaoh, "Indeed, this is a learned magician
110. Who wants to expel you from your land, so what do you instruct?"
111. They said, "Postpone the matter of him and his brother and send among the cities gatherers
112. Who will bring you every learned magician."
113. And the magicians came to Pharaoh. They said, "Indeed for us is a reward if we are the predominant."
114. He said, "Yes, and moreover, you will be among those made near to me."
115. They said, "O Moses, either you throw your staff, or we will be the ones to throw first."
116. He said, "Throw," and when they threw, they bewitched the eyes of the people and struck terror into them, and they presented a great feat of magic.
117. And We inspired to Moses, "Throw your staff," and at once it devoured what they were falsifying.

118. So the truth was established, and abolished was what they were doing.
119. And they were overcome right there and became debased.
120. And the magicians fell down in prostration.
121. They said, "We have believed in the Lord of the Worlds,
122. The Lord of Moses and Aaron." (Koran/Chapter 7)

Don Juan tells us in detail how sorcerers control human beings and manipulate their awareness. The sorcerers, who defied Prophet Moses, use this art that don Juan speaks of. And just like the old seers, who work for the sake of interest, they are coming before Prophet Moses for the sake of the Pharaoh's reward.

However, what the sorcerers do is always a product of human nature. In addition, since the sorcerers who came across Prophet Moses knew this science, they immediately understood that what Prophet Moses did was not really sorcery, but came from God Almighty. Hence, they instantly fell prostrate and believed in the Lord of the Worlds.

On the other hand, the Pharaoh is ignorant and does not have a slightest idea of what is happening. Therefore, he persists and denies Prophet Moses and threatens the sorcerers under his command with a terrible death:

123. Said Pharaoh, "You believed in him before I gave you permission. Indeed, this is a conspiracy which you conspired in the city to expel therefrom its people. But you are going to know.
124. I will surely cut off your hands and your feet on opposite sides; then I will surely crucify you all."
125. They said, "Indeed, to our Lord we will return.
126. And you do not resent us except because we believed in the signs of our Lord when they came to us. Our Lord, pour upon us patience and let us die in submission to You." (Koran/Chapter 7)

That's how the Pharaoh threatens the sorcerers. But because they have the knowledge, they understand that it is not a sorcery skill but comes from the Owner of the universe. So, they do not hesitate, nor do they take a step back in spite of Pharaoh's terrible threats.

The Art of Handling Awareness:

The sorcerers, who first defied Prophet Moses and then believed, were sorcerers from the class of the "seers of antiquity", don Juan mentioned. And when they're demonstrating their skills, they use "The Art of Handling Awareness" that don Juan speaks of:

- Ages before the Spaniards came to Mexico, there were extraordinary Toltec seers, men capable of inconceivable deeds. They were the last link in a chain of knowledge that extended over thousands of years.
- The Toltec seers were extraordinary men - powerful sorcerers, somber, driven men who unraveled mysteries and possessed secret knowledge that they used to influence and victimize people by fixating the awareness of their victims on whatever they chose.
- I have to emphasize an important fact that those sorcerers knew how to fixate the awareness of their victims. You didn't pick up on that. When I mentioned it, it didn't mean anything to you. That's not surprising. One of the hardest things to acknowledge is that awareness can be manipulated. [23]

Don Juan argues that these sorcerers uncover the mystery of human perception and know how to manipulate it. And the sorcerers, who stood out against Prophet Moses, did use this science to work their magic.

However, they still do some things by using the opportunity bestowed upon them by God Almighty. And when Prophet Moses comes to them directly with a might from God Almighty, they realize in no time that it is divine and prostrate.

A Messenger from the Lord of the Worlds:

104. And Moses said, "O Pharaoh, I am a messenger from the Lord of the Worlds
105. Who is obligated not to say about God except the truth. I have come to you with clear evidence from your Lord, so send with me the Children of Israel." (Koran/Chapter 7)

---

[23] CASTANEDA, The Fire from Within, Washington Square Press, The New Seers

Another important point about the sorcery mentioned in the Koran is that Prophet Moses introduces himself as a "Messenger of the Lord of the Worlds". Accordingly, this expression is always used in Koran together with Prophet Moses and is repeated persistently. And such conscious use is not preferred for any other prophets mentioned in Koran.

7. Mention when Moses said to his family, "Indeed, I have perceived a fire. I will bring you from there information or will bring you a burning torch that you may warm yourselves."
8. But when he came to it, he was called, "Blessed is whoever is at the fire and whoever is around it. And exalted is God, the Lord of the Worlds." (Koran/Chapter 27)

If you ask why this is important, that is because there are other realms which are accessible to man. And the jinns that the seers call inorganic beings reside there. The seers know these realms; moreover, they learn much of their knowledge through the jinns that live in these realms.

Therefore, the sorcerers, who confront Prophet Moses, are already specialized in these other realms and inorganic beings living in them. And Prophet Moses is sent to them, saying, "I am the Messenger of the Lord of the Worlds" since He is dealing with the sorcerers who possess this information.

In other words, God Almighty says to them, "You are familiar with some sort of science by establishing relations with entities live in other worlds, but I am the Owner of all those Worlds". And the magicians who understand this, use the same phrase as the Prophet Moses and say, "We have believed in the Lord of the Worlds".

<u>Sorcery as being a trouble</u>:

75. Then We sent after them Moses and Aaron to Pharaoh and his establishment with Our signs, but they behaved arrogantly and were a criminal people.
76. So when there came to them the truth from Us, they said, "Indeed, this is obvious magic."

77. Moses said, "Do you say thus about the truth when it has come to you? Is this magic? But magicians will not have salvation." (Koran/Chapter 10)

Although God Almighty created sorcery as a reality, He says it is evil and warns people against it. However, people often put aside this test to use sorcery in a negative way.

Don Juan says that the old seers use their knowledge in such a negative way that they influence people and call it "the evil fixation of the second attention". Don Juan also says that no one can stand before the sorcerers who have learned this, and that they eventually become hunters of men, ghouls.[24]

Don Juan, in turn, says that the new seers have surpassed these abusive practices of sorcery and are now turning to goals that are more sublime. But, the basis on which they are based is the same, hence, the results they achieve also.

Don Juan says, "it has no witchcraft, no evil, no devil, but only perception"[25] while speaking of his knowledge. However, finally, this information causes him to deny God Almighty and he turns into a denier of God, who is the Owner of all those things to be perceived. Therefore, despite of its glory, the knowledge of the seers is in fact, disconnected from the whole and does not help reach the target.

On the other hand, God Almighty makes a very interesting use in the Koran when talking about magic and sorcery. And He uses them many times together with the word "trouble":

101. When a messenger from God came to them confirming that which was with them, a party of those who had been given the Scripture threw the Scripture of God behind their backs as if they did not know.

---

[24] CASTANEDA, Eagle's Gift, Washington Square Press, The Fixation of The Second Attention

[25] CASTANEDA, The Power of Silence, Washington Square Press, Handling Intent: The Third Point

102. And they followed what the devils had recited during the reign of Solomon. It was not Solomon who disbelieved, but the devils disbelieved, teaching people 'magic' and that which was revealed to the two angels at Babylon, Harut and Marut. But these two do not teach anyone unless they say, "We are a 'trouble', so do not disbelieve." And they learn from them that by which they cause separation between a man and his wife. But they do not harm anyone through it except by permission of God. And they learn what harms them and does not benefit them. But they certainly knew that whoever purchased it would not have in the Hereafter any share. And wretched is that for which they sold themselves, if they only knew. (Koran/Chapter 2)

According to the Koran, this word has two uses. The first one means "trouble" and the second means "a trial which is made by means of this trouble". So, in the verse above the angels say, "We are a 'trial'. Therefore, do not lose this trial, and do not fall into trouble."

And as seen in this verse, the words magic and trouble are always used together in the Koran, and the angels who teach the spell do not teach anything to the devils without saying, "We are a trouble, so do not disbelieve." However, the devils prefer denial for the sake of learning spells, and then teach them to people.

As we have already said, the seers learned most of the things they have learned from the jinns, as they call them inorganic beings. What we did not say before was that, according to the Koran, Satan and the demons of his descendants were from the jinns.

In other words, the demons who teach the seers the science of sorcery are actually jinns, as this verse says. Since they have fallen into denial, they also tempt the seers to deny. And God Almighty states, "whoever purchased it would not have any share in the Hereafter." Hence, the seers are losing the universal trial in this world by falling into denial and finally they will fall into trouble in the Hereafter. [26]

---

[26] See Chapter 5- Inorganic Beings

The use of the words "Sorcery" and "Trouble" in Koran in equal numbers:

As seen in the above verse, the relationship between the words of magic and trouble is evident. And God Almighty uses these two words in equal numbers in the Koran, thereby strengthening this relationship between them. Accordingly, these two words and their derivatives are both mentioned 60 times in the Koran, thus, confirming "mathematically" that magic is both a trial and an obvious trouble.

Of course, you may say that this is a coincidence, but as we explained in more detail later in a separate chapter[27], there are dozens of relevant and pairing words in the Koran, which are used in equal numbers. In this way, the relations between these words are reinforced, and the Koran is encoded in hundreds of ways against possible alterations.

So, these are not random but highly conscious uses. And in this way, God Almighty puts his signature on every corner of the Koran. Being specific to our subject of sorcery, the Koran provides an objective evidence of a matter that seems relative to people of today and shows us that what don Juan tells is not a story.

[27] This topic is described under the title of "Eagle's Emanations – Worlds" in the mention of enciphering the Koran with the number 19 and word harmony.

2- The Eagle

- The Seers' Belief in God
- The Eagle
- The Eagle as being God
- Under-appreciation of God
- Return to the Eagle

THE SEERS' BELIEF IN GOD

Don Juan's disbelief:

82. They said, "When we have died and become dust and bones, are we indeed to be resurrected?
83. We have been promised this, we and our forefathers, before; this is not but legends of the former peoples." (Koran/Chapter 23)

Let us get straight to the point! Don Juan directly rejects religion and its belief in God and takes a stand against it. He does not believe in the existence of God; moreover, he sees them as mumbo jumbo of this world.

Don Juan also completely denies the life of the Hereafter and does not hesitate to make fun of Castaneda's belief in God. For example, one day Castaneda has trouble squatting. Don Juan, thereupon, pulls Castaneda's leg, saying that the latter finds it difficult to do so because he hasn't gone to confession during the years spent with him. After that, all the apprentices sitting around him begin to laugh at his joke.

At another time, don Juan says, "The Lord says that we should be good boys or He is going to punish us. The Lord has been threatening us for centuries and it does not make any difference."[28]

Though not a religious person, Castaneda firstly believes in God and is

---

[28] CASTANEDA, The Power of Silence, Washington Square Press, Intending Appearances

shocked by don Juan's salvos that he made to his faith. Don Juan makes more sinful interpretations than he has ever heard in comparison to his traditional Catholic upbringing. However, over the years, he comes to the same conclusion and, while speaking of Prophet Jesus in an interview, he says:

- Jesus and Buddha are ideal formations and they are too great to be true. They're gods. One is the Prince of Buddhism, the other is the Son of God. And ideal formations cannot be used for pragmatic movements.

Here, Castaneda complains about people's deifying of Prophet Jesus, resulting from their excessive praise. In other words, he suggests that they glorified him so much that they sent him away, having no practical benefit to them.

While this may be true at one point, he himself is swung to the other end, denying religion altogether and only pursuing practical benefits. However, God is nearer to us than our jugular vein, and it is He who gives to the seers all the practical benefits they obtain.

And as we shall see in the next chapters, most of the things that don Juan opposes in the name of religion are, in fact, those that God Almighty Himself opposes. Therefore, most of the arguments that the seers use against religion are not actually the things that belong to religion itself, but those added afterward by human beings.

Don Juan thinks religion is useless:

55. Mention when God said, "O Jesus, indeed I will take you and raise you to Myself and purify you from those who disbelieve and make those who follow you superior to those who disbelieve until the Day of Resurrection. Then to Me is your return, and I will judge between you concerning that in which you used to differ. (Koran/Chapter 3)

Due to the cultural environment in which he lives, don Juan is confronted with Christianity as religion, and there are two main points in which he criticizes this religion. Firstly, the useless nonsense, which he claims it contains—secondly, the absence of offering a better life.

However, the things don Juan criticizes are those later revealed as religion, as opposed to the religion that Prophet Jesus preached. And don Juan condemns Prophet Jesus of them.

For example, at one point, he asserts that the message brought by Prophet Jesus does not show people the life of righteousness as an example, not asserting itself seriously nor arousing respect. And he says, it leads people to act foolishly: playing the violin, dancing in Sunday service and putting on a mask.

Elsewhere, he says:

- Of course, there is a dark side to us. We kill wantonly, don't we? We burn people in the name of God. We destroy ourselves; we obliterate life on this planet; we destroy the earth. And then we dress in robes and the Lord speaks directly to us. [29]

However, all that don Juan says is related to the cultural transmissions made afterward and the result of misinterpretation of the religion. These things have nothing to do with the religion that God sent and Prophet Jesus preached.

The Prophet Jesus introduced by the Koran is one of the greatest prophets sent by God and has an exceptional place in His sight:

45. And mention when the angels said, "O Mary, indeed God gives you good tidings of a word from Him, whose name will be the Messiah, Jesus, the son of Mary – distinguished in this world and the Hereafter and among those brought near to God.
46. He will speak to the people in the cradle and in maturity and will be of the righteous."
47. She said, "My Lord, how will I have a child when no man has touched me?" God said, "Such is God; He creates what He wills. When He decrees a matter, He only says to it, 'Be,' and it is.
48. And He will teach him the Book and wisdom and the Torah and the Gospel
49. And will make him a messenger to the Children of Israel who says, 'Indeed I have come to you with a sign from your Lord in

[29] CASTANEDA, The Power of Silence, Washington Square Press, Intending Appearances

that I design for you from clay that which is like the form of a bird, then I breathe into it and it becomes a bird by permission of God. And I cure the blind and the leper, and I give life to the dead – by permission of God. And I inform you of what you eat and what you store in your houses. Indeed in that is a sign for you, if you are believers.

50. And I have come confirming what was before me of the Torah and to make lawful for you some of what was forbidden to you. And I have come to you with a sign from your Lord, so fear God and obey me.

51. Indeed, God is my Lord and your Lord, so worship Him. That is the straight path." (Koran/Chapter 3)

Don Juan knows what he is taught in the name of religion, in the cultural environment in which he grows. And it seems to him that those cannot compete with his own knowledge. However, that's not really the case.

In the Koran, God Almighty offers us not only his knowledge but much more, putting don Juan's knowledge to the test as a reference point. And He shows us that the religion, which he declared useless, is actually surrounding all his knowledge.

<u>The seers see the religion as a product of description</u>:

38. And We did not create the heavens and earth and that between them in play.

39. We did not create them except in truth, but most of them do not know. (Koran/Chapter 44)

Underneath such a blatantly rejection of religion by the seers lies the fact that they see this universe as a "description". They find out that this universe is only one of many possible realms, and then reach the point that the things in this universe do not matter. From their point of view, the idea of God and His religion are the concepts that are valid only in this universe. For the seers, who have managed to cross the boundaries of this universe, these concepts have already lost their significance.

Of course, that is only their assumption since God Almighty, just at the beginning of the Koran, introduces Himself as "the Lord of the Worlds". Therefore, all other realms discovered by the seers are created by God Almighty.

And God Almighty does not say, "This universe is worthless or it is just a description" due to the existence of these realms. On the contrary, He says, "We created this universe as a truth."

Therefore, this universe is the truth itself. But, as the seers see it as worthless, they also see its Owner as worthless. And by doing so, they are only duplicating their fallacy.

<u>The seers' chance of having faith in God</u>:

That is how the seers deny God and His religion. Although they, too, have the possibility to believe in God if they come face to face with a real annunciation, like sorcerers who struggled with Prophet Moses. Because their knowledge originally stems from sorcery and they are far more advanced than ordinary people in recognizing the universe, even if they bear false notions in religious matters.

That's why the sorcerers beside the Pharaoh saw the truth in front of them, despite him talking down to and arguing against Prophet Moses. And professed their faith in God, proclaiming, "In the Lord of the Worlds we trust".

23. Said Pharaoh, "What is the Lord of the Worlds?"
24. [Moses] said, "The Lord of the heavens and earth and that between them, if you should be convinced."
25. [Pharaoh] said to those around him, "Do you not hear?"
26. [Moses] said, "Your Lord and the Lord of your first forefathers."
27. [Pharaoh] said, "Indeed, your 'messenger' who has been sent to you is mad."
28. [Moses] said, "Lord of the east and the west and that between them, if you were to reason."
29. [Pharaoh] said, "If you take a god other than me, I will surely place you among those imprisoned."
30. [Moses] said, "Even if I brought you something manifest?"

31. "Then bring it, if you should be of the truthful."
32. So he threw his staff, and suddenly it was a serpent manifest.
33. And he drew out his hand; thereupon it was white with radiance for the observers.
34. [Pharaoh] said to the eminent ones around him, "Indeed, this is a learned magician.
35. He wants to drive you out of your land by his magic, so what do you advise?"
36. They said, "Postpone the matter of him and his brother and send among the cities gatherers
37. Who will bring you every learned, skilled magician."
38. So the magicians were assembled for the appointment of a well-known day.
39. And it was said to the people, "Will you congregate
40. That we might follow the magicians if they are the predominant?"
41. And when the magicians arrived, they said to Pharaoh, "Is there indeed for us a reward if we are the predominant?"
42. He said, "Yes, and indeed, you will then be of those near to me."
43. Moses said to them, "Throw whatever you will throw."
44. So they threw their ropes and their staffs and said, "By the might of Pharaoh, indeed it is we who are predominant."
45. Then Moses threw his staff, and at once it devoured what they falsified.
46. So the magicians fell down in prostration.
47. They said, "We have believed in the Lord of the Worlds,
48. The Lord of Moses and Aaron."
49. Pharaoh said, "You believed him before I gave you permission. Indeed, he is your leader who has taught you magic, but you are going to know. I will surely cut off your hands and your feet on opposite sides, and I will surely crucify you all."
50. They said, "No harm. Indeed, to our Lord we will return.
51. Indeed, we aspire that our Lord will forgive us our sins because we were the first of the believers." (Koran/Chapter 26)

These sorcerers are the first to believe in God through Prophet Moses, knowing that they will undergo a terrible torture. The reason being, they know and understand that what they witness is not a sorcery skill, but comes from the Owner of everything. This truth is so precise to them that even the bloodcurdling threats thrown by Pharaoh are not enough to turn them away from their faith. On the other hand, because of his ignorance, Pharaoh cannot understand what is happening and persists in being stubborn.

Supposing don Juan had experienced such a situation. In my opinion, his response would not have been any different from that of the sorcerers who consciously put their faith in God. Because don Juan knows as much as these sorcerers, if not better. And I believe that in such a case, with God's permission, his reaction would be the same as that of the sorcerers here.

THE EAGLE

In the previous chapter, we said that the seers do not believe in God, but that does not mean they do not know God. Because they know that there is a power that rules all the worlds, and they call it "Eagle". Yet, they do not believe that He is God.

The seers go beyond this visible realm and discover other realms, so they regard the universe only as an image and everything in it as worthless. And for them, religion is also a worthless product of this universe. So, they deny that the Eagle is God, as they reject the religion. And although they are cognizant of that supernal power, they are not willing to call it God.

> 66. He is the one who gave you life; then He causes you to die and then will again give you life. Indeed, mankind is ungrateful. (Koran/Chapter 22)

Don Juan says that the old seers, risking untold dangers, actually "saw" the indescribable force, which is the source of all sentient beings. They called it the Eagle, because in the few glimpses that they could sustain, they "saw" it as something that resembled a black-and-white eagle of infinite size.[30] They also "saw" that it is the Eagle who bestows awareness to the sentient beings, and in the same way, the entire universe is the product of the Eagle's emanations.

---

[30] CASTANEDA, The Fire from Within, Washington Square Press, The Eagle's Emanations

Castaneda quotes that this idea irritated him when he first heard of don Juan's statements about the "Eagle". And don Juan responds to him as follows:

- It is not just an idea; it is a fact. And a damn scary one if you ask me. The new seers were not simply playing with ideas.
- But what kind of a force would the Eagle be, don Juan?
- I wouldn't know how to answer that. The Eagle is as real for the seers as gravity and time are for you, and just as abstract and incomprehensible.
- Wait a minute, don Juan. Those are abstract concepts, but they do refer to real phenomena that can be corroborated. There are whole disciplines dedicated to that.
- The Eagle and its emanations are equally corroboratable. And the discipline of the new seers is dedicated to doing just that. [31]

Don Juan says, "The discipline of the new seers is dedicated to corroborate the Eagle and its emanations". Therefore, just as the science of matter confirms the existence of an atom, the science of the seers confirms the existence of the Eagle. And just as the existence of the atom is a fact, so is the existence of the Eagle for the seers.

"Seeing" the Eagle:

143. When Moses arrived at Our appointed time and his Lord spoke to him, he said, "My Lord, show me Yourself that I may look at You." He said, "You will not see Me, but look at the mountain; if it should remain in place, then you will see Me." But when his Lord appeared to the mountain, He rendered it level, and Moses fell unconscious. And when he awoke, he said, "Exalted are You! I have repented to You, and I am the first of the believers."
144. God said, "O Moses, I have chosen you over the people with My messages and My words. So take what I have given you and be among the grateful." (Koran/Chapter 7)

[31] CASTANEDA, The Fire from Within, Washington Square Press, The Eagle's Emanations

The seers' method of validating the Eagle is what they call "seeing": perceiving the energy directly as it flows in the universe. And don Juan explains this on a question from Castaneda as follows:

- Seers explain the act of "seeing" the Eagle in very simple terms: Because man is composed of the Eagle's emanations, man need only revert back to his components. The problem arises with man's awareness; it is his awareness that becomes entangled and confused. At the crucial moment when it should be a simple case of the emanations acknowledging themselves, man's awareness is compelled to interpret. The result is a vision of the Eagle and the Eagle's emanations. But there is no Eagle and no Eagle's emanations. What is out there is something that no living creature can grasp. [32]

And this action is not something the seers do whenever they feel like. That's because the emanations they use in this work belong to the "unknowable" parts of the Eagle's emanations and are outside the limits of normal human perception:

- By steadily practicing "seeing", the new seers found that the unknown and the known are really on the same footing, because both are within the reach of human perception. Seers, in fact, can leave the known at a given moment and enter into the unknown.
- Whatever is beyond our capacity to perceive is the unknowable. And the distinction between it and the knowable is crucial. Confusing the two would put seers in a most precarious position whenever they are confronted with the unknowable.
- When this happened to the ancient seers, thought their procedures had gone haywire. It never occurred to them that most of what's out there is beyond our comprehension. It was a terrifying error of judgment on their part, for which they paid dearly.
- Whenever what is taken to be the unknown turns out to be the unknowable, the results are disastrous. Seers feel drained, confused. A terrible oppression takes possession of them. Their bodies lose tone, their reasoning and sobriety wander away aimlessly, for the unknowable has no energizing effects whatsoever. It is not within

---

[32] CASTANEDA, The Fire from Within, Washington Square Press, The Eagle's Emanations

> human reach; therefore, it should not be intruded upon foolishly or even prudently. The new seers realized that they had to be prepared to pay exorbitant prices for the faintest contact with it. [33]

So, what the seers can do is pay a big price to get a glimpse of the "unknowable" by overcoming the big obstacles. They do this merely in order to acquire knowledge for their teachings, and then they do not repeat it again. Just like the case of Prophet Moses, they cannot see it directly but they know that the Eagle exists there, and behave accordingly.

What the seers call "we have seen" is actually nothing but witness the "Eagle", knowing its existence and transforming it into something they know. In fact, what is there, as don Juan says, is something that no living creature can grasp.

Even this information, which they are allowed to reach, is a very important discovery. Because they confirm the Almighty God to the extent that He allows. Even though they do not accept the Eagle as God, God Almighty reveals Himself to them as much as He wants and uses them as a channel, introducing Himself to mankind.

And just as the seers show us that life is real and reduce the materialist part of the evolution to nothing[34], this discovery of them confute the atheism that says there is no God.

Confutation of atheism by the Science of Seers:

Modern science works with the effort of explaining this universe without the need of a God. This means that they want to explain this universe without a living Supernal source and show that everything is self-created.

On the other hand, the seers show us that this is not the case and that there is a "supernal source". Thus, the science of the seers becomes the anti-thesis of the science of matter and allows us the opportunity to cross-check.

---

[33] CASTANEDA, The Fire from Within, Washington Square Press, The Eagle's Emanations

[34] See Chapter 13- Biological evolution

And the field into which the science of matter researches in terms of the knowledge held by the seers might be likened to the two-inch depth of the surface of a vast ocean. They only examine the "known", and take a look at the "unknown" using quantum physics, but the whole structure they erect is destined to decompose due to the fallacy of their basic assumptions.

They believe in the existence of some self-proclaimed nature's rules and laws. They accept it as an absolute truth, and that's how they make a start in everything they do. However, the science of the seers says that these rules consist of the "Eagle's emanations". Furthermore, says that the Eagle bestows awareness upon all living beings to spring to "life". From their perspective, what is essential is nothing but life, and matter and energy are the means to establish its environment.

The science of matter is, on the other hand, grounded on these agents that are responsible to create the environment and sees no other alternatives. And by doing so, it turns up its nose at life. In other words, the science of matter actually tells us, "You don't live," but we are not aware of it.[35]

---

35 See Chapter 13- Biological evolution

THE EAGLE AS BEING GOD

> 255. God – there is no deity except Him, the Ever-Living, the Sustainer of all existence. Neither drowsiness overtakes Him nor sleep. To Him belongs whatever is in the heavens and whatever is on the earth. Who is it that can intercede with Him except by His permission? He knows what is before them and what will be after them, and they encompass not a thing of His knowledge except for what He wills. His sovereignty extends over the heavens and the earth, and their preservation tires Him not. And He is the Most High, the Most Great. (Koran/Chapter 2)

According to the seers, the "Eagle" is responsible for every single thing in the universe, and in the same way, the source of all don Juan's teachings is, in fact, the Eagle. But even though it is the most fundamental thing in their teachings, the seers still do not call it God, because they do not know the true nature of God. However, many of the qualities of the Eagle that they describe belong to God Almighty Himself.

Eagle's Emanations:

In the early stages of don Juan's apprenticeship, his benefactor arranges for him an encounter with the inorganic beings they call allies. During this encounter, don Juan is terribly scared and promises God that he will now leave the path of knowledge and become a farmer.

On the other hand, his benefactor tells him "not to worry, that it had been a good promise, but that he didn't yet know that there is no one to hear such promises, because there is no God". According to him, all there is is the Eagle's emanations, and there is no way to make promises to them.[36]

Consequently, don Juan's benefactor says, "There is no God, there are only the Eagle's emanations". But as we explain in the next chapter, the emanations of the Eagle are the commandments of God Almighty Himself. And through those commands, God Almighty rules the entire universe at any moment.

His benefactor also tells don Juan that there is no one to hear his promise. But God Almighty says, "I am with you wherever you are and hear whatever you say". And He does this through the above-mentioned "Eagle's emanations":

6. On the Day when God will resurrect them all and inform them of what they did. God had enumerated it, while they forgot it; and God is, over all things, Witness.
7. Have you not considered that God knows what is in the heavens and what is on the earth? There is in no private conversation three but that He is the fourth of them, nor are there five but that He is the sixth of them – and no less than that and no more except that He is with them wherever they are. Then He will inform them of what they did, on the Day of Resurrection. Indeed God is, of all things, Knowing. (Koran/Chapter 58)

Therefore, there is no error in what the seers discover, but there is a mistake in the meanings they place on it. The seers rely on what they discover and make comments that go beyond their limits. And just like the scientists of matter, they fall into error.

<u>The Eagle's creation of living things</u>:

55. Unquestionably, to God belongs whatever is in the heavens and the earth. Unquestionably, the promise of God is truth, but most of them do not know.

[36] CASTANEDA, The Fire from Within, Washington Square Press, Inorganic Beings

56. He gives life and causes death, and to Him you will be returned. (Koran/Chapter 10)

According to the seers, living things have "awareness" and they are alive. Hence don Juan argues that it is the "Eagle", itself who blessed the living things with awareness. Accordingly, the Eagle creates living things, and at the end of their lives, takes away that awareness from them.

On the other hand, God Almighty proclaims in the Koran that, "I am the One who gives life to all living things", and in the end, "Unto Me is the final return". Therefore, what the seers call the Eagle is actually God Almighty Himself.

Don Juan also suggests that the Eagle is responsible for the lives of both organic and inorganic beings. And as we explain in the following chapters, what the seers call inorganic beings are the jinns that God Almighty created as the polar twin of man. And God Almighty is also responsible for their lives, and He says, "I created them as well", just as don Juan stresses.

Eagle's dominance on predestination:

120. Indeed, Abraham was a comprehensive leader, devoutly obedient to God, inclining toward truth, and he was not of those who associate others with God.
121. He was grateful for His favors. And God chose him and guided him to a straight path.
122. And We gave him good in this world, and indeed, in the Hereafter he will be among the righteous. (Koran/Chapter 16)

Don Juan says, "The world adjusts itself to itself"[37] and attempts to explain this with the concept "intent". And the term he connotes to as intent is solely the "Eagle's intent."

While expressing this term, don Juan says, "We are not players ourselves. We are mere pawns in its hands"[38] and harps on about Eagle

[37] CASTANEDA, Tales of Power, Washington Square Press, Having to Believe

[38] CASTANEDA, The Art of Dreaming, HarperCollins Publishers Inc., The Tenant

as "the power that governs the destinies of all living things"[39]. Thus, the "Eagle" guides all living beings in accordance with certain purposes at His disposal, and the seers who are aware of this fact organize their lives accordingly.

God Almighty, on the other hand, proclaims in His Holy Koran, "Indeed, upon Us is guidance. And indeed, to Us belongs the Hereafter and the first".[40] In other words, what don Juan refers to as intent is nothing but the guidance of God Almighty. Therefore, God Almighty provides all human beings with guidance, just as He did with Prophet Abraham. And we will explain this again in detail in the following chapters when we speak of intent.

The Eagle as being God:

Don Juan says, "All there is in universe is the Eagle's emanations", then he says, "He is the one who spares their lives to living beings", and adds, "The Eagle governs the destinies of all living things." Well, what remains of Him that He is unable to do? Nothing… Everything is at His disposal, and everything is happening at His command. So, what the seers call the Eagle, is the God that the Koran introduces to us.

For the reason the seers reject religion, they automatically deny that the Eagle is God and depict it as a power that rules over everything but is also "neutral" to everything. However, He is not neutral to anything and manifests this to us with His revelations. Since the seers reject the revelation, they do not know Him properly and come to inexact ideas about Him.

---

[39] CASTANEDA, The Eagle's Gift, Washington Square Press, The Rule of The Nagual

[40] Koran/Chapter 92, verses 12-13

UNDER-APPRECIATION OF GOD

91. They did not appraise God with true appraisal when they said, "God did not reveal to a human being anything." Say, "Who revealed the Scripture that Moses brought as light and guidance to the people? You make it into pages, disclosing some of it and concealing much. And you were taught that which you knew not – neither you nor your fathers." Say "God", then leave them in their empty discourse. (Koran/Chapter 6)

The seers know the existence of the "Eagle" as the power that reigns over everything, but they cannot get the picture of its true nature because they say, "God has revealed nothing to man." However, God Almighty supplies us with firsthand the things He wants to be known about Him, with the revelation He sends.

What the seers do is like viewing a planet in the sky with a telescope from afar. However, they have got a message sent from that planet. And this letter has been sent by the Owner of that planet.

The seers, on the other hand, rely on their own discoveries instead of reading this letter. So they cannot recognize God Almighty properly and come up with wrong ideas about Him.

67. They have not appraised God with true appraisal, while the earth entirely will be within His grip on the Day of Resurrection, and

the heavens will be folded in His right hand. Exalted is He and high above what they associate with Him.

68. And the Horn will be blown, and whoever is in the heavens and whoever is on the earth will fall dead except whom God wills. Then it will be blown again, and at once they will be standing, looking on.
69. And the earth will shine with the light of its Lord, and the Book will be placed, and the prophets and the witnesses will be brought, and it will be judged between them in truth, and they will not be wronged.
70. And every soul will be fully compensated for what it did; and He is most knowing of what they do. (Koran/Chapter 39)

When the seers ignore the revelations of God Almighty, they cannot avoid being driven away into two extremes of human nature. At one end, they say, "Everything in man's own little world is empty," starting from His greatness. On the other hand, they make humiliating interpretations that are incompatible with His greatness.

For example, don Juan's benefactor describes his actions as "a humble attempt to mirror the Eagle". In addition, since the Eagle is real and final, he states that all the things that people do are utter folly. [41]

In other words, he remarks, "The Eagle is so great and so real, that all the worldly endeavors of people are just madness that is condemned to be insignificant in the face of this greatness". So, for the seers, it does not matter what they are doing anymore, the only thing that matters is that the structure is done in a controlled and disciplined way. [42]

The Eagle neglecting men:

1. Whatever is in the heavens and whatever is on the earth is exalting God. To Him belongs dominion, and to Him belongs all praise, and He is over all things competent.

---

[41] CASTANEDA, The Eagle's Gift, Washington Square Press, The Nagual's Party of Warriors

[42] See Chapter 9- Stopping the Actions

2. It is He who created you, and among you is the disbeliever, and among you is the believer. And God, of what you do, is Seeing.
3. He created the heavens and earth in truth and formed you and perfected your forms; and to Him is the final destination.
4. He knows what is within the heavens and earth and knows what you conceal and what you declare. And God is Knowing of that within the breasts. (Koran/Chapter 64)

In their ground "Rule", the seers say that the Eagle does not care about man's actions and is indifferent to him. According to them, the Eagle is so big, and the human being is such an insignificant part of it, that it would be so humiliating for the Eagle to deal with people one-to-one.

However, God Almighty proclaims in the Koran, "God, of what you do, is Seeing". Therefore, there's no such thing as not being interested, unlike the allegations made by the seers.

He creates us in the most beautiful way, spreads His blessings before us, and then looks at what we will do. The seers misinterpret His grandeur and say that He will not condescend to such things.

131. And to God belongs whatever is in the heavens and whatever is on the earth. And We have instructed those who were given the Scripture before you and yourselves to fear God. But if you disbelieve – then to God belongs whatever is in the heavens and whatever is on the earth. And ever is God Free of need and Praiseworthy. (Koran/Chapter 4)

In His Holy Koran, God Almighty describes Himself as "Free of the need of the Worlds". So, He does not need our prayers nor our help. Yet, on the other hand, the seers interpret this as "You don't have to pray to the Eagle, it does not attend to us, etc." Notwithstanding, God Almighty tells us that is not the case.

On the contrary, in spite of all His Majesty, He takes care of us and then tries us to see if we will be thankful or be ungrateful to Him. As for the seers, they know of the greatness He has, but they absent themselves from worshipping Him. And by doing so, they show ingratitude to all His concern and blessings for us.

Therefore, just when the seers fail to pass on what they have witnessed and begin to comment, they hit the buffers, which brings God Almighty and us into contempt. Only God Himself can reveal us the truth behind their discoveries, and they never know God as He introduced Himself.

Naming and addressing the Eagle:

21. If We had sent down this Koran upon a mountain, you would have seen it humbled and splitting from fear of God. And these examples We present to the people that perhaps they will give thought.
22. He is God, other than whom there is no deity, Knower of the unseen and the witnessed. He is the Most Compassionate, the Most Merciful.
23. He is God, other than whom there is no deity. The Sovereign, the Pure, the Perfection, the Bestower of Faith, the Overseer, the Exalted in Might, the Compeller, the Superior. Exalted is God above whatever they associate with Him.
24. He is God, the Creator, the Inventor, the Fashioner; to Him belong the most beautiful names. Whatever is in the heavens and earth is exalting Him. And He is the Exalted in Might, the Wise. (Koran/Chapter 59)

God Almighty offers the seers an opportunity to testify in regard to the degree of maturity they have attained and allows them to know Him. On the other hand, the "Eagle" is the name they give for God, to whom belongs whatever is in the heavens and whatever is on the earth. The seers say this by taking a few short glances, which they can achieve under very difficult conditions, and define it simply as "the case of something unknowable vaguely resembling something known".[43]

The seers give this name by their reasons, and since the human mind is a product of this universe, they can only see its reflections and can only name the "unknowable" after the "known". Don Juan calls it "the

43 CASTANEDA, The Fire from Within, Washington Square Press, The Eagle's Emanations

temptation to ascribe human attributes to what is incomprehensible"[44], but there is nothing else the seers can do. They need to translate what they have witnessed into the syntax of this universe, but it's like telling someone color-blind the colors in words. It is merely like catching lightning in a bottle.

So, there is no "Eagle" in fact, but it is necessary to give a name to that undefined, incomparable thing, and finally, they decide to give it a name of something they know and fits their shaman origins.

On the other hand, in response to the name given by the seers that does not clarify anything, God Almighty introduces Himself to us in the Koran with nearly a hundred names.

Accordingly, God Almighty reveals Himself to the man in the Koran as the ever Knowing (knows everything), the Wise (everything He does is wise), the Exalted in Might (can afford everything), the Acquainted (He gets news from everything), the Most Compassionate (acts with compassion), the Prevailing (if necessary, He punishes), the Ever-Living (never dies), the Sustainer of all existence (all power belongs to Him), the Originator (originator of the heavens and earth), the Praiseworthy (all praise to Him), the Guide (guides everything in the universe), Seeing (of what you do), all-Encompassing (encompassing everything in the universe), Free of need, Forbearing, Forgiving, Honorable, Merciful, etc.

Therefore, God Almighty introduces himself to us in a hundred different ways with all these attributes, and as a reflection of these names, this universe consists of their diffraction.

> 53. We will show them Our verses in the horizons and within themselves until it becomes clear to them that it is the truth. Is it not sufficient concerning your Lord that He is, over all things, a Witness? (Koran/Chapter 41)

According to the Koran, God Almighty uses the term 'verse' for the chapters revealed in the Koran, as well as for a single cell in our bodies or the stars in the sky. From this point of view, everything in the

[44] CASTANEDA, The Fire from Within, Washington Square Press, The Eagle's Emanations

universe manifests His attributes and enables us to be acquainted with Him.

Therefore, God Almighty, whom the seers denote as "Eagle" in an attempt to gloss over and trumpet forth as "incomprehensible", introduces Himself to us at any time and everywhere with His approximately a hundred names and with their manifestations in the universe and in our selves. And the sole purpose of our coming to this universe is to identify and know Him in this way. On the contrary, the seers do not have an exact knowledge of Him because they do not take into account the revelation and try to content themselves with the slap-dash name they coined.

RETURN TO THE EAGLE

4. To Him is your return all together. It is the promise of God which is truth. Indeed, He begins the creation and then repeats it that He may reward those who have believed and done righteous deeds, in justice. But those who disbelieved will have a drink of scalding water and a painful punishment for what they used to deny. (Koran/Chapter 10)

In his statements about the "Eagle", don Juan asks Castaneda, in a semi-serious tone, whether he knows a good answer to the question that has always haunted man: the reason for our existence.

Castaneda tells him that it cannot be logically answered, and in order to discuss that subject, it is necessary to talk about religious beliefs and that turns it all into a matter of faith.

Upon this response, don Juan answers him back as follows:

- What I was trying to point out to you with that question, which has rattled you so badly, is that our rationality alone cannot come up with an answer about the reason for our existence. Every time it tries, the answer turns into a matter of beliefs. The old seers took another road, and they did find an answer which doesn't involve faith alone.
- One of the most dramatic legacies the old seers had left us was their discovery that the reason for the existence of all sentient beings is to enhance awareness; it was a colossal discovery.

- They "saw" that it is the Eagle who bestows awareness. The Eagle creates sentient beings so that they will live and enrich the awareness it gives them with life. They also "saw" that it is the Eagle who devours that same enriched awareness after making sentient beings relinquish it at the moment of death.
- For the old seers, to say that the reason for existence is to enhance awareness is not a matter of faith or deduction. They "saw" it. They "saw" that the awareness of sentient beings flies away at the moment of death and floats like a luminous cotton puff right into the Eagle's beak to be consumed. For the old seers, that was the evidence that sentient beings live only to enrich the awareness that is the Eagle's food. [45]

Don Juan says, "the reason for the existence of us is to enhance awareness," but what he actually means is that the Eagle creates us to consume this enriched awareness. In other words, the Eagle supposedly brings us into existence in order to consume us, which is our main raison d'être (the reason for being).

In the previous chapter, we stated that the seers had reached improbable results when they started to comment and not content themselves with what they have witnessed. And it's all just the same thing happening here.

In the Koran, God Almighty repeatedly says, "to Me is your return" and proclaims that people are returned to God after death. The ancient seers also discover that living beings return to the "Eagle" after death, but they explain it with something simple: "consuming". And they make comments that are incompatible with the greatness of God Almighty, whom they label as Eagle.

> 14. Say, "Is it other than God I should take as a friend, Creator of the heavens and earth, while it is He who feeds and is not fed?" Say, "Indeed, I have been commanded to be the first who submit to God." And do not ever be of the polytheists. (Koran/Chapter 6)

As we mentioned in the previous section, God Almighty is Free from

[45] CASTANEDA, The Fire from Within, Washington Square Press, The Eagle's Emanations

the needs of the Worlds. Therefore, He has nothing to do with eating or drinking. As the Creator of the heavens and the earth, it is He who creates and gives us today our daily bread. But when the seers begin to comment on things of which they have no idea, they reach such strange consequences.

In fact, don Juan does not give much credence to these statements made by the old seers, and he tells Castaneda that he finds it grotesque, because it turns an indescribable act into something as mundane as devouring:

- There is a definite laxness in that version, and that personally I did not appreciate the idea of something devouring us. For me, it would be more accurate to say that there is a force that attracts our consciousness, much as a magnet attracts iron shavings. At the moment of dying, all of our being disintegrates under the attraction of that immense force. [46]

<u>To God we shall return</u>:

8. Say, "Indeed, the death from which you flee–indeed, it will meet you. Then you will be returned to the Knower of the unseen and the witnessed, and He will inform you about what you used to do." (Koran/Chapter 62)

We have already said that the power that the seers call "Eagle" is God Almighty. Here proclaiming, “to the Eagle is our return", the seers confirm this once again.

The seers remark that our return is to the Eagle, and they affirm that at the time of death, it attracts our consciousness, much as a magnet attracts iron shavings.[47] And God Almighty proclaims in the Koran that "To God we shall return" and announces that the only place we will reach after death is His peace.

Therefore, there is no mistake in proclamations made by the seers, but there is a mistake in their comments on what they witness. Because in

---

[46] CASTANEDA, The Fire from Within, Washington Square Press, The Eagle's Emanations

[47] CASTANEDA, The Fire from Within, Washington Square Press, The Eagle's Emanations

this case, they stop being "unbiased witnesses"[48], and begin to make their personal remarks and depart from the straight and narrow path.

And as a result of it, the seers also deny resurrection after death. According to them, when we return to the "Eagle", everything is completed and there is no more. However, God Almighty proclaims in the Holy Koran, “We know what the earth diminishes of you"[49], and He heralds that we will be resurrected:

32. We sent among them a messenger from themselves saying, "Worship God; you have no deity other than Him; then will you not fear Him?"
33. The eminent among his people who disbelieved and denied the meeting of the Hereafter while We had given them luxury in the worldly life said, "This is not but a man like yourselves. He eats of that from which you eat and drinks of what you drink.
34. And if you should obey a man like yourselves, indeed you would then be losers.
35. Does he promise you that when you have died and become dust and bones that you will be brought forth once more?
36. How far, how far, is that which you are promised.
37. It is not but our worldly life – we die and live, but we will not be resurrected. (Koran/Chapter 23)

Like the deniers here, the seers deny that they will be resurrected and, instead, invent their own "hereafter". Accordingly, they claim that the Eagle offers them an exit according to the spiritual level they have reached.

The seers term it as the "Eagle's gift" and lays claim that "Any one of living thing, if Eagle so desires, has the power to keep the flame of awareness, the power to disobey the summons to die and be consumed."[50] Accordingly, by the will of the Eagle, the seers will not go to their final resting-place in the same way we make of, but they will

---

[48] CASTANEDA, The Fire from Within, Washington Square Press, The Shift Below

[49] Koran/Chapter 50, verse 4

[50] CASTANEDA, The Eagle's Gift, Washington Square Press, The Rule of The Nagual

retain their awareness for a while. And this is their ultimate aim in this universe.[51]

However, what the seers claim, contradicts with their own arguments since they assert the Eagle supposedly consumes the enriched awareness of us, and they add that it leaves as a gift their own awareness that has peaked in richness.

In fact, God Almighty sends us here so that our awareness can develop and become pure enough to enter heaven. And He bestows paradise upon those who He thinks deserve it. Therefore, this journey of awareness that the seers have discovered is actually a test of God Almighty, which we are all part of.

In the case of the seers, in order for their science to conclude, God Almighty gives them a temporary exit. As a result of the enrichment of awareness, as a preface to the Hereafter, He grants them the chance to retain their awareness for a while. Thus, He provides a suitable response for their efforts that cannot hit the nail on the head.

The disbelief of both sciences:

The seers know that sentient beings "live" and what gives them life is the "Eagle", but they don't admit that the Eagle is God. On the other hand, the science of matter accepts neither the awareness nor the "Eagle", which gives this awareness. In other words, they are cast in a different mold. Yet, there's only one point where both of them meet. That's the non-existence of God.

They both unite in disbelief, but the seers are one step ahead. At least they know the "life" and the "Eagle" that breaths it into the man. According to the scientists[52], there is no such thing as life, there is no power called Eagle, and ultimately you do not exist in reality.

---

[51] See Chapter 14- Evolution of Awareness

[52] I don't want to say that all scientists are the same, but some of them -especially Darwinists- are against the belief in God like the seers. Because, the unwritten rules of modern science say that there is no God and all their effort is on explaining this universe without the need of Him. So, when I am talking about the scientists and their disbelief in God, I mean this general acceptance of the science of matter.

19. Be not like those who forgot God, so He made them forget themselves. Those are completely off the road. (Koran/Chapter 59)

God Almighty proclaims in the Koran, "who forget God, so He makes them forget themselves". In other words, since God creates human beings as His own exemplar, you actually deny yourself when you deny Him. And as the science of matter denies the whole life and living things for the sake of denying God, it actually denies the human being and reduces it to a lifeless robot.

The seers, however, know life and awareness, and they are aware of the fact that people "live". What they don't know is why life was given. They go off the rails since they pin their faith and hopes on themselves, not on revelations from God. Otherwise, they know much more about this universe than the science of matter does; moreover, they reduce the materialist part of the science of matter to waste.

However, what both sciences do is actually nothing but witness the universe. Don Juan says, "The human mind witnesses this universe, but cannot say anything about it." And that goes for the things the seers bring to light. They are only witnesses, but when they start to comment on them, they fail. That is why the revelation sent by God Almighty is a mercy, as it teaches people "what they do not know" and shows us how to look at the universe that is "tabula rasa".

Both of these sciences look at the universe on the surface and setting themselves to make shallow comments on it. But in the revelation, God Almighty, as the Owner of the Worlds, speaks out from a very high place and tells us the truth. For example, the seers know that the return is to God, but they do not know the exact nature of this process. And God Almighty, as its Creator, tells us what this is all about.

So, what they comment about these discoveries does not matter. What's important here is what the seers have discovered. God, the Exalted in Might and the Wise, allows the seers to discover these things, and using them as a channel, makes them serve a sacred goal about which they do not have the slightest idea.

Thanks to them, He not only confirms the truth of what he proclaims in the Koran, but also demonstrates that this universe is not what the science of matter claims to be. Just as the anti-matter of matter exists, He allows the formation of an anti-thesis against the science of matter, thus revealing its polar twin and giving us the opportunity to cross-check.

3- The Eagle's Emanations

- The Eagle's Emanations
- The Worlds
- Breaking the Parameters of Normal Perception
- The Universe as being a Description
- The Universe as being a Mystery

THE EAGLE'S EMANATIONS

Don Juan says that the new seers are trying to understand how awareness works, and for this, they have developed a series of awareness facts. The seers call this sequence the "mastery of awareness". And when don Juan taught it to Castaneda, as the first truth he said:

- Our familiarity with the world we perceive compels us to believe that we are surrounded by objects, existing by themselves and as themselves, just as we perceive them, whereas, in fact, there is no world of objects, but a universe of the Eagle's emanations.
- Something out there is affecting our senses. This is the part that is real. The unreal part is what our senses tell us is there. Take a mountain, for instance. Our senses tell us that it is an object. It has size, color, form. We even have categories of mountains, and they are downright accurate. Nothing wrong with that; the flaw is simply that it has never occurred to us that our senses play only a superficial role. Our senses perceive the way they do because a specific feature of our awareness forces them to do so.
- Seers say that we think there is a world of objects out there only because of our awareness. But what's really out there are the Eagle's emanations, fluid, forever in motion, and yet unchanged, eternal. [53]

---

[53] CASTANEDA, The Fire from Within, Washington Square Press, The Eagle's Emanations

Accordingly, don Juan states that the universe is, above all, a universe of emanations of the Eagle, and he speaks of another tissue that exists beneath the universe of matter.

Don Juan also claims that the origin of these emanations is the "Eagle" and that its emanations cover everything that can be known and unknown. Thus, according to him, everything that exists is essentially the emanations of the Eagle, and the world of matter is only one of the thousands of forms it can take.

Moreover, in the previous section, we explained that what the seers call the Eagle is actually God Almighty. Therefore, what don Juan calls the Eagle's emanations are actually the emanations from God.

Arsh[54]:

84. Say, "To whom belongs the earth and whoever is in it, if you should know?"
85. They will say, "To God." Say, "Then will you not take advice?"
86. Say, "Who is Lord of the seven heavens and Lord of the Great Arsh?"
87. They will say, "God." Say, "Then will you not fear Him?"
88. Say, "In whose hand is the realm of all things – and He protects while none can protect against Him – if you should know?"
89. They will say, "God." Say, "Then how are you deluded?"
90. Rather, We have brought them the truth, and indeed they are liars. (Koran/Chapter 23)

In His Holy Koran, God Almighty introduces himself in three different ways: "Lord of the Heavens and Earth", "Lord of the Worlds" and "Lord of the Arsh". Accordingly, this universe is meant by the heavens and the earth, while the worlds are the countless other realms that the seers speak of. The Arsh, on the other hand, is the common texture of these realms, which the seers call the "Eagle's Emanations".

---

[54] One to one meaning of "arsh" is throne in English, but in the Koran, it makes a reflection from it and is used as the place from where God Almighty commands the universes.

In fact, as we will explain below, the seers also call the Eagle's emanations the "commands of the Eagle". And in the same way, the word "arsh" is used in many verses in the Koran with the word "command".

5. The Most Compassionate above the Arsh emanated.
6. To Him belongs what is in the heavens and what is on the earth and what is between them and what is under the soil. (Koran/ Chapter 20)

Another important phrase used in the Koran in relation to the Arsh is to "emanate". This is usually translated as God Almighty's establishing Himself on the Arsh, but in fact, the main meaning of the word is "to spread and invade, to cover". In other words, an expression fully describing the Eagle's emanations and their dominant power, which don Juan mentions.

So, what the seers call the "Eagle's emanations" is referred to as the "Arsh" in the Koran, and God Almighty also introduces Himself as "Lord of the Arsh". And through this Arsh, God Almighty reigns over all these realms.

<u>The likeness of emanations to the filaments of light</u>:

35. God is the Light of the heavens and the earth. The example of His light is like a niche within which is a lamp; the lamp is within glass, the glass as if it were a pearly white star lit from a blessed olive tree, neither of the east nor of the west, whose oil would almost glow even if untouched by fire. Light upon light. God guides to His light whom He wills. And God presents examples for the people, and God is Knowing of all things.
36. It is in houses which God has permitted to be raised and that His name be mentioned therein. They exalt Him therein in the morning and the evenings. (Koran/Chapter 24)

Don Juan describes the Eagle's emanations as filaments of light that spread in all directions, vibrate and are aware of themselves. However, he still opposes their acceptance as a one-to-one filament of light and says, "That would be too simple. They are something indescribable.

And yet, my personal comment would be to say that they are like filaments of light."[55]

Castaneda explains these emanations by using the expressions of shamans:

- What the shamans of ancient Mexico found out when they focused their seeing on the dark sea of awareness was the revelation that the entire cosmos is made of luminous filaments that extend themselves infinitely. Shamans describe them as luminous filaments that go every which way without ever touching one another. They saw that they are individual filaments, and yet, they are grouped in inconceivably enormous masses… The energetic fact of the universe being composed of luminous filaments gave rise to the shamans' conclusion that each of those filaments that extend themselves infinitely is a field of energy. [56]

Therefore, these "luminous filaments", which the seers call the Eagle's emanations, are the common texture of all realms, and the seers assert that the source of these luminous filaments is the "Eagle".

Similarly, God Almighty introduces himself in the Koran as "the Light of the heavens and the earth". So, these luminous emanation filaments referred by don Juan originate from God Almighty, who introduces himself as the “the Light of the heavens and the earth". And God Almighty guides His servants, who live in His way, to His light.

Emanations as the commands:

52. Thus, We have revealed to you a Spirit of Our command. You did not know what the Scripture is or what faith is, but We have made it a light by which We guide whom We will of Our servants. And indeed, you guide to a straight path –

---

[55] CASTANEDA, The Fire from Within, Washington Square Press, The Eagle's Emanations

[56] CASTANEDA, The Teachings of Don Juan, Washington Square Press, Author's Commentaries on the Occasion of the Thirtieth Year of Publication

53. The path of God, to whom belongs whatever is in the heavens and whatever is on the earth. Unquestionably, all commands return to God. (Koran/Chapter 42)

Don Juan affirms that nagual Julian[57] and many other seers often call the Eagle's emanations "commands". Don Juan himself reportedly chose to call them emanation because of his respect for his benefactor having a strong character, but says that, in fact, they are commands. Therefore, the universe actually is a universe of the "Eagle's commands" rather than the emanations of the Eagle.

- Seers who "see" the Eagle's emanations often call them commands. I wouldn't mind calling them commands myself if I hadn't got used to calling them emanations. It was a reaction to my benefactor's preference; for him they were commands. I thought that term was more in keeping with his forceful personality than with mine. I wanted something impersonal. "Commands" sounds too human to me, but that's what they really are, commands. [58]

In explaining this situation, don Juan uses a term called "the compelling power of the emanations". What he means by this is the commands imposed on Eagle's emanation. Thus, these emanations "physically" exist, but there are commands imposed on them. And the Eagle, through these orders, sustains all the worlds.

Elsewhere, don Juan refers to these commands as the "intent of the Eagle's emanations" and remarks that we perceive as a result of the "pressure and intrusion of intent". And we also have professed in the next chapter that what don Juan calls "intent" is actually the intent of God Almighty.

Therefore, what don Juan calls the commands of the Eagle are actually the commandments of God Almighty. And the Almighty God recreates this universe each moment with these orders named by the science of matter; "rules of physics." And except for His will, there is

---

[57] Nagual turns out to be used as a name given by the seers to the "World of Commands", and they also call their teachers as "nagual" because they guide themselves to it.

[58] CASTANEDA, The Fire from Within, Washington Square Press, The Eagle's Emanations

no force in this universe that can sustain these rules for even a second.

5. He arranges the command from the heaven to the earth; then it will ascend to Him in a Day, the extent of which is a thousand years of those which you count.
6. That is the Knower of the unseen and the witnessed, the Exalted in Might, the most Merciful, (Koran/Chapter 32)

It is God Almighty who arranges the command and returns it to Himself. So the Islamic Sufis call it the "World of Command", the world behind this visible world that don Juan speaks of. According to this, behind the material reality we see ahead, there is a huge World of Commands and the Almighty God informs us firsthand about it as the Knower of the unseen and the witnessed.

The seers perceive this situation with their own discoveries and summarize it with the words "tonal" and "nagual". They describe the tonal as a "witnessed" aspect of the universe and the nagual as a huge ocean surrounding and holding the tonal island. In other words, "nagual" is the name given to the "World of Commands" by the seers.

String Theory:

Firstly, "String Theory", then "Superstring Theory" and now added "The Theory of Everything"...! And one of the most famous defendants of this theory is the recently passed physicist Stephen Hawking. He says, "I have spent the last twenty years of my life finding answers to the questions of why we exist and how we came to being."

According to String Theory, the substances that make up the universe, which we call the particle, are actually one-dimensional vibrating strings that resemble a violin string. According to this, even though they are short in length, they are like the Milky Way galaxy and the Earth when compared to an atom. And different particles emerge according to the different vibrations of these strings.

Similarly, the seers say that "the essence of the universe resembles incandescent threads stretched into infinity in every conceivable direction", and those threads also vibrate as the scientists have stated:

- The most significant act of sorcery is to "see" the essence of the universe. Don Juan's version was that the sorcerers of antiquity, the first ones to "see" the essence of the universe, described it in the best manner. They said that the essence of the universe resembles incandescent threads stretched into infinity in every conceivable direction, luminous filaments that are conscious of themselves in ways impossible for the human mind to comprehend. [59]

So, both sciences mention similar things. For now, it appears that the only thing they do not agree with each other is the length of the strings and awareness.

And both sciences are actually experiencing the same difficulties in describing what they find. For example, String Theory says that strings are unidimensional, but no one has ever seen anything one-dimensional. However, mathematical equations claim, "They exist."

Likewise, don Juan says:

- Notice that when I talk about "seeing", I always say "having the appearance of" or "seemed like". Everything one "sees" is so unique that there is no way to talk about it except by comparing it to something known to us. [60]

In other words, both sciences actually assert, "there is something there and the description of it looks like this". The descriptions they make are also very similar, but the main distinction hides in "awareness".

"We are perceivers, and the 'strings' are aware of themselves as well," says don Juan. But the science of matter does not accept awareness and still maintains its main question; "Is God really necessary?" They are trying to explain "a mechanical universe without God", but in fact, they are trying to find a "lifeless universe".

---

[59] CASTANEDA, The Art of Dreaming, HarperCollins Publishers Inc., Sorcerers of Antiquity: An Introduction

[60] CASTANEDA, The Art of Dreaming, HarperCollins Publishers Inc., Sorcerers of Antiquity: An Introduction

Awareness of the Eagle's emanations:

Don Juan says, "What is incomprehensible to normal awareness is that the filaments are aware," and states, "The filaments are aware of themselves, alive and vibrating." Therefore, according to the seers, there is no static dead universe, as the science of matter claims. On the contrary, what is essential in the universe is life. And the universe exists as its carrier platform.

- What's incomprehensible to normal awareness is that the filaments are aware. I can't tell you what that means, because I don't know what I am saying. All I can tell you with my personal comments is that the filaments are aware of themselves, alive and vibrating, that there are so many of them that numbers have no meaning and that each of them is an eternity in itself. [61]

The seers discover that this is the case, but they cannot express it fully and cannot make all the connections of the pieces of truths they found since their information does not come from God Almighty. On the other hand, God Almighty proclaims that everything in the heavens and the earth praises Him:

24. He is God, the Creator, the Inventor, the Fashioner; to Him belong the most beautiful names. Whatever is in the heavens and earth is exalting Him. And He is the Exalted in Might, the Wise. (Koran/Chapter 59)

Therefore, there is also a vector in the "awareness" that don Juan refers to. In other words, this awareness is not a scholastic one, but an awareness towards God Almighty, who owns everything.

115. And to God belongs the east and the west. So wherever you turn, there is the Face of God. Indeed, God is all-Encompassing and Knowing. (Koran/Chapter 2)

Just as the whole being glorifies God, the Face of God is there, wherever we turn our faces. In addition, as everything heads toward Him, He is with us at all times. God Almighty is not far off the universe, as some think. He is here with us at all times.

---

[61] CASTANEDA, The Fire from Within, Washington Square Press, The Eagle's Emanations

Therefore, this texture, which the seers call the "Eagle's emanations", is not independent of God Almighty; on the contrary, is a place of His manifestation. So, la Gorda[62] names it "the kingdom of heaven" and wishes her soul to reach there.

- I was a religious woman. I could tell you what I used to repeat without knowing what I meant. I wanted my soul to enter the kingdom of heaven. I still want that, except that I'm on a different path. The world of the nagual is the kingdom of heaven. [63]

La Gorda cannot make the connection because she does not have a deep knowledge of the Holy Books and thinks that her heavenly nagual floor is something separate from God Almighty, but it is not. On the contrary, God Almighty brings all creation into being as a window opening to Him and commands, "Wherever you look, there you will see the Face of God".

Therefore, everything around us stated by the seers as "unspeakable of" tells us about God Almighty in a great manner with their own body language. Furthermore, when a human being perceives the energy essence of such beings, he/she also energetically confirms God Almighty. Hereof, don Juan is incredibly afraid of losing "it":

- Compared with losing the nagual, death is nothing. My fear of losing the nagual is the only real thing I have, because without it I would be worse than dead. [64]

Thus, when the seers adhere to the nagual, they actually adhere to God Almighty. They perceive the kingdom of the heavens and the earth, and establish a connection with God Almighty; who is in fact, its Owner. And the loss of this connection with the origin of everything is worse to them than death.

---

[62] One of the apprentices of don Juan

[63] CASTANEDA, The Second Ring of Power, Washington Square Press, The Art of Dreaming

[64] CASTANEDA, The Art of Dreaming, HarperCollins Publishers Inc., Flying On The Wings of Intent

The universe as the energy itself:

- The energetic fact of the universe being composed of luminous filaments gave rise to the shamans' conclusion that each of those filaments that extend themselves infinitely is a field of energy. [65]

The seers consider these luminous filaments that make up the emanations of the Eagle as an energy field and claim that the whole universe is actually an energy universe:

- Everything is energy. The whole universe is energy. The social base of our perception should be the physical certainty that energy is all there is. [66]

Hence the seers say, "This is first a world of energy; then it's a world of objects". According to them, there is a sea of energy behind this world of matter, and the greatest skill of the seers is to perceive the energy essence of objects.

"Is it possible to train people in such a fashion?" Castaneda asks don Juan. And he replies that it is possible and that this is precisely what he is doing with Castaneda and his other apprentices.[67] Therefore, the seers call the act of perceiving the energy in the universe "seeing" and suggest that this is the highest skill they have developed after a lifetime of discipline and training.

The scientists, on the other hand, are trying to discover the realities that the seers have found by means of awareness, utilizing the means of the material world, and they do not put forward anything quite different from the seers. They also state that matter is a condensed form of energy. And according to the formula of $E=mc^2$, energy can be transformed into matter and matter into energy.

---

[65] CASTANEDA, The Teachings of Don Juan, Washington Square Press, Author's Commentaries on the Occasion of the Thirtieth Year of Publication

[66] CASTANEDA, The Art of Dreaming, HarperCollins Publishers Inc., Sorcerers of Antiquity: An Introduction

[67] CASTANEDA, The Art of Dreaming, HarperCollins Publishers Inc., Sorcerers of Antiquity: An Introduction

Therefore, both sciences speak the same language. Since one side handles the universe from the viewpoint of matter, it formulates $E = mc^2$ and remarks that the universe is energy. And the other side deals with the universe from the viewpoint of awareness, perceiving the energetic essence of objects and says that the whole universe is made up of energy.

The methods and worldviews of these two sciences are totally different, but they reach the same conclusions in the end, which is not actually a surprise. This is the reflection of the unity of God Almighty. And God Almighty uses these two opposite twins to make the crosscheck each other and show the truth. Even if the truth is different from what they think.

THE WORLDS

According to don Juan,

- Our world, which we believe to be unique and absolute, is only one in a cluster of consecutive worlds, arranged like the layers of an onion.
- Even though we have been energetically conditioned to perceive solely our world, we still have the capability of entering into those other realms, which are as real, unique, absolute, and engulfing as our own world is.
- Their existence is constant and independent of our awareness, but their inaccessibility is entirely a consequence of our energetic conditioning. In other words, simply and solely because of that conditioning, we are compelled to assume that the world of daily life is the one and only possible world. [68]

So, the seers are aware of the other worlds. And as we mentioned before, God Almighty introduces Himself in the Koran as the "Lord of the Worlds":

2. All praise is due to God, Lord of the Worlds (Koran/Chapter 1)

<u>Humanity as the unaware of the other worlds</u>:

---

[68] CASTANEDA, The Art of Dreaming, HarperCollins Publishers Inc., Authors Note

"Human beings think that their interpretation system is all that exists, and they are unaware of the other realms", says don Juan.

Although this is true for humanity in general, don Juan thinks that only the seers know it because he is not aware of the Koran. Yet God Almighty begins the Koran in the second verse by saying, "I am the Lord of the Worlds" and besides accepting the existence of those realms, He says "I am the Owner of them all".

Don Juan tells Castaneda about these other realms as follows:

- I know how difficult it is for the mind to allow mindless possibilities to become real. But new worlds exist! They are wrapped one around the other, like the skins of an onion. The world we exist in is but one of those skins. [69]

As you can see, don Juan is obliged to call these realms "mindless possibilities" in the face of Castaneda's prejudices, but as the Koran teaches us, these are not mindless possibilities but absolute truths.

On the other hand, the science of matter has only recently begun to speak of these realms, which the seers discovered centuries ago. And especially after the discovery of the expansion of this universe with the Big Bang, they began to produce theories involving other realms. However, these theories are still up in the air and they must be built on solid grounds.

<u>The realms system of humans and jinns</u>:

49. And of all things We created two counterparts; perhaps you take advice. (Koran/Chapter 51)

Don Juan says the seers have realized that the universe consists of opposing forces that complement each other. God Almighty expresses the truth that they have discovered, "We created everything in pairs". And as a reflection of this, He creates the "jinn" as the polar twin of mankind in our system of realms.

---

[69] Carlos CASTANEDA, The Art of Dreaming, , HarperCollins Publishers Inc., The Fixation of The Assemblage Point

Don Juan says that although there are too many realms to be counted, only eight of them are accessible to human beings. And mankind lives in the realm system of these eight worlds, along with the jinns that the seers call inorganic beings.

Accordingly, don Juan names the seven realms other than our cosmos as "unknown". And he affirms that although we cannot reach them under normal circumstances, they are within human coverage and can communicate with the beings of these realms if the right techniques are used. And this dimension of existence is already the expertise of the seers.

Therefore, those who seek "foreign living forms" in the universe do not need to go too far. They are with us at any moment, but because of our energetical conditioning, it is not possible to reach them without applying the special techniques known to the seers.

On the other hand, don Juan calls the countless other realms as "unknown" outside these eight realms, saying that these are completely outside the human talent circle.

<u>Bearing "eight" on them</u>:

13. Then when the Horn is blown with one blast,
14. And the earth and the mountains are lifted and leveled with one blow,
15. Then on that Day, the Occurrence will occur.
16. And the heaven will split and open, for that Day it is infirm.
17. And the angels are at its edges. And the "eight" will bear the Arsh of your Lord in that Day. (Koran/Chapter 69)

God Almighty describes the Day of Resurrection, and the stages of the Resurrection that take place after the last Horn having been blown out are given in these verses. Accordingly, the ground and the mountains are torn to pieces, and after that, the sky is split and the door to the "Arsh World"[70] is opened by losing its function. And the angels take their places, and on that day, the "eight" bear the Lord's

[70] The World of Command/Nagual/Energy Universe

Arsh. So, if you ask about this number "eight", it refers to the eight realms that don Juan mentioned above.

According to the Koran, not only humans but also the jinn, the polar twin of mankind, are being gathered on the Day of Resurrection. And as described above, when the sky split and the world of continuity in the meaning we know now comes to an end, the first real meeting of the jinn and humans is realized. And these eight realms that don Juan speaks of are gathered together into an assembly in the presence of God Almighty.

We have already said that Arsh is the common texture of the realms system of humans and jinn. Therefore, the word "eight", which is mentioned here together with the Arsh, expresses these "eight realms" that the seers are talking about and confirms their discovery.

<u>There is "nineteen" on it</u>:

> 9. Indeed, it is We who sent down this message, and indeed, We will be its guardian. (Koran/Chapter 15)

The phrase about Arsh that we mentioned above is important because in the Koran, there is one more similar expression, and it is said that "There is nineteen on it". And we have learned today that the Koran is enumerated mathematically in hundreds of different ways with the number 19.

Accordingly, there are verses with only a few letters at the beginning of some Koran chapters. But what they really are, were not understood for centuries, and although many predictions were made, it was unknown until it was discovered in the last century. The secret of these letters was solved in 1974[71], and it was found that there was a mathematical encryption coded with the number 19 in the Koran.

---

[71] The code 19 in the Koran was discovered for the first time in the year 1974. And what is interesting that the name of the chapter that includes the verse "There is nineteen on it" is "The Hidden", and the chapter number of it is 74. And when you put the chapter number besides 19, it gives the discovery year of this "hidden" code, 1974.

Thus, the chapters in the Koran starting with these letters are encoded in connection with 19. And in addition to this, there are also dozens of numerical ciphers in connection with 19 in other sections of the Koran as well. Below are a few examples: [72]

The code 19 and H-M letters:[73]

1. H, M,
2. A, S, Q
3. Thus has He revealed to you and to those before you – God, the Exalted in Might, the Wise. (Koran/Chapter 42)

The first example is the seven chapters starting with the letters H and M. Accordingly, in these seven chapters, the letters H and M are used 2147 times (19x113), and it is precisely the times of 19. What's more, if you add up the digits of the usage numbers, this gives the product coefficient of 113.

Chapter #	H #	M #	The total of digits
40	64	380	6+4+3+8+0 = 21
41	48	276	4+8+2+7+6 = 27
42	53	300	5+3+3+0+0 = 11
43	44	324	4+4+3+2+4 = 17
44	16	150	1+6+1+5+0 = 13
45	31	200	3+1+2+0+0 = 6
46	36	225	3+6+2+2+5 = 18
Total	292	1855	113
General Total	292 + 1855 = 2147		19 x 113 = 2147

Of course, you may think this might be a huge coincidence, so let's look at the next step given below:

---

[72] Caner Taslaman, The Quran: Unchallengeable Miracle, Nettleberry Publications. 2006, p. 330-332, 381

[73] Caner Taslaman, The Quran: Unchallengeable Miracle, Nettleberry Publications. 2006, p. 392-394

Chapter 42 is unique in Koran since it is the only chapter having relevant code letters of 19 in its second verse. Accordingly, it has "A-S-Q" letters in its second verse, and again the sum of the usage of these letters in this chapter is exactly the full multiple proportion of 19:

A (98) + S (54) + Q (57) = 209 (19x11)

Moreover, this unique chapter divides the table above into two parts by giving the two tables below. In these tables again, the sum of the numbers of H and M are full multiple proportions of 19, and the sum of the digits is equal to the product coefficients.

Chapter #	H #	M #	The total of digits
40	64	380	6+4+3+8+0 = 21
41	48	276	4+8+2+7+6 = 27
42	53	300	5+3+3+0+0 = 11
Total	165	956	59
General Total	165 + 956 = 1121		19 x 59 = 1121

Chapter #	H #	M #	The total of digits
43	44	324	4+4+3+2+4 = 17
44	16	150	1+6+1+5+0 = 13
45	31	200	3+1+2+0+0 = 6
46	36	225	3+6+2+2+5 = 18
Total	127	899	54
General Total	127 + 899 = 1026		19 x 54 = 1026

I believe this speaks for itself: this mathematics equation leads the role and shows this is not a coincidence, but a product of consciousness.

<u>The code 19 and the Chapter Mary</u>:

1. K, H, Y, A, S,
2. This is a mention of the mercy of your Lord to His servant Zechariah (Koran/Chapter 19)

The first verse of Chapter Mary consists of the letters "K-H-Y-A-S". And according to this, in Chapter Mary, these letters appear a total of 798 times (19x42):

K (137) + H (175) + Y (343) + A (117) + S (26) = 798 (19x42)

Let us also say that in the Arabic language, each letter has a number value, and if you put the number values of the letters (K, H, Y, A, S) consecutively in the verse (20 5 10 70 90), the formed number 205107090 is also a full multiple proportion of 19. (19x10795110)

Moreover, God Almighty has determined the Chapter Mary as the 19th chapter of the Koran. So, it is very unique and important. And Prophet Jesus was also mentioned once in this chapter, and this was also the 19th usage of Prophet Jesus in the Koran. Thus, it is clear that this is a very purposeful use.

The code 19 and God's Mercy:

In the Koran, there are a total of 114 Chapters (19 x 6) and the phrase "In the name of God, the Most Compassionate, the Most Merciful" is also used 114 times (19 x 6) in the Koran. The importance of this word is that it is found at the head of all Chapters except one.[74] It is, therefore, very important and is also coded with 19.

Firstly, this sentence consists of 19 letters. In addition, each of the four words that make up is repeated in the Koran as the exact multiples of 19.

Name 19 (19x1) God 2698 (19x142) the Most Compassionate 57 (19x3) the Most Merciful 114 (19x6)

The Most Compassionate, the Most Merciful and God are among the names of God Almighty. And interestingly, only four of nearly a hundred names of God in the Koran are used as the exact multiples of 19. These are:

---

[74] This incomplete usage is also a conscious one, and "the lost one" is used in another chapter several pages later and creates a separate coding. Please check Caner Taslaman, The Quran: Unchallengeable Miracle, Nettleberry Publications. 2006, p. 351-353

Witness (19x1) God (19x142) The Most Compassionate (19x3) the Most Merciful (19x6)

So the word "Witness", which is used in the same number in the table, is used instead of the word "Name". And with this relation, apparently God Almighty proclaims, "Be a witness that God is the Most Compassionate and the Most Merciful". Should you have heard before that God's blessings could be proven mathematically, you probably wouldn't believe it.

"I really want to believe in God, but I wish we had an objective evidence", says Carl Sagan. Today, hundreds of relationships with this coding have been discovered in the Koran, and there are things that even human memory cannot take. Moreover, anyone can see them at any time. Therefore, God Almighty has sent the objective proof that Carl Sagan wanted.

Also, let alone changing a word of the Koran, it is not possible to change the location of one letter. Thus, God Almighty has coded the Koran in hundreds of ways, protecting it against any distortion.

<u>His Arsh is upon water</u>:

There is another statement in the Koran regarding the Arsh (nagual), which also confirms the seers and has not yet been fully understood. According to this, the Koran says that "His Arsh is upon water"[75] and we think that this expression can be better understood in the light of the discoveries made by the seers.

Don Juan says that water had been given to us not only for life, but also as a link to the other seven realms:

- In the instance of the water practices, the old seers were convinced that it was humanly possible to be transported bodily by the fluidity of water anywhere between this level of ours and the other seven levels below; or to be transported in essence anywhere on this level, along the watercourse of a river in either direction. They used, accordingly, running water to be transported

[75] Koran/Chapter 11, verse 7

> on this level of ours and the water of deep lakes or that of waterholes to be transported to the depths.[76]

Accordingly, the seers can use water as a gate and communicate with the jinns they call inorganic beings or allies. Don Juan calls this technique "a knock on their door", and the seers have their apprentices practice this technique during their "ally training".

Therefore, don Juan takes Castaneda to some water sources to communicate with inorganic beings in the early days of his apprenticeship; where the former helps the latter make contact with inorganic beings that make water the gateway.

Later on, he arranged for him to meet an "ally" with the help of a mirror on a river, giving him another experience of direct encounter with inorganic beings.

In other words, as the seers have discovered, God Almighty brings into being, water; not only as a source of life, but also as a gateway to the common texture of the worlds: enabling it to communicate with the beings living in other realms.

However, there is still a nuance between the seers and the statements used by God Almighty. Although don Juan uses a passive phrase, saying "water had been given to us as a link, a road", he does not declare who gave it.

On the other hand, God Almighty introduces himself as "the Owner of the Arsh" and proclaims, "I am the Owner of all these realms and the window between them". Therefore, the seers are discovering the existing once again, and Almighty God is the only Owner of that existing.

<u>The "ambiguous" verses in the Koran</u>:

7. It is He who has sent down to you the Book; in it are verses that are precise – they are the foundation of the Book – and others ambiguous ones. As for those in whose hearts is deviation from truth, they will follow that of it which is unspecific, seeking

[76] CASTANEDA, The Fire from Within, Washington Square Press, Inorganic Beings

> discord and seeking an interpretation. And no one knows its true interpretation except God and who are deep in knowledge. They say, "We believe in it. All of it is from our Lord." And no one takes advice except those of understanding. (Koran/Chapter 3)

The examples we have given above are some of the "ambiguous" verses of the Koran, that is, the verses which might only be comprehended with time. So, God Almighty sends His Koran together with ambiguous verses, as well as other main basic ones, to be read at all times. And these verses are being clarified by humanity as time goes on.

Some of them are the subject of the science of the seers, and the seers make them clear. And some of them are the subject of the science of matter, and Almighty God authorizes the science of matter to explain them.

For example, God Almighty announces in the following verses: "We constructed the heaven and indeed, We are expanding it" and proclaims that the universe is expanded by God Almighty:

47. And the heaven We constructed with strength, and indeed, We are its expander.
48. And the earth We have spread out, and excellent is the preparer.
49. And of all things We created two counterparts; perhaps you take advice.
50. So flee to God. Indeed, I am to you from Him a clear warner. (Koran/Chapter 51)

As you know, our universe is expanding every moment. But until the 20th century, there is not even the slightest piece of information produced by humanity that the universe is expanding. Even Einstein is not convinced - although his own equations tell him otherwise - and he tries to invent a "universal constant" to adapt the universe to his own ideas. And he says that it is the biggest mistake of his career.

However, the Koran made this clear in the 7th century, and this truth it declares could only be confirmed by modern science in the 20th century.

30. Have those who disbelieved not considered that the heavens and the earth were a joined entity, and We separated them and made from water every living thing? Then will they not believe?
31. And We placed firm mountains on earth lest it would shake them, and We made therein passes as roads that they might be guided.
32. And We made the sky a protected ceiling, but they, from its signs, are turning away.
33. And it is He who created the night and the day and the sun and the moon; all in an orbit are swimming. (Koran/Chapter 21)

In these verses, the Koran declares that the heavens and the earth were once united and separated by God Almighty, just like today's Big Bang theorists who say that the universe starts from a single point.

Almighty God also refers to the sky as a protected ceiling. To understand what this means, just look at the surface of the moon. If we did not have a protective atmosphere, the earth would be exposed to meteor bombings just as it did on the moon. Also, if harmful rays from the sun were not prevented, not living things would be able to live on earth.

And the last verse says, "He created the sun and the moon, all in an orbit are swimming". As you know, every object bends space-time and every celestial body swims in that space-time pattern. So, as the Owner of the realms, God Almighty takes a picture of it and tells us centuries ago, not only stating that they have trajectories, but also proclaims that they are "swimming" in it.

88. And you see the mountains, thinking them rigid, while they pass as the passing of clouds. It is the art of God, who perfected all things. Indeed, He is Acquainted with that which you do. (Koran/Chapter 27)

Among the verses of the Koran, which might be understood in the course of time, the most interesting one for me is the verse above. During my university years, I read a book called "The Great Misconceptions in Science", and one of the twenty events described in this book was about the discovery of plate tectonics.

Accordingly, it is Alfred Wegener who first put forward the idea of plate tectonics in the early 20th century, saying that earth is not a single land, but rather a combination of various land pieces. However, this idea is not accepted in his time and even considered ridiculous.

Wegener dies before seeing that his theory is accepted as the technology that can prove this idea has not yet been developed. Years later, it is discovered that the land is actually composed of 15 plates and that they act as an island, albeit slowly on the magma.

Today, these are obvious facts, but now, please put yourself in the place of the Prophet Muhammad and think for a moment: You are in the middle of a desert, there are only barren rigid hills around you, and the verse comes and declares that these hills act just as clouds move. What would you do, how would you explain this to those around you? And you have to wait 1400 years before what you say is proved to be right.

So, the prophecy is such a thing, but we have no excuse anymore. As mentioned above, God Almighty gives these examples and asks: "Then will they not believe?" But in the next verse, He gives the answer: "They are turning away from the signs of the sky".

Then, what does the science of matter do? Does it turn away from these signs even though it sees all this order, perfection and design? Yes, it does. Then, is it possible to say that despite all these signs, they still use their minds? Up to you to decide.

BREAKING THE PARAMETERS OF NORMAL PERCEPTION

"Breaking the parameters of normal perception is the obsession of every man on Earth," says don Juan, and names it "the unavoidable issue of mankind". Also, he announces that this is the reason for the profusion of drugs, stimulants, religious rituals and ceremonies among modern men. [77]

According to don Juan, breaking the parameters of normal perception means "the entrance into unthinkable worlds of a pragmatic value in no way different from the value of our world of everyday life".

"But why would I want to enter into those worlds?" Castaneda asks. Don Juan answers him:

- Because you are a creature of awareness, a perceived like the rest of us. Human beings are on a journey of awareness, which has been momentarily interrupted by extraneous forces. Believe me, we are magical creatures of awareness. If we don't have this conviction, we have nothing.
- Take my word, because mine are not arbitrary statements. My word is the result of corroborating, for myself, what the shamans

[77] CASTANEDA, Magical Passes, HarperCollins Publishers Inc., Introduction

> of ancient Mexico found out: that we human beings are magical beings." [78]

Don Juan's answer to the question "What are you?" is "We are perceivers". Then don Juan continues by saying, "Human beings are magical creatures of awareness." In other words, human magic comes from being a perceiver and from being able to use it, unlike animals.

Being condemned to this world:

Don Juan avers that the certainty of this world is regarded as an unquestionable fact, but it is actually a "trap" into which mankind, capable of perceiving many realms, falls.

The seers say that we were forced into this system by being born into it. But the seers learn to perceive objects as energy and overcome this limitation. And according to them, not being aware of this deliberately reduces the scope of what can be perceived and makes us believe that the mold into which we fit our perception is all that exists. [79]

On the other hand, the seers describe the universe as follows:

- It could physically be described as a tunnel of infinite length and width; a tunnel with reflective furrows. Every furrow is infinite, and there are infinite numbers of them. Living creatures are compulsorily made, by the force of life, to gaze into one furrow. To gaze into it means to be trapped by it, to live that furrow. [80]

Therefore, the seers try to change this situation, which they see as a "trap" by crossing these boundaries. And for this, they try to break the mirror of this realm and move to the other realms.

---

78 CASTANEDA, Magical Passes, HarperCollins Publishers Inc., Tensegrity

79 CASTANEDA, The Art of Dreaming, HarperCollins Publishers Inc., Sorcerers of Antiquity: An Introduction

80 CASTANEDA, The Eagle's Gift, Washington Square Press, The Plumed Serpent

Breaking the parameters of worlds:

Don Juan speaks of the fact that we were forced into this universe

because we were born into it, and he describes it as a "jail". The seers of antiquity have opposed it entirely and chose to perceive the energy directly, thus opening the door to other realms.

However, God, the Lord of the Worlds, creates man with these potentials but does not want them to use it in this way. Because the mission He imposes on human beings is certain and wants the nature He gave to man to be used accordingly. Moreover, when one starts to turn away from this, one actually starts to persecute oneself. And we can see much of Castaneda's sufferings during his education.

Therefore, human beings have no mission to relate to other realms and learn from the jinns that live there. And in the Koran, God Almighty warns them: "This is a trial, do not do it", but the seers do not listen to Him and walk straight in.

Actually, the reason they do this is not as "the obsession of breaking the parameters of normal perception" as claimed by don Juan, but the "desire for immortality" that God has placed in man. And as we will explain later, in more detail, the main reason the seers are interested in other realms is that they do not want to die. They are primarily trying to overcome this realm to get rid of death, but ultimately God Almighty does not give them immortality, because they are trying to do it in a way that He does not want.

THE UNIVERSE AS BEING A DESCRIPTION

"This universe is nothing more than a description", says don Juan. And he asserts that the first job of a benefactor is to pass on this idea to his apprentice:

- The first act of a teacher is to introduce the idea that the world we think we see is only a view, a description of the world. Every effort of a teacher is geared to prove this point to his apprentice. But accepting it, seems to be one of the hardest things one can do; we are complacently caught in our particular view of the world, which compels us to feel and act as if we knew everything about the world. [81]

As the seers reach the common fabric of the realms system and other realms that are accessible to human beings, they are not based on this universe, but the energy universe behind it, and they declare this world a description. Therefore, they say that this is first a world of energy, then it is a world of matter, and they take energy as their base and say that this visible world is insignificant.

<u>The insignificance of the universe</u>:

Castaneda maintains that the main proposition of the seers is that "our

---

[81] CASTANEDA, Tales of Power, Washington Square Press, The Strategy of a Sorcerer

reality is merely one of many descriptions".[82] According to this, the seers discover other realms that are accessible to human beings, but since they do not have any knowledge from God, they make a wrong interpretation and consider this universe and everything in it as insignificant. According to them, this universe is only one of many possible realms and therefore, an ordinary one that is no different from the others.

Thus, seeing all the human values, ideas, and religious beliefs of this universe as an obstacle, dump them into the garbage. Supposedly, they reach such a great reality that our world remains beside it in the desert like dust, and they no longer take what is going on in this world seriously.

According to them, love and morality are insignificant, like everything else in this universe. There is no difference between charity and evil, and they are all equal in the face of absolute eternity. Moreover, these are the ties of socialization that nailed us to our place, and it is not possible to reach other realms without getting rid of them.

1. Blessed is God in whose hand is dominion, and He is over all things competent
2. He created death and life to test which of you is best in deed. And He is the Exalted in Might, the Forgiving.
3. He created seven heavens in layers. You can't see in the creation of the Most Compassionate any inconsistency. So return your vision to the sky; do you see any breaks? (Koran/Chapter 67)

In response to the allegations of the seers, God, the Lord of the Worlds proclaims, "We created death and life to test which of you is best in deed". So, this universe and its contents are not such useless things, but they are all tests. And when the time comes, they will all be questioned upon.

31. And to God belongs whatever is in the heavens and whatever is in the earth – that He may recompense those who do evil with the penalty of what they have done and recompense those who do good with the best reward (Koran/Chapter 53)

---

[82] CASTANEDA, Journey to Ixtlan, Washington Square Press, Introduction

God Almighty creates the heavens and the earth, in the same way, to determine who will do better work; and says that in the Hereafter, everyone will get in return for what they are doing in this world. According to this, whoever exhibits beauty in this world, will receive beauty by God in the Hereafter, and whoever does cruelty will taste the same.

Therefore, the seers are again missing the point of equilibrium. As they have discovered other realms, they declare useless everything in this world. But God, the Lord of the Worlds, creates this world with an aim and examines us here. He adorns the heavens and the earth with signs that will introduce Himself and asks us to find Him. Consequently, this universe is not insignificant or useless. On the contrary, it is the manifestation place of God Almighty, our introduction to Him.

<u>Considering the universe as insignificant, but seeing what they are doing as important</u>:

- For me the world is weird because it is stupendous, awesome, mysterious, and unfathomable. My interest has been to convince you that you must assume responsibility for being here, in this marvelous world, in this marvelous desert, in this marvelous time. I wanted to convince you that you must learn to make every act count, since you are going to be here for only a short while, in fact, too short for witnessing all the marvels of it. [83]

Don Juan says, "the world we think we see is only a view, a description of the world"[84] and deems its contents insignificant. On the other hand, he tells Castaneda that everything he does in this universe is his "last battle" and is very important. And he formulates this as "controlled folly". In other words, he knows that he's doing something empty, but on the other hand, in order to gain energy due to human nature, he has to pretend to be the most important thing in the world.

---

83 CASTANEDA, Journey to Ixtlan, Washington Square Press, The Last Battle on Earth

84 CASTANEDA, Tales of Power, Washington Square Press, The Strategy of a Sorcerer

Therefore, the seers here again operate the rules of the universe set by God, but because they have not learned it from revelation, they go to extremes and fall into contradiction. They need to pay attention to everything they do due to human nature, but on the other hand, they say that what we do does not really matter.

29. Say, "Whether you conceal what is in your breasts or reveal it, God knows it. And He knows that which is in the heavens and that which is on the earth. And God is over all things competent.
30. The Day every soul will find what it has done of good present and what it has done of evil. It will wish that between itself and that evil was a great distance. And God warns you of Himself, and God is Kind to His servants." (Koran/Chapter 3)

According to the Koran, human beings are here to win or lose an eternal life. Therefore, as don Juan said, everything we do here is incredibly important.

But on the other hand, the blessings of this world are temporary. And here, besides the life of the Hereafter, which is the main life, there is only a small blessing and a test arena where only the samples of those blessings are found. Therefore, clinging to the blessings of this world and struggling for them is without cause.

20. Know that the life of this world is but amusement and diversion and adornment and boasting to one another and competition in increase of wealth and children – like the example of a rain whose resulting plant growth pleases the tillers; then it dries and you see it turned yellow; then it becomes scattered debris. And in the Hereafter is severe punishment and forgiveness from God and approval. And what is the worldly life except the enjoyment of delusion. (Koran/Chapter 57)

So, without being deceived by this world's ornament, praise, and wealth, we need to ask for the everlasting one. And in doing so, God Almighty says to us, "Compete for good deeds with each other". Therefore, there is no "controlled folly" in this world, even though this world is not permanent. However, the seers cannot make this connection, and they level down to insignificance all that they do, while

God Almighty demands us to turn this world into heaven just like the Hereafter.

The triviality of the universe for the science of matter:

64. It is God who made for you the earth a place of settlement and the sky a structure with multi layers and formed you and perfected your forms and provided you with good things. That is God, your Lord; then blessed is God, Lord of the Worlds. (Koran/Chapter 40)

We have explained above the thoughts of the seers regarding the insignificance of this universe, they have concluded as a result of their discovery of other realms. And what is interesting is that the scientists have these similar ideas. Although they have just begun to speak of the existence of other realms that the Koran spoke of 1400 years ago, their philosophical inferences are not very different from the seers.

According to the recently discussed view in the science of matter, our universe is not unique. And it is one of many universes created by a mother universe that could produce millions of possible Big Bang explosions. Based on this, some scientists who make philosophical inferences say almost the same things as don Juan. For them, our universe is not special, because there are many others out there, and our universe is just an ordinary one.

Of course, since these scientists are not free of ego like don Juan, they also enjoy a secret pleasure in handling it this way:

- Humanity has in the course of time had to endure from the hands of science two great outrages upon its naive self-love. The first was when it realized that our earth was not the center of the universe, but only a tiny speck in a world-system of a magnitude hardly conceivable; this is associated in our minds with the name of Copernicus, although Alexandrian doctrines taught something very similar. The second was when biological research robbed man of his peculiar privilege of having been specially created, and relegated him to a descent from the animal world, implying an ineradicable animal nature in him. (Sigmund Freud)

Just as Freud, today's scientists present these realms as a great discovery and between the lines, they imply that all human efforts are nothing against this greatness. In other words, just like the seers, man is lost to the size of the realms system, reducing him to a desperate, idle being.

On the other hand, God Almighty is the Owner of all these worlds they have just started to discover. And He declares all of them as truth. Therefore, there is no such thing as triviality, but those who deny God Almighty, also deny His universe.

He reveals these realms that have been found, as the result of thousands of years of efforts by the seers and scientists, just as in the second verse of the Koran and introduces himself as the "Lord of the Worlds". Therefore, He says, "I am the Owner of all these Worlds", in which these two sciences only bear witness to their existence.

THE UNIVERSE AS BEING A MYSTERY

1. H, M. [85]
2. The revelation of the Book is from God, the Exalted in Might, the Wise.
3. We did not create the heavens and earth and what is between them except in truth and for a specified term. But those who disbelieve, from that of which they are warned, are turning away. (Koran/Chapter 46)

The seers call their constitution where they combine the basic principles of their teachings with the name "Rule". And the first two principles of this Rule say that this universe is a "mystery":

- The first precept of the rule is that everything that surrounds us is an unfathomable mystery.
- The second precept of the rule is that we must try to unravel these mysteries, but without ever hoping to accomplish this. [86]

According to the seers, this universe is an unfathomable mystery and there is no way to unravel it. Therefore, the most basic proposition from them is the inexplicability of this universe.

---

[85] Letters related with the numeric code of 19 that we told in previous pages

[86] CASTANEDA, The Eagle's Gift, Washington Square Press, Florinda

They supposedly reach the vastness of this universe, accepting it only as a "mystery that can be witnessed, but never explained." Since they have discovered other realms and beings living in them, the explanations of this world are no longer sufficient to them, and they ignore the explanations and use the existing in practice:

- It is monstrous to think that the world is understandable or that we ourselves are understandable. What we are perceiving is an enigma, a mystery that one could only accept in humbleness and awe. [87]

As the seers go beyond this universe, they are supposedly exceeding the explanations of this universe and describe it as something "witnessable but unspeakable of". But this is true only for the human mind, and what they overlook is the fact that God Almighty teaches people what they do not know:

1. Read in the name of your Lord who created –
2. Created man from an attached embryo.
3. Read, and your Lord is the most Generous –
4. Who taught by the pen –
5. Taught man what he did not know. (Koran/Chapter 96)

Almighty God uses this expression in the first revelation of the Koran, and explains what He actually intended by His revelation. With the revelation He sent, He opens the talisman of this universe witnessed by human beings and answers the question, "What is this?" The seers call it an unknown enigma, but God Almighty proclaims, "It is not an enigma, on the contrary, it is the truth itself".

<u>The universe as being truth</u>:

5. He created the heavens and earth in truth. He wraps the night over the day and wraps the day over the night and has subjected the sun and the moon, each running for a specified term. Unquestionably, He is the Exalted in Might, the Perpetual Forgiver. (Koran/Chapter 39)

---

87 CASTANEDA, The Eagle's Gift, Washington Square Press, The Nagual Woman

The seers call this universe a mystery, but as God Almighty repeated many times in the Koran, he declares that he created this universe as a truth. So, this realm is not a description or an unknown enigma, but a truth. And it is not created in vain:

38. We did not create the heavens and earth and that between them in play.
39. We did not create them except in truth, but most of them do not know. (Koran/Chapter 44)

God Almighty creates the heavens and the earth for a specified term and to show the truth. He puts his signature all over them, then sends His revelation and asks us to read the "universe book" by it. But the seers are enigmatic because they deny the revelation which God has sent down. However, there is no enigma in the universe and it is the truth itself.

31. Say, "Who provides for you from the heaven and the earth? Or who controls hearing and sight and who brings the living out of the dead and brings the dead out of the living and who arranges every matter?" They will say, "God," so say, "Then will you not fear Him?"
32. For that is God, your Lord, the Truth. And what can be beyond truth except aberration? So how are you averted? (Koran/Chapter 10)

The word "truth" is so essential in the Koran that it acts as a litmus paper. Accordingly, God Almighty creates the heavens and the earth as truth and introduces himself as the "Truth". And again, God Almighty sends His Books and His messengers as truth.

Therefore, this universe is overflowing with "truth", and God Almighty Himself, His Books and His Prophets are truth itself. And, as the above verse says, nothing remains of the aberration after the truth, and what the seers call mystery vanishes into thin air.

<u>All things in the universe as being a verse</u>:

99. It is He who sends down rain from the sky. And We produce thereby the growth of all things. We produce from it greenery from which We

> produce grains arranged in layers. And from the palm trees – of its emerging fruit are clusters hanging low. And gardens of grapevines and olives and pomegranates, similar yet varied. Look at each of its fruit when it yields and at its ripening. Indeed in that are verses for a people who believe. (Koran/Chapter 6)

As a reflection of the fact that the universe is the truth, God Almighty proclaims that everything He creates in this universe is a verse just like the verses He sent down to His prophets, and He introduces Himself to us by means of their help.

He creates all things in a magnificent way, puts his signature all over them and wants us to ponder over them. Therefore, this universe and its contents are not created in vain; on the contrary, they are signs for each of us.

3. Indeed, within the heavens and earth are verses for the believers.
4. And in the creation of yourselves and what He disperses of moving creatures are verses for people who are certain in faith.
5. And in the alternation of night and day and in what God sends down from the sky of provision and gives life thereby to the earth after its lifelessness and in His directing of the winds are verses for a people who reason.
6. These are the verses of God which We recite to you in truth. Then in what statement after God and His verses will they believe? (Koran/Chapter 45)

We all go on holiday, go around the sea or trek in the mountains, etc. In fact, all of what we see in those trips is a "verse" of God. Even though we are not aware of it, we actually go on vacation to see the verses of God, not the mountains themselves. When we see them, we say, "Nature is wonderful here", but in fact, there is no nature. They are all products of the great art of the Almighty God.

In the same way, we comb our hair in front of the mirror, we take photos and find ourselves beautiful. In fact, it is God Almighty who gives us this beauty, but we do not think much about it. God Almighty gives them to us, so we can think of Him and comprehend His greatness.

Therefore, as the seers claim, this universe is not a description or a mystery, but a fact, which shows us God Almighty. And God, the Lord of the Worlds, has created it for a specific term and for a specific aim. We witness it for a very short time, and then we leave this realm. But its vastness and our smallness in front of it do not require us to disappear. On the contrary, it shows us the greatness of God Almighty.

1. E, L, R… This is a Book which We have revealed to you, that you might bring mankind out of darknesses into the light by permission of their Lord – to the path of the Exalted in Might, the Praiseworthy –
2. To God, whom belongs whatever is in the heavens and whatever is on the earth. And woe to the disbelievers from a severe punishment. (Koran/Chapter 14)

God equips the heavens and the earth with glorious arts and makes it an exhibition for us. But most people can't see them, and they pass by without realizing it. Yet in the verse, God Almighty says that the way to go out of the darkness to see the light is to see the magnificence of the art of God in the universe.

Therefore, seeing the gloriousness actually illuminates our inner self and fills us with beauty. At the same time, we establish our connection with God, and thus we understand the greatness of Him, the Owner of all Praises. But those who cannot see them are unfortunately trapped in their own narrow world, and in the end, they are addressed by the name of God, the Exalted in Might.

Running after certainty while describing the universe as a mystery:

"The sorcerers' struggle for assuredness is the most dramatic struggle there is. It's painful and costly. Many, many times it has actually cost sorcerers their lives,"[88] says don Juan. According to him, the most precious thing for the seers is to attain this certainty. Therefore, he warns Castaneda, who overindulges his doubts, like this once:

[88] CASTANEDA, The Power of Silence, Washington Square Press, The Ticket To Impeccability

- You feel that indulging in doubts and tribulations is the sign of a sensitive man. Well, the truth of the matter is that you're the farthest thing from being sensitive. [89]

It is one of the main goals of the seers in this world to be free from doubts and become a determined person. But according to them, this world is an unknown mystery. Then, is it possible both of them? In other words, can something that is pursued on an individual basis be the opposite of truth on a universal basis?

Of course it cannot be, because God is one and the truth is one. And from micro to macro, its reflection is unique. In other words, as planets move around the sun, electrons circulate around the atom. And just as God Almighty created man in need of certainty, there is certainty in the universe and there is no mystery.

Therefore, as the methods discovered by the seers do not come from God, they again make mistakes and their teachings contradict each other. And the truth is told to us by God Almighty only, who Himself is the Truth.

[89] CASTANEDA, Tales of Power, Washington Square Press, The Dreamer and The Dreamed

4- The Eagle's Intent

- Intent
- Abstract Cores
- Sorcery Stories
- Fate
- Rely Upon God
- Prayer

INTENT

Don Juan says, "In the universe there is an unmeasurable, indescribable force which sorcerers call intent, and that absolutely everything that exists in the entire cosmos is attached to intent by a connecting link."[90] And according to him, this force is guiding everything in the universe:

- What put you and me together was the intent of infinity. It is impossible to determine what this intent of infinity is, yet it is there, as palpable as you and I are. Sorcerers say that it is a tremor in the air. The advantage of sorcerers is to know that the tremor in the air exists, and to acquiesce to it without any further ado. For sorcerers, there's no pondering, wondering, or speculating. They know that all they have is the possibility of merging with the intent of infinity, and they just do it. [91]

"Intent" is the guiding force for us, and the seers build whole their lives on understanding this power. And don Juan says, "Without it, there could be no warrior's path, nor any warriors in search of knowledge."[92]

---

90 CASTANEDA, The Power of Silence, Washington Square Press, Introduction

91 CASTANEDA, The Active Side of Infinity, HarperCollins Publishers Inc., Who Was Juan Matus, Really?

92 CASTANEDA, The Power of Silence, Washington Square Press, The Knock of The Spirit: The Abstract

Intent as being God's guiding force:

12. Indeed, upon Us is guidance.
13. And indeed, to Us belongs after and before. (Koran/Chapter 92)

Don Juan says that intent is a force found in everything that exists and is actually the intent of the Eagle's emanations, which is the underlying fabric of the universe. And according to the seers, since the origin of these emanations is "Eagle", it is the intent of what the seers call Eagle. Therefore, don Juan says that "the power that governs the destinies of all living things" is called Eagle.[93]

In the previous chapters, we have explained that what the seers call Eagle is God Almighty Himself. So, what don Juan calls intent is the intent of God Almighty. And as can be seen from the above verse, God Almighty says, "Guidance belongs to Me".

Therefore, it is God Almighty Himself who guides us and tests us in this guidance. And the belonging of the intent to God reveals what the seers call the Eagle is the God Almighty Himself.

Intent as being God's command:

1. E, L, M.
2. The Byzantines have been defeated
3. In the nearest land. But they, after their defeat, will overcome
4. Within a few years. To God belongs the command before and after. And that day the believers will rejoice
5. With the help of God. He helps to whom He wills, and He is the Exalted in Might, the Most Merciful.
6. It is the promise of God. God does not fail in His promise, but most of the people do not know. (Koran/Chapter 30)

During World War II, the Americans, subjected to a sudden raid on Pearl Harbor by the Japanese, found themselves involved in a war.

The Japanese believe they will eliminate the Americans with this sudden attack, but God Himself also has a plan to make the Japanese

93 CASTANEDA, The Eagle's Gift, Washington Square Press, The Rule of the Nagual

pay the price of this unjust attack six months later, during the Midway War.

Under normal circumstances, it is almost impossible for the Americans to defeat the Japanese in this battle. Because the Japanese have more aircraft carriers, their planes are in better condition and have experienced pilots who have fought for years. But God Almighty brings such a moment that when the Japanese prepare to bomb Midway Island, they discover American aircraft carriers and decide to change the type of bombs. The American planes that came at that time were blasting Japanese aircraft carriers with bombs and fuel everywhere, like fireworks. Even with years of elaborate plans, the Americans could not have made this possible without the help of God's plan.

Although the Japanese are a very noble nation, they are governed by a bad administration at this time. And God Almighty sends the Americans who have knowledge from the Scriptures to restrain them. And like Pearl Harbor, He does a raid in such a way that eliminates the question of legitimacy. The Japanese fall into their own trap, and the Americans, subjected to this task, become the world's superpower. God Almighty leads them to a position they cannot even imagine.

The verses above also describe the defeat of the Eastern Roman Empire, which is the equivalent of the US at that time, to the Zoroastrian Sassanid Empire, and say that even if defeated, they will soon be victorious. As the verse says, although experiencing one of the most significant defeats in its history, Eastern Rome is recovering to become victorious in a few years. Just as Americans experienced in World War II, God Almighty helps them and makes the believers victorious after their defeat.

God Almighty explains this in the Koran 1400 years ago and says, "To God belongs the command before and after". In both cases, the main reason of this entire outcome is through the wants of God Almighty: what the seers call "intent".

The seers know of this, but modern-day people don't. For example, whatever documentary I have seen on Pearl Harbor or the Battle of Midway, there is no mention of this "intent" of God. They always talk about bombs, planes, and ships. We also hear of how the warning telegram about the attack arrived to Pearl Harbor late because of the storm. Yet God Almighty wanted that raid to occur that way. And whatever they did could not have stopped it.

ABSTRACT CORES

The seers recognize the "intent" through their own experiences as they do not have any knowledge coming from God. Based on this, they say that a recurrent pattern appears when intent indicates something meaningful:

- Sorcerers understood this abstract core to be a blueprint for events, or a recurrent pattern that appeared every time intent was giving an indication of something meaningful. Abstract cores, then, were blueprints of complete chains of events. [94]

The seers call these patterns "abstract cores". And don Juan says that these abstract cores are best noticed during the initiation of an apprentice.

The Manifestations of the Spirit:

Don Juan explains the manifestations of the Spirit[95] as follows:

- Every act performed by sorcerers, especially by the naguals, is either performed as a way to strengthen their link with intent or as a response triggered by the link itself. Sorcerers, and specifically

---

[94] CASTANEDA, The Power of Silence, Washington Square Press, The Manifestations Of The Spirit: The First Abstract Core

[95] Don Juan sometimes uses the word "Spirit" instead of the Eagle or its intent but again, what he refers is the Eagle and its intent.

the naguals, therefore has to be actively and permanently on the lookout for manifestations of the spirit. Such manifestations are called gestures of the spirit or, more simply, indications or omens.

- The spirit manifests itself to a sorcerer, especially to a nagual, at every turn. However, this is not the entire truth. The entire truth is that the spirit reveals itself to everyone with the same intensity and consistency, but only sorcerers, and naguals in particular, are attuned to such revelations. [96]

For example, when Nagual Elias found Julian, a hawk suddenly made him a dive and his horse was startled. After which, Elias immediately got off his horse and started to look around, because the hawk said to him, "Stop here!" Then he saw a young urban man wearing expensive clothes, very improbable to be seen in the cornfields. According to him, the falcon's flight and the man's appearance were the obvious manifestations of the spirit. And that's how he found his apprentice Julian.

<u>The Knock of the Spirit</u>:

According to the seers, the manifestation of the spirit is sometimes in the form of clearly laid out commands. For example, in Nagual Julian's story, Nagual Elias saw the manifestations of intent, but Julian was not aware of them. Finally, he suffered a major crisis and hit the shore, so that the "knock of the spirit" occurred and he had to surrender himself to Nagual Elias.

In the case of don Juan, after he was shot and bleeding from his chest, he met nagual Julian on his way. Before this happened, nagual Julian was thinking it was time to have an apprentice and miraculously, he found don Juan lying on the road.

Thus, the events that occur in the form of an explosion after the manifestations of the spirit are called the knock of the spirit. God Almighty uses them as a seal and creates a moment of breaking in existence and declares His judgment to everyone. Hence, those living

---

[96] CASTANEDA, The Power of Silence, Washington Square Press, The Impeccability Of The Nagual Elias

this moment realize that they are on the right path, so they undoubtedly continue on their way.

<u>Omens and Agreements</u>:

27. And recite to them the story of Adam's two sons, in truth, when they both offered a sacrifice to God, and it was accepted from one of them but was not accepted from the other. Said the latter, "I will surely kill you." Said the former, "Indeed, God only accepts from the righteous.
28. If you should raise your hand against me to kill me – I shall not raise my hand against you to kill you. Indeed, I fear God, Lord of the Worlds.
29. Indeed, I want you to obtain my sin and your sin so you will be among the companions of the fire. And that is the recompense of wrongdoers."
30. And his soul permitted to him the murder of his brother, so he killed him and became among the losers.
31. Then God sent a crow scratching in the ground to show him how to hide the body of his brother. He said, "O woe to me! Have I failed to be like this crow and hide the body of my brother?" And he became of the regretful. (Koran/Chapter 5)

In his book the Journey to Ixtlan, Castaneda frequently mentions the "omens" and the "agreements" that are the other manifestations of the spirit.

According to don Juan, the crows flying or cawing are one of these omens. And by looking at these crows on his trips, don Juan may decide whether to stay or where to go. Hence, crows are very exceptional animals for the seers.

In the above verses, the story of Prophet Adam's two sons is told. And the necessity of the burial of a dying man is taught by a crow, sent by God Almighty.

This is important because it is one of the most fundamental features of human beings to bury their dead in a grave, and this tradition begins with the sons of Prophet Adam. And the sending of a crow to teach it shows us that it is an exceptional animal. In the Koran, there is no other situation where an animal teaches a man something. And the seers have discovered this particular case in crows that they see them as a messenger.

> 40. If you do not aid him– God has already aided him when those who disbelieved had driven him out as one of two, when they were in the cave and he said to his companion, "Do not grieve; indeed God is with us." And God sent down His tranquility upon him and supported him with armies you did not see and made the word of those who disbelieved the lowest, while the word of God– that is the highest. And God is Exalted in Might and Wise. (Koran/Chapter 9)

Don Juan's "agreement" means something similar to a rolling stone in the middle of silence or a bush the wind blows to our feet; adding something extra to the current situation. Their function is to show us we are onto something right or wrong at that moment.

Sometimes, when we are about to tempt a sin, our child runs and sits on our lap, or when a negative thought passes through our minds, our head slams against the closet. There are dozens of things like that happening to us every day, which we see as coincidental happenings in daily bustles. But in fact, God Almighty is with us at all moments and gives us instant help.

However, the term don Juan uses for these agreements is the "world". And he tells Castaneda, "A man can get agreements from everything around him"[97]. But it is not actually the world that confirms him, but God Almighty. And Almighty God, the Owner of the "armies" of the heavens and the earth, guides us through them.

Since the seers know this truth in the universe, they pay close attention to these manifestations and arrange all their behaviors accordingly. And as those manifestations come from the Owner of everything, they always make the right decisions.

---

[97] CASTANEDA, Journey to Ixtlan, Washington Square Press, Reaffirmations From The World Around Us

Silent Knowledge:

About the manifestations that the seers follow, Castaneda wants to know if sorcerers could misinterpret an omen. Don Juan, on the other hand, tells Castaneda that his question is irrelevant, as most of the questions he asks, even if it seems to be quite logical:

- When a sorcerer interpreted an omen, he knew its exact meaning without having any notion of how he knew it. This was one of the bewildering effects of the connecting link with intent. Sorcerers had a sense of knowing things directly. They were sure of the strength and clarity of their connecting link.
- The feeling everyone knows as "intuition" is the activation of our link with intent. And since sorcerers deliberately pursue the understanding and strengthening of that link, it could be said that they intuit everything unerringly and accurately. Reading omens is commonplace for sorcerers - mistakes happen only when personal feelings intervene and cloud the sorcerers' connecting link with intent. Otherwise, their direct knowledge is totally accurate and functional. [98]

The seers call the direct information they receive from intent "silent knowledge". And, thanks to it, they directly know the designs of God, that they call the "arrangements of the abstract".

Don Juan says, "Silent knowledge is something that all of us have. Something that has complete mastery, complete knowledge of everything".[99] And as the link of the human beings with intent intensifies, this direct knowledge increases over time, and the seers begin to direct their lives accordingly.

However, not all people are equally open to it. "The more he clings to the world of reason, the more ephemeral intent becomes," don Juan says. And maintains that "Man gave up silent knowledge for the world

---

[98] CASTANEDA, The Power of Silence, Washington Square Press, The Impeccability Of The Nagual Elias

[99] CASTANEDA, The Power of Silence, Washington Square Press, The Place Of No Pity

of reason."[100] But according to him, it does not bring happiness to mankind; because moving away from silent knowledge means losing our connection with the "source of everything".

Don Juan likens this to the story of Adam's expulsion from heaven and thus says that sorcery means returning to its original place, Paradise.

- Sorcery is a journey of return. We return victorious to the spirit, having descended into hell. And from hell we bring trophies. Understanding is one of our trophies. [101]

Don Juan calls "impeccability" as behaving according to the way that the silent knowledge tells warriors. For example, in his meetings with Castaneda, he always leaves the course of events to the spirit in order to convey his teachings in the most appropriate way. And from the moment the spirit appears, the events proceed to a satisfactory end with great ease.

Therefore, it is necessary to do what silent knowledge says. However, don Juan says that most people don't want to understand that we can know without using words or thoughts:

- I am just considering how our rationality puts us between a rock and a hard place. Our tendency is to ponder, to question, to find out. And there is no way to do that from within the discipline of sorcery. Sorcery is the act of reaching the place of silent knowledge, and silent knowledge can't be reasoned out. It can only be experienced. [102]
- Sorcerers believe that when man became aware that he knew, and wanted to be conscious of what he knew, he lost sight of what he knew. This silent knowledge, which you cannot describe, is, of course, intent - the spirit, the abstract. Man's error was to want to

---

[100] CASTANEDA, The Power of Silence, Washington Square Press, The Place Of No Pity

[101] CASTANEDA, The Power of Silence, Washington Square Press, The Requirements Of Intent: Breaking The Mirror Of Self-Reflection

[102] CASTANEDA, The Power of Silence, Washington Square Press, Intending Appearances

> know it directly, the way he knew everyday life. The more he wanted, the more ephemeral it became. [103]

However, this does not mean that the seers do not use logical thinking. On the contrary, they see a combination of silent knowledge and reason in their lives, and they use the one which is applicable for that moment. Therefore, silent knowledge and reason do not actually reject each other, but they complement each other. And as a result of the Almighty God's creation of all things in this universe as opposed twins, silent knowledge and logical thinking take their place in human nature as opposing twins that complement each other. And the most sensible thing to do is to use both together.

---

[103] CASTANEDA, The Power of Silence, Washington Square Press, The Place Of No Pity

SORCERY STORIES

3. We tell you the best of stories in what We have revealed to you of this Koran. Indeed you were, before it, among the unaware. (Koran/ Chapter 12)

Don Juan tells Castaneda short stories about the seers of Antiquity as best he can. And the main reason for it, not to speak of people but "intent".

Through these stories, the seers notice the "abstract cores" embodied in the lives of the old seers and have the chance to understand the intent. Don Juan says, "Nothing can give sorcerers a better view of intent than examining stories of other sorcerers battling to understand this force." [104] As an example, he tells the story of Nagual Elias:

- The nagual Elias's story is another matter. Although it seems to be a story about people, it is really a story about intent. Intent creates edifices before us and invites us to enter them. This is the way sorcerers understand what is happening around them.
- As you can see, the story of the nagual Elias was more than merely an account of the sequential details that made up the event. Underneath all that was the edifice of intent. And the story was meant to give you an idea of what the naguals of the past were like,

104 CASTANEDA, The Power of Silence, Washington Square Press, The Place Of No Pity

so that you would recognize how they acted in order to adjust their thoughts and actions to the edifices of intent. [105]

With such nagual stories, don Juan tries to tell Castaneda what the intent is and asks him to reflect upon it. At first, it is incomprehensible and beyond Castaneda's knowledge; but as time passes, he begins to see it more clearly.

Stories of the Prophets:

111. There is certainly in messengers' stories a lesson for those of understanding. Never is this Koran a narration invented, but a confirmation of what was before it and a detailed explanation of all things. And a guidance and mercy for a people who believe. (Koran/ Chapter 12)

When the seers teach the intent to their apprentices, they make use of the stories which is the way of God's nature. And instead of prophets, they try to give lessons to their apprentices relating the life stories of the old naguals.

On the other hand, God Almighty sends each of His prophets to humanity with a different mission, and the life story of each prophet contains information to shed light on a different dimension of human existence. Then, God Almighty reveals the essence of these stories with His revelation:

163. Indeed, We have revealed to you, as We revealed to Noah and the prophets after him. And We revealed to Abraham, Ishmael, Isaac, Jacob, the Descendants, Jesus, Job, Jonah, Aaron, and Solomon, and to David We gave the Book of Psalms.
164. And We sent messengers about whom We have related their stories to you before and messengers about whom We have not related to you. And God spoke to Moses with direct speech.
165. We sent messengers as bringers of good tidings and warners so that mankind will have no argument against God after the messengers. And ever is God Exalted in Might and Wise. (Koran/Chapter 4)

---

[105] CASTANEDA, The Power of Silence, Washington Square Press, The Knock of The Spirit: The Abstract

The Koran includes the life stories of some 25 prophets, particularly Abraham, Jesus, Moses, Muhammad, Joseph, Jacob and Noah. And God Almighty documented the life stories of these prophets in the Koran and presented them for our benefit. In other words, the knowledge that dozens of prophets have lived and experienced for centuries is formulated in the Koran and set before humanity like a healer.

However, the stories of the prophets in the Koran, unlike those of don Juan's, are not merely a narrative; and when one reads them, it is as if they themselves are experiencing that event. Because Almighty God, who created them, transfers the emotions experienced by those prophets to the stories in the best way. So, one feels through these stories to be the prophet himself and knows how to behave when experiencing a similar situation. In other words, the things that are wanted to be taught are taught to people by "doing" it.

Moreover, along with these stories, a lot of moral and ontological information is given to people in a very intricate way without realizing it. Therefore, these stories are not only related to the intent of God Almighty; but when one reads them, also learns the intent.

"Intent" in the stories of the Prophets:

4. When Joseph said to his father, "O my father, indeed I have seen in a dream eleven stars and the sun and the moon; I saw them prostrating to me."
5. He said, "O my son, do not relate your dream to your brothers or they will contrive against you a plan. Indeed Satan, to man, is a manifest enemy.
6. And thus will your Lord choose you and teach you the interpretation of narratives and complete His favor upon you and upon the family of Jacob, as He completed it upon your fathers before, Abraham and Isaac. Indeed, your Lord is Knowing and Wise." (Koran/Chapter 12)

In the Koran, the part in which the intent is explained in the most obvious way is the story of Prophet Joseph. God Almighty refers to it as "the best of the stories". And with this story, God Almighty reveals a clear statement that the thing don Juan mentions as intent is actually His own guidance.

According to this, Prophet Jacob perceives Joseph's greatness when he is younger and inevitably shows more attention to him, but he is also afraid that his brothers will be jealous of him. And as a matter of fact, what Prophet Jacob feared, happens to him. Joseph's brothers' first intention is to kill him, but then, they decide to leave him at the bottom of a well.

19. There came a company of travelers; then they sent their water drawer, and he let down his bucket. He said, "Good news! Here is a boy." And they concealed him, taking him as merchandise; and God was Knowing of what they did.
20. And they sold him for a reduced price – a few cents – and they were, concerning him, of those content with little.
21. And the one from Egypt who bought him said to his wife, "Make his residence comfortable. Perhaps he will benefit us, or we will adopt him as a son." And thus, We established Joseph in the land that We might teach him the interpretation of narratives. And God is predominant over His affair, but most of the people do not know.
22. And when Joseph reached maturity, We gave him judgement and knowledge. And thus We reward the doers of good. (Koran/Chapter 12)

As can be seen, everyone has an intent here. Joseph's brothers' intent is different, the intent of those who sell him is different, and the intent of those who receive him is different... But also, there is the "intent" of God Almighty. And only God is predominant over His affairs.

In this way, while everyone desires something, they are actually serving Him as a servant of God Almighty; and Prophet Joseph is being sent through them, to the place where God Almighty will educate him. In other words, what Prophet Jacob feared, is actually turning into a reward for him.

Prophet Joseph stays here for a while and the lady of the house wants to amuse herself with him. But when he avoids this, she has him thrown into the dungeon, where he stays for years. But at last, God

Almighty takes him out of the dungeon and makes him a governor in Egypt. In other words, the dream, which frightened Prophet Jacob, has come reality when his brothers cheat Prophet Joseph. And in the end, he goes to Egypt as a governor.

And very interestingly, Prophet Joseph himself made an attempt to get out of prison and told a prisoner to be released, "Remember me with the King". But God Almighty takes Joseph out of jail, not when Joseph would like to, but when God Almighty chooses: so that the King may realize he is unjustly imprisoned and gives him a good position.

In other words, like the intentions of the other people mentioned above, Prophet Joseph's "intent" is not, in reality, good for him. Therefore, God Almighty does not carry it out in order to give him in the end, the reward he deserves.

99. And when they entered upon Joseph, he embraced his parents and said, "Enter Egypt, if God willing, safe and secure."
100. And he raised his parents upon the throne, and they bowed to him in prostration. And he said, "O my father, this is the explanation of my dream of before. My Lord has made it reality. And He was certainly good to me when He took me out of prison and brought you here from desert after Satan had induced estrangement between me and my brothers. Indeed, my Lord is Subtle in what He wills. Indeed, it is He who is the Knowing, the Wise.
101. My Lord, You have given me something of sovereignty and taught me of the interpretation of dreams. Creator of the heavens and earth, You are my protector in this world and the Hereafter. Cause me to die in submission to You and join me with the righteous." (Koran/Chapter 12)

As it is seen in the whole story, God Almighty guides Prophet Joseph according to His intention. And in the Koran, He formulates this guidance under His names, the Knowing and the Wise.

So what don Juan calls intent is actually a manifestation of His attributes, the Knowing and the Wise. Accordingly, God Almighty, who is the Knowing, has an awareness of the big picture better than anyone, and guides us to whatever is good for us. And with the attribute the Wise, He does this guidance in the wisest ways we couldn't even imagine. Therefore, the seers who submit to "intent" do nothing but submit to God, the Knowing and the Wise.

89. He said, "Do you know what you did with Joseph and his brother when you were ignorant?"
90. They said, "Are you indeed Joseph?" He said, "I am Joseph, and this is my brother. God has certainly favored us. Indeed, he who fears God and is patient, then indeed, God does not allow to be lost the reward of those who do good."
91. They said, "By God, certainly has God preferred you over us, and indeed, we have been sinners."
92. He said, "No blame will there be upon you today. God forgives you; and He is the most merciful of the merciful. (Koran/Chapter 12)

Lastly, if you should ask why God Almighty is performing this guidance to Prophet Joseph, God Almighty answers in the above verses: "God does not allow the reward of those who do good, to be lost". In other words, God Almighty does not give us this guidance for nothing, but because of our good intentions and deeds. And to those who want to take a step towards Him, He answers with ten steps and makes their way easier with His guidance.

FATE

- I am already given to the power that rules my fate.
- And I cling to nothing, so I will have nothing to defend. [106]

Don Juan says that the power that determines our fate is outside us, having nothing to do with our actions and our will. According to him, this power, which governs the fate of all living beings, is "Eagle".

As we said earlier, the Eagle that don Juan mentions in his narratives is actually God Almighty. And as we explained before, what the seers call intent was actually the intent of God Almighty. So, what don Juan calls our fate is, in fact, nothing more than the governance of our destinies by the intent of God Almighty.

34. Indeed, God alone has knowledge of the Hour of Resurrection. He sends down the rain and knows what is in the wombs. And no soul perceives what it will earn tomorrow, and no soul perceives in what land it will die. Indeed, God is the Knowing and the Acquainted. (Koran/Chapter 31)

In the famous Matrix movie, when the wise man Morpheus asks Neo, who is the main character of the film, "Do you believe in fate?", Neo replies: "No". And when the former asks, "Why not?", the latter says, "I don't like the idea that I am not in control of my life". But is the

[106] CASTANEDA, The Eagle's Gift, Washington Square Press, The Plumed Serpent

domination of our destinies by God Almighty really what Neo thinks?

First of all, there is no such thing as absolute freedom in the universe, and the living things exist within the boundaries that God Almighty sets to them.

On the other hand, Neo says, "I don't like the idea that I am not in control of my life", but there is no such thing. Because God Almighty gives us a "limited will" and offers us a choice. If there were no such choice, there would be no meaning for the test, heaven and hell.

But God Almighty also owns the "Total Will" and knows us better than us. He is the only one dominant over the things both witnessed and unseen. Therefore, He knows what's good for us and what's bad for us. Thus, the Koran says, "You have no other friend or helper than God."

According to the Koran, there is no static conception of fate; but there is a dynamic sense of destiny, which interacts with human beings at any moment, but ultimately the last word of God Almighty is determinant and dominant. And God Almighty's last word is given according to what we have done and it offers us what we deserve.

- Sorcerers, although they seem to make nothing else but decisions, make no decisions at all. I didn't decide to choose you, and I didn't decide that you would be the way you are. Since I couldn't choose to whom I would impart my knowledge, I had to accept whomever the spirit was offering me. And that person was you. [107]

That's how God Almighty leads us to His will. Since God Almighty encompasses everything with His knowledge, the decisions He makes for us are the right decisions, and obeying them is the smartest thing on earth.

In other words, what Neo feels disgusted about, and what Castaneda turns his nose up at the beginning of his apprenticeship, in fact, becomes the best choice for us, and the deeds, which the intent paves the way for a start, easily come to a conclusion. That's why don Juan uses the phrase "the top of the teachings" to submit to destiny. And indeed, the submission of the seers to their fate is incredible.

---

107 CASTANEDA, Magical Passes, HarperCollins Publishers Inc., Introduction

Don Juan also says, "The art of sorcerers is not really to choose, but to be subtle enough to acquiesce". And indeed, those who "submit" to the decisions that God Almighty sees fit for them, become the happiest people on earth.

It's not because they're stupid or they don't use their minds. On the contrary, they use their minds. Their minds are always working, they are sensitive to everything around them, and they try to feel the decisions that the "Total Mind" makes for them. And with the help of God, they usually achieve the most accurate results for themselves.

RELY UPON GOD

67. Jacob said, "O my sons, do not enter the city from one gate but enter from different gates. Actually I cannot avail you against the decree of God at all, the decision belongs only to God. Upon Him I have relied, and let those who would rely, rely upon Him."
68. And when they entered from where their father had ordered them, it did not avail them against God at all except a need within the soul of Jacob, which he satisfied. And indeed, he was a possessor of knowledge because of what We had taught him, but most of the people do not know. (Koran/Chapter 12)

Relying upon God means full trust in Him about our future. According to this, believers do their best on a subject they believe is good for them, and then trust in God and leave the final judgment to Him.

Similarly, Steve Jobs, who has made Apple the world's biggest brand, devotes one of the three stories he told to "rely upon something" in his famous Stanford speech and calls what he describes as "connecting the dots".

In his speech, Jobs talks about the typography class he took when he dropped out of university and says:

- None of this had even a hope of any practical application in my life. But ten years later, when we were designing the first Macintosh computer, it all came back to me. And we designed it all into the Mac… If I had never dropped out, I would have never dropped in on this calligraphy class, and personal computers might not have the wonderful typography that they do.

And he explains it this way:

- You can't connect the dots looking forward, you can only connect them looking backwards. So you have to trust that dots will somehow connect in your future. You have to trust in something; your gut, destiny, life, karma, whatever. Because believing that the dots will connect down the road, it will give you the confidence to follow your heart even when it leads you off the well-worn path. And that will make all the difference.

Of course, Steve Jobs -as a hippie- says, "Trust anything, no matter what", but God Almighty commands in His Koran, "Let the believers rely upon God." Because the decision belongs only to Him.

Therefore, God Almighty paves the way for us in advance by connecting the dots Steve Jobs is referring to. And although we do not notice them as they are being laid, we can see that they have connected in a meaningful way when we take a look back. And this is the "intent" that God Almighty sees fit for us.

Considering planning them, we cannot think of many of these points, but since God Almighty knows better what is good for us, He ranks them in accordance with our intentions. And that is why it is wise to trust in God Almighty and perform complete submission to His supernal mind. Although he does not do it consciously, that's also what Steve Jobs exactly does. And he says, "That will make all the difference".

On the other hand, don Juan explains how warriors behave in such situations as follows:

- The warriors do their utmost, and then, without any remorse or regrets, they relax and let the spirit decide the outcome. [108]

Of course, since don Juan knows this world better than Steve Jobs does, he makes a more appropriate explanation of the universal truth;

---

[108] CASTANEDA, The Power of Silence, Washington Square Press, The Ticket To Impeccability

and by doing his best, he expects the "spirit" to decide on his behalf. In other words, don Juan ultimately trusts God Almighty, which is named as "spirit" by the seers.

In his speech, Steve Jobs said, "Trust your gut, destiny, life, karma, whatever." So, Jobs has discovered that he has to trust something by human nature, and he does it, but he does not know what to trust. Trust one thing, and the rest will come.

Don Juan makes a more accurate explanation than Steve Jobs does, but unfortunately, since he does not have any knowledge coming from God, he also misses the target and cannot call God to be the one who makes the decision. However, although they cannot hit the bull's eye, God Almighty rewards them both for operating the laws of human nature.

Two other issues in Steve Jobs' speech:

Interestingly enough, Steve Jobs, who founded the most successful company in the world, talks about two more issues in his historic speech, which are both about the teachings of don Juan.

For example, in his second story, Jobs talks about listening to the heart no matter what:

- Don't let the noise of others' opinions drown your own inner voice. And most important, have the courage to follow your heart and intuition. [109]

And don Juan says the same things to Castaneda from the very first moments of his apprenticeship and asks him to take a "path with heart":

- I have said this to you countless times. One must always choose the path with heart in order to be at one's best, perhaps so one can always laugh. [110]

---

[109] See Chapter 7- Stopping The Self for more detailed explanation

[110] CASTANEDA, A Separate Reality, Washington Square Press, Chapter 4

The third story Steve Jobs mentions in his speech is about "taking death as an advisor", which is the fundamental teaching of the seers. And like don Juan, Steve Jobs considers himself dead:

- Remembering that you are going to die is the best way I know to avoid the trap of thinking you have something to lose. You are already naked. There is no reason not to follow your heart.

And with the courage he gets from his "death", he realizes his dreams one by one.

Therefore, these three basic teachings that Steve Jobs has followed as a guide are actually the teachings of don Juan. What do you say; Steve Jobs, a former hippie, was following don Juan? Or, do we all owe our iPhones to the seers?

Of course not; but because every success in the universe is by enforcing the rules that God Almighty has put in human nature, Steve Jobs makes them his guide and thus succeeds. And there is no distinction in these rules between worldly or otherworldly. Whatever it takes for success in this world, it is for spirituality. And even something that everyone uses, the latest wonder of technology, is based on the teachings of don Juan and ultimately on God Almighty.

"The mood of a warrior is not so far-fetched for yours or anybody's world. You need it in order to cut through all the guff"[111] says don Juan. And Steve Jobs is successful because he managed to cut through all the guff and did the things nobody dared to.

---

[111] CASTANEDA, Journey to Ixtlan, Washington Square Press, The Mood of a Warrior

PRAYER

60. Your Lord says, "Call upon Me; I will respond to you." Indeed, those who disdain My worship will enter Hell rendered contemptible. (Koran/Chapter 40)

The Almighty God, the owner of the "Total Intent", also gives man a particular intent, as a reflection of His own intent. And human beings, sometimes with actual effort, sometimes with direct prayer, offer their intent to God Almighty. And if God Almighty considers it appropriate, He accepts it and does as it should be done.

"If we encounter a fortuitous occurrence, we talk about it in terms of accident or coincidence, rather than in terms of our attention having beckoned the event,"[112] says don Juan. And in another dialogue, he explains this situation as "Our command can become the Eagle's command":

- The explanation is simplicity itself. You willed it, and thus you set a new intent, a new command. Then your command became the Eagle's command. This is one of the most extraordinary things that the new seers found out that our command can become the Eagle's command. [113]

---

[112] CASTANEDA, The Art of Dreaming, HarperCollins Publishers Inc., Dreaming Together

[113] CASTANEDA, The Fire From Within, Washington Square Press, The Position of the Assemblage Point

In fact, our strong intentions have the force of a prayer and are accepted and realized by God Almighty. However, don Juan does not accept the term "prayer" for this and says:

- The Eagle- the power that governs the destinies of all living things- reflects equally and at once all those living things. There is no way, therefore, for man to pray to the Eagle, to ask favors, or to hope for grace. The human part of the Eagle is too insignificant to move the whole. [114]

In other words, don Juan means that in the midst of all this greatness, what is the importance of our prayer and our worship? When there are so many living things, will God stand up and deal with trivial beings like us?

In fact, the seers do not accept prayer in the sense of worship because they do not accept the Eagle as God; otherwise, prayer is actually present in their own lives.

186. When My servants ask you concerning Me – indeed I am near. I respond to the invocation of the supplicant when he calls upon Me. So let them respond to Me and believe in Me that they may be rightly guided. (Koran/Chapter 2)

First of all, God is Free of need, who will not need the worlds. So, He does not need our prayer nor our worship. However, He creates man with a special purpose and defines prayer as the method of communication between man and Himself.

13. We have already created man and know what his soul whispers to him, and We are closer to him than his jugular vein. (Koran/Chapter 50)

The seers do not know God properly because they deny revelation; and because of that they do not recognize Him, they are positioning the human beings wrongly. However, God Almighty is closer to us than our jugular vein and gives immediate answers to our prayers. The greatness of God Almighty, or the abundance of creatures that He

---

[114] CASTANEDA, The Eagle's Gift, Washington Square Press, The Rule of the Nagual

dominates their fates, has nothing to do with it. He sends us here as His representative, and therefore He is particularly interested.

On the other hand, don Juan is trying to portray human being as an ordinary living being, but there is no creature other than man who can accomplish what the seers have accomplished. And in this context, they are well aware of the uniqueness of human beings. But when it comes to appreciating the Almighty God, who gave them all these abilities, move away from this. And whenever they deny God Almighty, they actually deny themselves.

Prayer of the Seers:

87. And mention Jonah, when he went off in anger and thought that We would not decree anything upon him. And he called out within the darkness "There is no deity except You; exalted are You. Indeed, I have been of the wrongdoers."
88. So We responded to him and saved him from the distress. And thus do We save the believers. (Koran/Chapter 21)

Even though don Juan says that the Eagle cannot be prayed, the seers sometimes ask for something from the Spirit; in other words, from the God they call the Eagle. Hence, they actually pray, but they don't call it prayer.

For example, don Juan wants Castaneda to express his intentions on a matter and to do this in the form of loud exclamations. Initially, Castaneda is surprised by this, but don Juan wants him to speak aloud, whatever his intention is, and he names it "calling intent". [115]

According to the seers, the most indispensable part of calling intent is a "total concentration" on what is intended. And even though don Juan abandoned the rituals, the old seers, including his benefactor, used various rituals to achieve this concentration. But even if they worked, don Juan says, they had side effects and made the mind obsessed.

However, since the Almighty God is "closer to man than his jugular vein", there is no such thing as ritual in Islam. "Call upon Me; I will

115 CASTANEDA, The Power of Silence, Washington Square Press, Intending Appearances

respond to you," says our Lord. Knowing this and behaving accordingly, there is no need to resort to artificial means with such side effects.

7. Those who believe and do righteous deeds – We will surely remove from them their misdeeds and will surely reward them according to the best of what they used to do. (Koran/Chapter 29)

According to don Juan, "sincerity" is another requirement in calling intent. In one of his dialogues, he tells Castaneda, "You were sincere; you really intended to voice your request. To be sincere is all that was required." [116] So, without sincerity, there is no intent.

In terms of Islam, sincerity means everything. And very interestingly, in the Koran, God Almighty predicates righteous deeds, that is sincere behaviors specific to God, upon worship as an inevitable condition to go to Heaven. And in this way, impure behaviors, even worship, are not accepted. Therefore, Prophet Muhammad proclaims, "Intention is superior to the deeds."

As a result, although don Juan opposes it, their call for intent is actually a prayer, and God Almighty gives them what they want, based on their intention. In fact, they do not accept God's divinity; but whenever they need, they only ask of God Almighty.

---

[116] CASTANEDA, The Art of Dreaming, HarperCollins Publishers Inc., The Third Gate of Dreaming

5- Inorganic Beings

- Inorganic Beings
- Allies
- Satan and Man
- Satan and Angels
- Predator
- Prophet Solomon and Demons

INORGANIC BEINGS

36. Exalted is He who created all pairs– from what the earth grows and from themselves and from that which they do not know. (Koran/ Chapter 36)

The shamans of ancient Mexico believed that everything in the universe is composed of dual forces, which are opposite but at the same time complementary. And according to them, human beings are subjected to that duality in every aspect of their lives. [117]

The arguments discovered by the science of matter, which is the "opposite twin" of the science of seers, also bolster this polar structure. Matter-antimatter, positive-negative charges, etc., are always the outcomes of this binary structure.

And so is our daily life. We were brought into being in two opposite sexes - man and woman, there is hot versus cold or high versus low, etc. We can give numerous examples for this fact.

So, everything in this universe coexists with their opposite and gain meaning with their opposite twins. God Almighty calls this situation "creating in pairs", and as the Owner of all things, manifests in His Holy Koran, "And of all things We created two counterparts."

---

[117] CASTANEDA, Magical Passes, HarperCollins Publishers Inc., The Second Group: The Recapitulation

The discovery of inorganic beings by the seers of Antiquity:

47. And the heaven We constructed with strength, and indeed, We are its expander.
48. And the earth We have spread out, and excellent is the preparer.
49. And of all things We created two counterparts; perhaps you take advice. (Koran/Chapter 51)

Don Juan says that another important discovery by the seers of Antiquity who discovered this twin creation in the universe is that they found out the existence of other realms that are opposing, but also complementary to our world.

Thus, in these realms "inorganic beings" which are the opposite of us, but at the same time complementary for us, are reportedly living. And essentially the whole universe is crammed to the brim with worlds of awareness, organic and inorganic.[118] Even though we don't notice, they are always around us, but since our attention is hooked on this world, we tend to ignore this, even if we recognize them from time to time.

- The old shamans discovered that the entire universe is composed of twin forces. Forces that are at the same time opposed and complementary to each other. It is inescapable that our world is a twin world. Its opposite and complementary world is one populated by beings that have awareness, but not an organism. For this reason, the old shamans called them inorganic beings.
- This world is here, where you and I are sitting. I told you that it's our twin world, so it's intimately related to us. The sorcerers of ancient Mexico didn't think like you do in terms of space and time. They thought exclusively in terms of awareness. Two types of awareness coexist without ever impinging on each other, because each type is entirely different from the other. The old shamans faced this problem of coexistence without concerning themselves with time and space. They reasoned that the degree of awareness of organic beings and the degree of awareness of inorganic beings were so different that both could coexist with the most minimal interference.

---

118 CASTANEDA, The Active Side of Infinity, HarperCollins Publishers Inc., Inorganic Awareness

- We certainly can perceive those inorganic beings. Sorcerers do it at will. Average people do it, but they don't realize that they're doing it because they are not conscious of the existence of a twin world. When they think of a twin world, they enter into all kinds of mental masturbation, but it has never occurred to them that their fantasies have their origin in a subliminal knowledge that all of us have: that we are not alone. [119]

Don Juan also remarks that the inorganic beings who populate our twin world, were considered by the sorcerers of his lineage, to be "our cousins." According to him, these two "species" are the children of two sisters who live next door to each other. They are exactly alike, although they look different. [120]

Inorganic beings as being "jinn" in fact:

130. "O company of jinn and mankind, did there not come to you messengers from among you, relating to you My verses and warning you of the meeting of this Day of yours?" They said, "We bear witness against ourselves." The worldly life had deluded them, and they beared witness against themselves that they were disbelievers. (Koran/Chapter 6)

About the discovery of inorganic beings, don Juan says, "If we take as our clue what seers see, life is indeed extraordinary."[121] Of course, this may be the case for Castaneda, but the seers actually discover the "jinn" created by the Almighty God, as the polar twin of mankind in this system of realms. So, there's nothing unusual about it, and God Almighty already informs us about them in the Koran.

Koran calls the inorganic beings "jinn" and places them as the "equivalent" of human beings. Therefore, jinns are the equivalent of

---

[119] CASTANEDA, The Active Side of Infinity, HarperCollins Publishers Inc., Inorganic Awareness

[120] CASTANEDA, The Active Side of Infinity, HarperCollins Publishers Inc., Inorganic Awareness

[121] CASTANEDA, The Fire From Within, Washington Square Press, Inorganic Beings

human beings as species in this system of realms; not animals, not monkeys, or whatever.

God Almighty gives elaborate information about them in the Koran and uses jinns and human beings in many verses together, since He places them in a position of the polar twin and "proof" of man.

Jinn as being the servants of God:

56. I did not create the jinn and mankind except to worship Me. (Koran/Chapter 51)

In one case, Castaneda asks don Juan about the reason for the existence of inorganic beings. Don Juan answers this question as follows:

- This is like asking me what we men do in the world. I really don't know. We are here, that's all. And the allies are here like us; and maybe they have been here before us. [122]

Don Juan does not know, "What do allies and men do in this world?" But God Almighty commands in His Koran, "I did not create the jinn and mankind except to worship Me". Therefore, God Almighty does not create jinn and mankind in vain and sends both of them to recognize and know Him in this system of realms.

29. We once directed to you a few of the jinn, listening to the Koran. And when they attended it, they said, "Listen quietly." And when it was concluded, they went back to their people as warners.
30. They said, "O our people, indeed we have heard a Book revealed after Moses confirming what was before it which guides to the truth and to a straight path.
31. O our people, respond to the Caller of God and believe in him; He will forgive for you your sins and protect you from a painful punishment.
32. But he who does not respond to the Caller of God will not cause failure to Him upon earth, and he will not have besides Him any friends. Those are in manifest aberration." (Koran/Chapter 46)

---

122 CASTANEDA, A Separate Reality, Washington Square Press, Chapter 2

In the Koran, God Almighty declares that a group of jinn, who are His own servants, listen to the Koran and return to their communities as warners. Hence, God Almighty sends messengers to the jinn who are polar twins of men in the same manner that He commissions messengers to warn people to return to His righteous path. And He says they will be put on trial in the same way. In other words, no one will be exempt from the final judgment in this system of realms.

1. Say, "It has been revealed to me that a group of the jinn listened and said, 'Indeed, we have heard an amazing Koran.'
2. 'It guides to the right course, and we have believed in it. And we will never associate with our Lord anyone.' (Koran/Chapter 72)

By the Koran He has sent down, God Almighty addresses Himself not only to the people of this universe, but also to the inorganic beings that the seers have discovered through thousands of years of efforts and inform them of the truth.

The seers associate with these inorganic beings created and guided by God Almighty, learn much from them and build their knowledge on what they have learned. In other words, like naughty cousins, they come together and keep messing around, but God Almighty is aware of them all and does not actually create them for that purpose.

Jinn as being the proof of man:

When Castaneda first hears of the inorganic beings from don Juan, he immediately opposes it and makes a long argument about the definition of life and being alive. He talks about reproduction, metabolism, and growth, the processes that distinguish live organisms from inanimate things. But don Juan says, "You're drawing from the organic, but that's only one instance. You shouldn't draw all you have to say from one category alone" and adds:

- For seers, to be alive means to be aware. For the average man, to be aware means to be an organism. This is where seers are different.[123]

[123] CASTANEDA, The Fire From Within, Washington Square Press, Inorganic Beings

Thus, the inorganic beings also lead a life, but in broad terms, they don't have a body we are aware of. Or more precisely, their bodies, like ours, are formed according to the conditions of their realms.

Then Castaneda asks if those inorganic beings have life like we have life? Don Juan answers him with these words:

- If you think that life is to be aware, then they do have life. I suppose it would be accurate to say that if life can be measured by the intensity, the sharpness, the duration of that awareness, I can sincerely say that they are more alive than you and I. [124]

Therefore, what is essential in this universe is "life", and our bodies are carriers of it. But, as the objection made by Castaneda, the greatest dilemma of the science of matter is that it does not treat man as a "living being".

The science of matter examines our bodies and does not go further. Awareness is none of its business. However, these bodies are carriers of us, and we are being sent to this universe with these body capsules. Just as jinn are sent to their own universes with other types of capsules. And if we existed in the realm of jinn, then we would have a suitable body there, but "we" would still be the same "we".

Therefore, God Almighty creates mankind and jinn as two counterparts with different kind of bodies, so that it is possibly understood that life is the main thing and that the bodies are the means of this life.

Yet the science of matter denies this, the seers go to the other end because they discover the life in the other realms, and come to the point that this universe does not matter. However, both of these sciences do not know that, God Almighty creates them as "two counterparts in different bodies" and thus makes them cross-check each other.

Consequently, the jinns are the opposite twins of man in this system of realms, and as living individuals, they make the "existential" proof of

---

124 CASTANEDA, The Active Side of Infinity, HarperCollins Publishers Inc., Inorganic Awareness

mankind. At this point, the universal dual creation principle of God Almighty transcends the science of matter. And modern science, which only examines the polarity in matter, falls short over against life being polar.

And of course, the universal polarity law set by God Almighty is not limited to this, and further on, we will see together the point where the science of the seers, the polar twin of the science of matter, also remains.

ALLIES

50. Mention when We said to the angels, "Prostrate to Adam," and they prostrated, except for Iblees. He was of the jinn and departed from the command of his Lord. Then will you take him and his descendants as allies other than Me while they are enemies to you? Wretched it is for the wrongdoers as an exchange.
51. I did not make them witness to the creation of the heavens and the earth or to the creation of themselves, and I would not have taken the misguiders as assistants. (Koran/Chapter 18)

For the seers, jinns which they call inorganic beings, are of great importance and occupy a large part in Castaneda's books. The seers learn almost all they know through these inorganic beings and do their training using them. Because of these benefits, the seers call them "allies", as also the Koran says.

Earlier in his education, don Juan gives Castaneda "power plants" and, with the help of these herbs, gets him to connect with inorganic beings. Later, with the help of these allies, he teaches him to "see" and occasionally uses them to scare Castaneda into a tight corner.

Don Juan labels the relationship of the seers with inorganic beings as "a fair exchange of energy", and thus establishes a relationship for the interests of both species.[125] In other words, inorganic beings become

---

[125] CASTANEDA, The Fire From Within, Washington Square Press, Inorganic Beings

the partners of the seers in this system of realms, and therefore they call them "allies", just as God Almighty proclaims in the Koran.

<u>Relations with allies as being dangerous</u>:

128. At that Day He gathers them together and says, "O company of jinn, you have misled many of mankind." And their allies among mankind say, "Our Lord, some of us made use of others, and we have now reached our term which You appointed for us." He says, "The Fire is your residence, wherein you will abide eternally, except for what God wills. Indeed, your Lord is Wise and Knowing." (Koran/Chapter 6)

Don Juan announces that the relationship with inorganic beings is the legacy of the old seers. And he does not really like it because he asserts that they're stuck up in this relationship and can't get over it.

He is of the opinion that the old seers were very impressed by the dedication of inorganic beings to them, and therefore each of them possessed hordes of "allies". They could get these allies to do whatever they wished, but there was a price for this, and they made the old seers addicted to them. Accordingly, as soon as the seers contacted them, they became a potential prey for them, and as mentioned in the above verse, some jinns made use of their human allies, who tried to use them and misled them.

Therefore, don Juan warns Castaneda many times during his training against allies, tells him that he is now in the most dangerous part of the sorcerers' knowledge and wants him to be careful.[126]

However, don Juan still does not give up his education with allies. Because the new seers, although they deny most of what the ancients did, are from their lineage and continue to take the useful parts of their techniques.

"I refused that part of the sorcerers' knowledge, because I don't want to be at the mercy of any entity" says don Juan and lets Castaneda get

---

126 CASTANEDA, The Art of Dreaming, HarperCollins Publishers Inc., The Second Gate of Dreaming

connected with them just as much as necessary.[127] That's because the new seers have defined their main purpose as "freedom" and their relationship with inorganic beings is no longer a goal, but a means for it.

Relation with allies as being prohibited:

6. Indeed there were men from mankind who sought refuge in men from the jinn, but they only increased them in burden.
7. And they had thought, as you thought, that God would never resurrect anyone. (Koran/Chapter 72)

Don Juan declares that both jinn and mankind are trying to take advantage of each other. And God Almighty knows that this will be the case and proclaims, "Do not do this", because He does not create jinn and mankind for this purpose. He bestows this potential upon them as a test, yet He warns saying, "Don't come near that". But human beings are always tempted to what is prohibited, and as a result, it is he who has come out a loser in this relationship.

"Every sorcerer has to face it,"[128] says don Juan, despite the fact that God Almighty has banned it and all the dangers he has experienced. That's because the seers owe their knowledge to this relationship and it is not possible for a new seer to gain experience without this relationship.

Don Juan sees this communication only as an expansion of human perception and the use of our hidden talents. According to him, there is no evil, no devil, but only perception in this. But at the last point, we see that all the great information they have gained is a trouble for them and they end up denying God. And God Almighty asks us in the Koran, "Will you leave Me and make them allies for yourselves?"

---

[127] CASTANEDA, The Art of Dreaming, HarperCollins Publishers Inc., The Second Gate of Dreaming

[128] CASTANEDA, The Art of Dreaming, HarperCollins Publishers Inc., The Second Gate of Dreaming

<u>God Almighty as being the true ally</u>:

22. You can not cause failure to God upon the earth or in the heaven. And you have not other than God any ally or any helper. (Koran/ Chapter 29)

The seers acknowledge them as allies since they take advantage of inorganic beings, and then they disacknowledge their faithful ally, God Almighty. Thus, inorganic beings are actually their false allies that they replace with their true ally, God Almighty.

According to the Koran, man has neither an ally nor a helper other than God. That is why the dervishes in Islamic Sufism refer to God Almighty as "Friend" and see Him as their loyal ally.

In contrast, don Juan says, "I am alone in a hostile universe, and I have learned to say: So be it!"[129] When man drifts away from God Almighty in this way, he remains all alone in the whole universe and sees it as hostile.

However, no matter where you look in the universe, all that you see are the masterpieces of God Almighty. God gives us our sustenance, our water, our oxygen, our minds, our spouses, and our friends. He is with us at every moment, fulfills all our needs, and answers us when we pray... Therefore, there is not a hostile universe around us but a real Friend supporting us. But just like don Juan, those who lose the true "Ally" are also being deprived of the friendship of the universe.

On the other hand, the remedy don Juan found out is to learn to say, "So be it!" He does not care about anything, and whenever something happens to him, he shrugs it off. So, does it work? Yes, partially it does, but it's not innate or inborn. He is trying to stand alone in a vast "hostile universe" instead of leaning on the Owner of everything and saying, "Sufficient for us is God, and He is the best Disposer of affairs."[130]

---

[129] CASTANEDA, The Art of Dreaming, HarperCollins Publishers Inc., The World of Inorganic Beings

[130] Koran/Chapter 3, verse 173

SATAN AND MAN

The story of Prophet Adam described in the Koran is a very important one. And in this parable, God Almighty distributes their existential duties to different types of beings He created in this system of worlds, and introduces them to us.

61. Mention when We said to the angels, "Prostrate to Adam," and they prostrated, except for Iblees. He said, "Should I prostrate to one You created from clay?"
62. And said, "Do You see this one whom You have honoured above me? If You delay me until the Day of Resurrection, I will surely bring his descendants under my sway, except for a few."
63. God said, "Go, for whoever of them follows you, indeed Hell will be the recompense of you - an ample recompense." (Koran/Chapter 17)

When God Almighty creates man out of clay and breathes into him from His soul, He commands the angels and Iblees to prostrate to Adam. However, the Iblees, full of pride and arrogance, refutes to be with those who prostrate. Like the Darwinists of our time, he stumbles upon the material side of human being and rebels against his Lord saying, "Should I prostrate to one You created from clay?" And God Almighty commissions him and some of the jinn who follows him to make disobedience attractive to men on earth and mislead them all until the Day of Resurrection.

According to the Koran, demons are descended from Iblees, originally a jinn,[131] and they are human beings' blatant enemies. As a matter of fact, after the event of refusal, God Almighty begins to call the Iblees as "Satan" and warns Prophet Adam against him.

God Almighty then put Prophet Adam in heaven, but Satan tricks him into rebelling against God. Then the heaven throws Prophet Adam out, as if the stomach throws out a bad meal: "You're not pure enough for the place. Go and clean yourself." And upon this, Prophet Adam is being sent to this world, a place of refinement and purgation.

<u>Desire for Immortality</u>:

19. "O Adam, dwell, you and your wife, in Paradise and eat from wherever you will but do not approach this tree, lest you be among the wrongdoers."
20. But Satan whispered to them to make apparent to them that which was concealed from them of their private parts. He said, "Your Lord did not forbid you this tree except that you become angels or become of the immortal."
21. And he swore to them, "Indeed, I am to you from among the sincere advisors."
22. So he made them fall, through deception. And when they tasted of the tree, their private parts became apparent to them, and they began to fasten together over themselves from the leaves of Paradise. And their Lord called to them, "Did I not forbid you from that tree and tell you that Satan is to you a clear enemy?"
23. They said, "Our Lord, we have wronged ourselves, and if You do not forgive us and have mercy upon us, we will surely be among the losers."
24. God said, "Descend, being to one another enemies. And for you on the earth is a place of settlement and enjoyment for a time."
25. He said, "Therein you will live, and therein you will die, and from it you will be brought forth." (Koran/Chapter 7)

[131] Koran/Chapter 18, verse 50

The way Satan deceives Prophet Adam in heaven is very interesting. God Almighty shows Adam a tree as a test and says, "Dwell in Paradise and eat from wherever you will but do not approach this tree, lest you be among the wrongdoers." But Satan uses the desire for immortality of them and makes them fall through the deception, saying: "Your Lord did not forbid you this tree except that you become angels or become of the immortal."

In other words, Prophet Adam opposes the commandment of God with the desire for immortality, which God Almighty put in his nature. But God Almighty says to him, "You can become immortal only by following Me, not by going against My commandment," and expels him from the heaven and sends him down to this world to purify.

And this short story also summarizes the whole story of the seers. Their real purpose is to become immortal, but like Prophet Adam, they are trying to do so against the rules set by God. All the things they do are for this purpose, but they are trying to be eternal in spite of God, using the opportunities that God has given to them.

Therefore, the story of Prophet Adam described in the Koran is not a mythological story, but a fundamental one that sheds light on one aspect of human existence with every word. And with this story, God Almighty both teaches us the existential duties of the "species" He created in this universe, and informs us of the most basic "genetic codes" of human nature.

SATAN AND ANGELS

In this system of realms, God Almighty creates angels as the opposite twins of devils, just as He creates jinns as the opposite twins of humans, and brings them to the stage of existence as another important figure of this universe.

In other words, while the jinns are existentially the opposite twins of mankind, their mischievous mob is given a special name and is called the devil, and they are the opposite twins of the angels from the standpoint of good and evil.

According to the Koran, angels are the manifestations of the first name of God Almighty, the Most Compassionate. For this reason, the angels are called "the servants of the Most Compassionate" in the Koran and are used many times together with this name of God.

The name of Most Compassionate means "treating with compassion" and constitutes the first feature of God's relationship with creatures. Therefore, in angels, unlike devils, the manifestation of "compassion" is dominant.

63. The servants of the Most Compassionate are those who walk upon the earth in humility, and when the ignorant address them, they say, "Peace".
64. And those who spend the night to their Lord prostrating and standing in prayer.

65. And those who say, "Our Lord, avert from us the punishment of Hell. Indeed, its punishment is ever adhering;
66. Indeed, it is evil as a settlement and residence."
67. And those who, when they spend, are neither wasteful nor stingy, but choose a middle course between that.
68. And those who do not invoke with God another deity or kill the soul which God has forbidden to be killed, except by right, and do not commit adultery. And whoever should do that will meet a penalty.
69. Multiplied for him is the punishment on the Day of Resurrection, and he will abide therein humiliated –
70. Except for those who repent, believe and do righteous work. For them God will replace their evil deeds with good. And ever is God Forgiving and Merciful.
71. And he who repents and does righteousness does indeed turn to God with accepted repentance.
72. And those who do not testify to falsehood, and when they pass near ill speech, they pass by with dignity.
73. And those who, when reminded of the verses of their Lord, do not fall upon them deaf and blind.
74. And those who say, "Our Lord, grant us happiness from our wives and children and make us a leader for the righteous."
75. Those will be awarded the chamber for what they patiently endured, and they will be received therein with greetings and peace,
76. Abiding eternally therein. Good is the settlement and residence.
77. Say, "What would my Lord care for you if not for your supplication? You have denied and there will be the punishment." (Koran/Chapter 25)

Just like the angels, God Almighty calls the prototype human He proposed to us in the Koran as "the servants of the Most Compassionate". And that actually means a person who has managed to "angelize" himself.

What is interesting is that not any similar expressions are used for each of about one hundred names of the Almighty God in the Koran, and the term "servant of the Most Compassionate" is used concerning the point where man is meant to reach. In other words, the devotees who manage to distance themselves from Satan and transform themselves into angels are blessed with the Love of God Almighty, and they become prepared to be accepted into the heaven.

> 30. When your Lord said to the angels, "Indeed, I will make upon the earth a successor." They said, "Will You place upon it one who causes corruption therein and sheds blood, while we declare Your praise and sanctify You?" He said, "Indeed, I know that which you do not know." (Koran/Chapter 2)

Of course, there is an important anecdote here: it is optional for human beings to become angelized, whereas this is compulsory for the angels. So human beings have the freedom to choose both sides, as opposed to the angels, and this is one of the reasons why God Almighty made the angels prostrate before Adam.

And when they ask the Almighty, "Will You place upon it one who causes corruption therein and sheds blood, while we declare Your praise and sanctify You?"; He replies, "Indeed, I know that which you do not know."

In other words, God Almighty means that there will be people who will unjustly shed blood, as you have stated. However, there will be also my servants standing out and going back to heaven which they had to leave since they were not sufficiently refined and innocent. So, God Almighty stands with human beings and does not give up hope of them. And He wants them to be here the servants of the Most Compassionate.

The use of the terms Angel and Devil in Koran in equal numbers:

> 64. We have revealed to you the Book only to make clear to them that wherein they have differed and as guidance and mercy for a people who believe. (Koran/ Chapter 16)

In the mention of sorcery, we have already said that the words "sorcery" and "trouble" are used in equal numbers in the Koran. Here again, the Almighty God, who created the devils and the angels as opposing mates, uses both of them 88 times in the Koran. And by using them in equal numbers, He emphasizes the relationship between the two and also shows that the things He says in the Koran are truths.

Of course, you might say that this is a coincidence. However, we can give you an example that in the Koran, the words "World" and "Hereafter" are both mentioned 115 times, "mother" and "father" both 117 times, and the word "day" is used 365 times.

Hence, these are very conscious usages, and in this way, God Almighty has imprinted its seal on every point of the Koran. And in the Koran, there are dozens of words like this, as well as the coding of the number 19 mentioned earlier. Thanks to all these codings, God Almighty has provided objective and logical evidence to the "men of reason" of our age. According to this: [132]

- The word "Day" is mentioned 365 times in the Koran.
- The word "Days" is 30 times.
- The word "Moon" is 12 times.
- The "World" and the "Hereafter" are both 115 times.
- "That day" and "The day of Resurrection" are both 70 times.
- "Final destination" and "Forever" are both 28 times.
- "Mother" and "Father" are both 117 times.
- The "Angels" and the "Devil" are both 88 times.
- "Showing mercy" and "The Most Merciful" are both 114 times. "The Most Compassionate" 57 times. (114/2)
- "Guidance" and "Mercy" are both 79 times.
- "People" and the "Messengers" are both 368 times.
- "Adam" and "Jesus" are both 25 times.
- "Say" and "They said" are both 332 times.
- "Language" and "Advise" are both 25 times.
- "A few" and "Appreciate" are both 75 times.
- "Annoyance" and "Rejoice" are both 13 times.

Caner Taslaman, The Quran: Unchallengeable Miracle, Nettleberry Publications. 2006, p. 271-332

- "Benefit" and "Corruption" are both 50 times.
- "Sexual crime", "Transgression" and "Wrath" are both 24 times, and "Sin" is 48 times. (2x24)
- "Recompense" is 117 times and "Forgive" is 234 times. (2x117)
- "Sorcery" and "Trouble" are both 60 times.
- "Hope" and "Fear" are both 8 times.
- "Hot" and "Cold" are both 4 times.
- "Harm" and "Benefit" are both 9 times.
- "Act" and "Response" are both 108 times.
- "Poor" is 13 times and "Rich" is 26 times. (2x13)
- "Justice" and "Injustice" are both 15 times.
- "Tree" and "Plant" are both 26 times.
- "Sow", "Grow" and "Fruit" are both 14 times.
- "Sun" and "Light" are both 33 times.
- And so on…

PREDATOR

21. O you who have believed, do not follow the footsteps of Satan. And whoever follows the footsteps of Satan – indeed, he enjoins immorality and wrongdoing. And if not for the favor of God upon you and His mercy, not one of you would have been pure, ever, but God purifies whom He wills, and God is Hearing and Knowing. (Koran/Chapter 24)

In one of his narratives, don Juan tells Castaneda, "We have a predator that came from the depths of the cosmos and took over the rule of our lives". And he adds that this predator is an inorganic being.

- We have a predator that came from the depths of the cosmos and took over the rule of our lives. Human beings are its prisoners. The predator is our lord and master. It has rendered us docile, helpless. If we want to protest, it suppresses our protest. If we want to act independently, it demands that we don't do so. [133]
- What I'm saying is that what we have against us is not a simple predator. It is very smart, and organized. It follows a methodical system to render us useless. Man, the magical being that he is destined to be, is no longer magical. He's an average piece of meat. There are no more dreams for man but the dreams of an animal who

---

133 CASTANEDA, The Active Side of Infinity, HarperCollins Publishers Inc., Mud Shadows

> is being raised to become a piece of meat: trite, conventional, imbecilic. [134]

The shamans of ancient Mexico called this the topic of topics. For them, it was an energetic fact, and down in the depths of every human being, there was an ancestral, visceral knowledge about the predators' existence.

"It is, of course, an inorganic being", says don Juan about this predator and refers to it as an essential part of the universe. On the other hand, Castaneda says he has made extensive anthropological inquiries on predators, but couldn't find any references to them anywhere.[135]

However, in the Koran, God Almighty calls them the "devil" and, as we have already mentioned, says that some of the jinns, the seers call inorganic beings, turn into devils that haunt and seduce human beings. The seers label these special inorganic beings, which the Koran calls the devil, as "predator".

<u>Time allocation to Satan</u>:

14. Satan said, "Reprieve me until the Day they are resurrected."
15. Said, "Indeed, you are of those reprieved."
16. Satan said, "Because You have put me in error, I will surely sit in wait for them on Your straight path.
17. Then I will come to them from before them and from behind them and on their right and on their left, and You will not find most of them grateful."
18. God said, "Depart from it, reproached and expelled. Whoever follows you among them – I will surely fill Hell with you, all together." (Koran/Chapter 7)

"They are the means by which the universe tests us", says don Juan about the predators[136]. And in the Koran, Satan, the father of the

[134] CASTANEDA, The Active Side of Infinity, HarperCollins Publishers Inc., Mud Shadows

[135] CASTANEDA, The Active Side of Infinity, HarperCollins Publishers Inc., Mud Shadows

[136] CASTANEDA, The Active Side of Infinity, HarperCollins Publishers Inc., Mud Shadows

devils, asks the Almighty to grant him time until the Day of Judgment and says, "I will mislead them all, except your devoted servants."[137]

God Almighty, who established the system of the worlds and distributed their roles to everyone in this system, replies: "This is the truth, and I only say the truth". Therefore, God Almighty, as don Juan says, creates devils as testing means of humans, and through them, while making some people stray away from the righteous path, increases the maturity of others.

But there is a very important nuance between what don Juan says and what the Koran says. Even the Satan in the Koran says, "You have put me in error", don Juan says when mentioning the predators, "They are the means by which the universe tests us."

In other words, don Juan knows the wisdom of existence from the universe, as well as the scientists of matter who invent some self-existent physics rules. But in Koran, even Satan himself says that God Almighty has led him astray. Therefore, the depravement and unruliness of the predators and their haunting on human beings are all happening in the knowledge of God Almighty. And don Juan does nothing but witness these "means to test" who were created by Him.

The predator as being the enemy and his whispering into our ears:

> 53. Tell My servants to say that which is best. Indeed, Satan induces dissension among them. Indeed Satan is ever, to mankind, a clear enemy. (Koran/Chapter 17)

"The predators are monstrous and implacable challengers and not benevolent to us", says don Juan. In the same way, God Almighty warns us about them and says, "They are to you a clear enemy".

Of course, these might be "absurd stuff" for modern people. So, they continue living without having an idea of their greatest enemy. However, results are not good for them.

> 27. O children of Adam, let not Satan tempt you as he removed your parents from Paradise, stripping them of their clothing to show them

[137] Koran/Chapter 38, verses 82-84

their private parts. Indeed, he sees you, he and his tribe, from where you do not see them. Indeed, We have made the devils allies to those who do not believe. (Koran/Chapter 7)

Regarding inorganic beings, don Juan says, "When compared to them, we are only energetic kids. We learned what we knew from them, and they were the first to invite us." Moreover, he says, they're always one step ahead of us.

In the Koran, God Almighty comments the devils, "Indeed, they see you from where you do not see them". Also He says, these devils whisper evil and suspicions into the breasts of mankind, from where we do not see them.

64. "Incite whoever you can among them with your voice and assault them with your horses and foot soldiers and become a partner in their wealth and their children and promise them." But Satan does not promise them except delusion.
65. Indeed, over My servants there is for you no authority. And sufficient is your Lord as Disposer of affairs. (Koran/Chapter 17)

Don Juan says, "The predators inject into the lives of human beings whatever is convenient for them."[138] Accordingly, the devil whispers something into our thoughts, and we accept it as our own thought. So, we do the things suggested by the devil, but which are actually harmful to ourselves.

- In order to keep us obedient and meek and weak, the predators engaged themselves in a stupendous maneuver-stupendous, of course, from the point of view of a fighting strategist. A horrendous maneuver from the point of view of those who suffer it. They gave us their mind! Do you hear me? The predators give us their mind, which becomes our mind. The predators' mind is baroque, contradictory, morose, filled with the fear of being discovered any minute now.
- You see, the predators' mind has no competitors. When it proposes something, it agrees with its own proposition, and it makes you believe that you've done something of worth. The predators' mind

[138] CASTANEDA, The Active Side of Infinity, HarperCollins Publishers Inc., Mud Shadows

will say to you that whatever Juan Matus is telling you is pure nonsense, and then the same mind will agree with its own proposition, 'Yes, of course, it is nonsense,' you will say. That's the way they overcome us. [139]

Don Juan says that these whispers are possible thanks to a "foreign installation" and explains the mechanism as follows:

- Human beings have six main centers of energy… But the sixth center of energy doesn't quite belong to man. You see, we human beings are under siege, so to speak. That center has been taken over by an invader, an unseen predator. And the only way to overcome this predator is by fortifying all the other centers.
- Isn't it a bit paranoiac to feel that we are under siege, don Juan?
- Well, maybe for you, but certainly not for me. I 'see' energy, and I 'see' that the energy over the center on the top of the head doesn't fluctuate like the energy of the other centers. It has a back-and-forth movement, quite disgusting, and quite foreign. I also 'see' that in a sorcerer who has been capable of vanquishing the mind, which sorcerers call a foreign installation, the fluctuation of that center has become exactly like the fluctuation of all the others. [140]

Don Juan says these are discoveries that took the seers thousands of years, and just like the scientists, the seers reveal the mechanism of what is happening in the universe. On the other hand, God Almighty tells us the meaning of these discoveries made by the seers, and tells us how a person who leads a normal daily life should understand them.

Predators having no authority over human beings:

22. And Satan said when the matter has been concluded, "Indeed, God had promised you the promise of truth. And I promised you, but I betrayed you. But I had no authority over you except that I invited you, and you responded to me. So do not blame me; but blame

---

[139] CASTANEDA, The Active Side of Infinity, HarperCollins Publishers Inc., Mud Shadows

[140] CASTANEDA, Magical Passes, HarperCollins Publishers Inc., The Third Series>The First Group>The Center for Decisions

yourselves. I cannot be called to your aid, nor can you be called to my aid. Indeed, I deny your association of me with God before. Indeed, for the wrongdoers is a painful punishment." (Koran/Chapter 14)

In the above verse, Satan says, "I had no authority over you except that I invited you, and you responded to me". So, we have the freedom not to accept the whispers of Satan. However, only those whom God calls "My true and sincere servants" can achieve this:

39. Said, "My Lord, because You have put me in error, I will surely make attractive to them on earth, and I will mislead them all
40. Except, among them, Your sincere servants." (Koran/Chapter 15)

Don Juan says that the whispering of the predators is unrivaled and can only be avoided by the "disciplined seers". According to him, the only thing that can be done against the predators is "discipline" ourselves to the point where they will not touch us:

- The only alternative left for mankind is discipline. Discipline is the only deterrent. But by discipline I don't mean harsh routines. I don't mean waking up every morning at five-thirty and throwing cold water on yourself until you're blue. Sorcerers understand discipline as the capacity to face with serenity odds that are not included in our expectations. For them, discipline is an art: the art of facing infinity without flinching, not because they are strong and tough but because they are filled with awe.
- The grand trick of those sorcerers of ancient times was to burden the predators' mind with discipline. They found out that if they taxed the predators' mind with inner silence, the foreign installation would flee, giving to any one of the practitioners involved in this maneuver the total certainty of the mind's foreign origin. The foreign installation comes back, I assure you, but not as strong, and a process begins in which the fleeing of the predators' mind becomes routine, until one day it flees permanently. A sad day indeed! That's the day when you have to rely on your own devices, which are nearly zero. There's no one to tell you what to do. There's no mind of foreign origin to dictate the imbecilities you're accustomed to. [141]

---

141 CASTANEDA, The Active Side of Infinity, HarperCollins Publishers Inc., Mud Shadows

What the seers understand from this disciplinary maneuver is the ability to face the odds with serenity, which are not included in our expectations. And for them, discipline is an art, the art of facing infinity without flinching.

According to the Koran, every unexpected event that the seers eliminate with discipline, is actually a test from God. And in such a case, the chosen servants of God know that this is a test from their Lord, and they say: "Indeed we belong to God, and indeed to Him we will return."

155. We will surely test you with something of fear and hunger and a loss of wealth and lives and fruits, but give good tidings to the patient,
156. Who, when disaster strikes them, say, "Indeed we belong to God, and indeed to Him we will return."
157. Those are the ones upon whom are blessings from their Lord and mercy. And it is those who are the rightly guided. (Koran/Chapter 2)

So, the rightly guided servants say, "We have nothing to lose in this world. We have come from God, and we will return to God again", and they welcome every event that happens to them with "inner silence". And what the seers call "discipline", comes spontaneously as a byproduct of acting in accordance with His will.

What the seers do again is to discover a mechanism that God puts in human nature and use it for their own benefits. So why are these demons? Why are they haunting people? And why does the discipline keep them away from us? The seers have no answer to these questions, but they discover and use all of them.

<u>Not bringing down the religion by predators</u>:

At one point, don Juan asks Castaneda how to explain the contradiction between the intelligence of man the engineer and the stupidity of his systems of beliefs. And answers this question himself: "Sorcerers believe that the predators have given us our systems of beliefs, our ideas of good and evil, our social mores."[142] And he shows

---

[142] CASTANEDA, The Active Side of Infinity, HarperCollins Publishers Inc., Mud Shadows

it as a way for predators to make us passive, selfish and coward. In other words, as communism says, he means to say, 'Religion is opium', but he replies in a way they cannot accept: "It is the predators who gave it to us."

Don Juan makes such a comment, but there is nothing of his own knowledge, which might be a counterpart in the Koran that is so delicate and correspondent with human nature. And the Almighty God's Koran is so encompassing that it does not leave even this claim of him without an answer.

210. And the devils have not brought it down.
211. It is not allowable for them, nor would they be able. (Koran/Chapter 26)

With regards to the Koran, God Almighty says the devils did not bring the revelation down. In other words, He commands that predators did not bring it down as don Juan claimed, and they would not be able to do this. What's more, He challenges them and all people at this point and says:

88. Say, "If mankind and the jinn gathered in order to produce the like of this Koran, they could not produce the like of it, even if they were to each other assistants."
89. And We have certainly diversified for the people in this Koran from every kind of example, but most of the people refused except disbelief. (Koran/Chapter 17)

It is interesting to note that in the above verses, God Almighty does not only call upon the human beings, but also includes the jinns the devils belong to, and says: "If mankind and the jinn gathered in order to produce the like of this Koran, they could not, even if they were to assist each other." With these words, He challenges both human beings and jinn altogether and gives the best response to don Juan.

So, where do these controversies in religions come from? Alternatively, in don Juan's words, how do these "stupidities" come into being? Almighty God answers this also in the Koran:

118. God has cursed Satan. For he had said, "I will surely take from among Your servants a specific portion.

119. And I will mislead them, and I will arouse in them sinful desires, and I will command them so they will slit the ears of cattle, and I will command them so they will change the creation of God." And whoever takes Satan as an ally instead of God has certainly sustained a clear loss. (Koran/Chapter 4)

There is no conflict in the essence of the religion, which God has sent down to His prophets; however, these superstitions, rituals, etc., are the products of Satan's whispering and attempts to deceive man. According to the Koran, all the prophets are brothers and were sent to declare the existence and oneness of God. In addition, each of them swept away these superstitions at the time they were sent.

136. The polytheists assign to God from that which He created of crops and livestock a share and say, "This is for God," by their claim, "and this is for our 'partners' associated with Him." But what is for their "partners" does not reach God, while what is for God – this reaches their "partners." Evil is that which they rule.
137. And likewise, to many of the polytheists their partners have made to seem pleasing the killing of their children in order to bring about their destruction and to cover them with confusion in their religion. And if God had willed, they would not have done so. So leave them and that which they invent.
138. And they say, "These animals and crops are forbidden; no one may eat from them except whom we will," by their claim. And there are those whose backs are forbidden and those upon which the name of God is not mentioned – all of this an invention of untruth about Him. He will punish them for what they were inventing.
139. And they say, "What is in the bellies of these animals is exclusively for our males and forbidden to our females. But if it is born dead, then all of them have shares therein." He will punish them for their description. Indeed, He is Wise and Knowing.
140. Those will have lost who killed their children in foolishness without knowledge and prohibited what God had provided for them, inventing untruth about God. They have gone astray and were not rightly guided. (Koran/Chapter 6)

In the society where Prophet Muhammad was sent, the "stupidities" made in the name of religion are clearly seen in the verses above. And even if these people have female babies at first, they are deviated enough to bury them alive. That is what the Koran calls them the steps of the devil and sweeps them all away.

The Koran calls these acts "foolishness", but on the other hand it says, "If God had not willed, they would not have done so". In other words, the things that don Juan calls foolishness and throws the blame on the predators are the things that happen with the permission of God and are set as a test before man.

Therefore, the predators are to blame for this, but they are also servants of God, and they will be judged for what they did on the Day of Judgment. The thing to do against them is not to give an ear to what the devils say, but to hearken to what God says:

221. Shall I inform you upon whom the devils descend?
222. They descend upon every sinful slanderer.
223. They pass on what is heard and most of them are liars. (Koran/ Chapter 26)

The devils do not bring religion down, but they descend upon the sinners, become their allies, and lead them astray. As a result, they bring those "stupidities" into being. Don Juan looks at them and says, "There is no religion", but in fact, it is he himself who falls into the trap of the predators.

66. Man says, "When I have died, am I going to be brought forth alive?"
67. Does man not remember that We created him before, while he was nothing?
68. So by your Lord, We will surely gather them and the devils; then We will bring them to be present around Hell upon their knees.
69. Then We will surely extract from every sect those of them who were worst against the Most Compassionate in insolence.
70. Then, surely it is We who are most knowing of those most worthy of entering it.
71. And there is none of you except he will come to there. This is upon your Lord an inevitability decreed.

72. Then We will save those who feared God and leave the wrongdoers there, on their knees. (Koran/Chapter 19)

God Almighty says in the Koran that He will gather up both men and devils and will question them for what they have done. Therefore, there are no human beings created for no reason and creatures that haunt them, as the seers claim. There is a plan created by God and a distribution of tasks in accordance with this. And God Almighty is testing us in this environment and says, "To Me is your return". However, the seers are on the wrong side of existence by renouncing the religion.

PROPHET SOLOMON AND DEMONS

15. We had certainly given to David and Solomon knowledge, and they said, "Praise is due to God, who has favored us over many of His believing servants." (Koran/Chapter 27)

We have already mentioned that God Almighty has given each prophet the task of illuminating a dimension of existence. And just as we are given information about the sorcerers in the story of Prophet Moses, the jinns are mentioned in Prophet Solomon's parable. And God Almighty, as the Owner of the property, says that He has given him something from His property.

30. And to David We gave Solomon. An excellent servant, indeed, he was one repeatedly turning back to God.
31. When the beautiful horses were paraded before him in the afternoon.
32. He said, "Indeed, I have preferred the love of goods to mention my Lord." Then the sun disappeared into the curtain of darkness.
33. He said, "Return them to me," and set about caressing their legs and necks.
34. And We certainly tried Solomon and placed on his throne a dead body, then he returned to Us.
35. He said, "My Lord, forgive me and grant me a kingdom such as will not belong to anyone after me. Indeed, You are the Bestower."
36. So We subjected to him the wind blowing by his command, gently, wherever he directed,

37. And the devils of jinn – every builder and diver,
38. And others bound together in shackles.
39. This is Our gift, so grant or withhold without account.
40. And indeed, for him is nearness to Us and a good place of return. (Koran/Chapter 38)

There are many examples in Castaneda's books about how the seers make use of jinns. They used this method, especially to frighten their apprentices and straighten them up. Also, the "Mescalito"[143] experiences told in his early books and the exercises of "seeing" he made with a "moth" are all about the use of these allies.[144]

However, they are always the things that the seers discover over time, and they can only use them after a long training. But here, this knowledge is given directly to Prophet Solomon by God Almighty. In other words, Almighty God, the Owner of the creation, sets Prophet Solomon as an example to show the essence of the knowledge used by the seers and gives the jinns directly to his command.

Don Juan, for example, once set the "wind" upon la Gorda and does not relieve her from it until she gets exhausted and gives up, or likewise, teaches Castaneda "willful wind" early in his training. He tries to teach him "to be available or unavailable" with this, and at the same time he attacks his rationality.

Of course, don Juan is not using the wind here, but the jinns. Essentially, he sets his jinns on his apprentices, and they manifest themselves in the form of wind.

In the case of Prophet Solomon, the jinns that help him do this by God's command, not as a result of mutual benefit, as in the case of the seers. As for the wind, God Almighty directs it to his command and says, "This is Our gift, so grant or withhold without account."

In other words, Prophet Solomon's property and reign is a blessing from the Almighty, an exceptional situation. Moreover, God Almighty, as the Owner of all things, gives him an exceptional grace to show the

---

[143] Peyote is one of the psychotropic plants that the seers use and don Juan calls it "Mescalito".

[144] See Chapter 10- Stopping The World

nature of the relationship between the seers and jinns, and tells them; "I am the source of what you have discovered and used."

<u>Prophet Solomon's faith and the devils' disbelief:</u>

101. When a messenger from God came to them confirming that which was with them, a party of those who had been given the Scripture threw the Scripture of God behind their backs as if they did not know.
102. And they followed what the devils had recited during the reign of Solomon. It was not Solomon who disbelieved, but the devils disbelieved, teaching people magic and that which was revealed to the two angels at Babylon, Harut and Marut. But these two do not teach anyone unless they say, "We are a trouble, so do not disbelieve." And they learn from them that by which they cause separation between a man and his wife. But they do not harm anyone through it except by permission of God. And they learn what harms them and does not benefit them. But they certainly knew that whoever purchased it would not have in the Hereafter any share. And wretched is that for which they sold themselves, if they only knew. (Koran/Chapter 2)

These verses reject false superstitions fabricated by former communities about Prophet Solomon's property. According to this, Prophet Solomon is not an infidel and what he possesses is given to him as a blessing from God. However, the demonic jinns who teach people the spell deny God. And these jinns are also the demons that communicate with the seers and teach them what they know.

In addition, this explains why don Juan, whose knowledge is based on what these demonic jinns teach, is so strict about denial of God. While Prophet Solomon, who received the blessing from God and took the information from the source, did not deviate into denial; the demons who took their knowledge from two angels assigned by God as a test, bought the denial in return. Also, the seers who followed them, are too in denial.

So, Prophet Solomon's property is not a randomly granted thing, but rather a litmus paper on the science of the seers. While the seers learn their knowledge from these demonic jinns, it is unrequitedly given to Solomon by God Almighty. And while the seers deviate into denial because of their knowledge, Prophet Solomon does not do such a thing. On the contrary, he gives thanks to God Almighty for His blessing.

<u>The jinns unaware of the unseen:</u>

> 14. When We decreed for Solomon death, nothing indicated to them his death except a creature of the earth eating his staff. But when he fell down, it became clear that if jinns had known the unseen, they would not have remained in a humiliating punishment. (Koran/Chapter 34)

In verse #102 above, it was said that people learned from these demonic jinns the things that would cause separation between the man and his wife. This means that intimate information about humans is told to other people by these demonic jinns. And don Juan was learning from them all the secrets of their own apprentices. So much so that in Castaneda's life, he even explained to him what he had forgotten.

However, the verse here sets a limit to this, and says that although there were so many jinns around Prophet Solomon, they did not know when he would die. And it tells us that the jinns do not know the "unseen", they only know what exists. In other words, they are maneuvering within the limits set by God Almighty and they cannot know the outside of it.

> 51. I did not make demons witness to the creation of the heavens and the earth or to the creation of themselves, and I would not have taken the misguiders as assistants. (Koran/Chapter 18)

Therefore, there is a limit to the science of the seers established through communication with the jinns. They know what God Almighty has taught them within the limits set by Him. Yet, like modern Darwinists, they rely on their knowledge and begin to patronize Him. However, God Almighty is entirely encompassing of them.

6- Energy Body

- Energy Body
- The Assemblage Point
- Magical Passes

ENERGY BODY

8. O you who have believed, repent to God with sincere repentance. Perhaps your Lord will remove from you your misdeeds and admit you into gardens beneath which rivers flow. That Day God will not disgrace the Prophet and those who believed with him. Their light will proceed before them and on their right; they will say, "Our Lord, perfect for us our light and forgive us. Indeed, You are over all things competent." (Koran/Chapter 66)

"With the body as an object one tackles the known, with the body as a luminous egg one tackles the unknown", says don Juan and explains this as follows:

- Human alternatives are everything we are capable of choosing as persons. They have to do with the level of our day-to-day range, the known; and owing to that fact, they are quite limited in number and scope. Human possibilities belong to the unknown. They are not what we are capable of choosing but what we are capable of attaining.
- An example of human alternatives is our choice to believe that the human body is an object among objects. An example of human possibilities is the seers' achievement in viewing man as an egglike luminous being. With the body as an object one tackles the known,

> with the body as a luminous egg one tackles the unknown; human possibilities have, therefore, nearly an inexhaustible scope. [145]

In addition, don Juan explains the discovery of the energy body by the seers as follows:

- From 'seeing' the essence of the universe, the sorcerers of antiquity went on to 'see' the energy essence of human beings. And they depicted human beings as bright shapes that resembled giant eggs and called them luminous eggs. [146]

According to the seers, this luminous egg constitutes the "energy body" of man. So, they discover what is called "aura body" by some other cultures.

The seers depict the energy body as a luminous sphere that surrounds the human being, and according to them, this luminous sphere constitutes all energetic possibilities of human beings. And the seers are committed to discovering these possibilities.

Existence of two energy spheres on a human being:

In one of his speeches, don Juan says that for the shamans who lived in Mexico in ancient times, the concept that a human being is composed of two complete functioning bodies, one on the left and one on the right, was fundamental to their endeavors as sorcerers.

Castaneda, on the other hand, counters that modern biologists have the concept of bilateral symmetry, which means "a basic body plan in which the left and right sides of the organism can be divided into approximate mirror images of each other along the midline."

In answering this, don Juan emphasizes his own science and says: "The classifications of the shamans of ancient Mexico were more profound than the conclusions of modern scientists, because they stemmed from perceiving energy directly as it flows in the universe."

---

145 CASTANEDA, The Fire From Within, Washington Square Press, The First Attention

146 CASTANEDA, The Art of Dreaming, HarperCollins Publishers Inc., Sorcerers of Antiquity: An Introduction

Accordingly, he claims that when the human body is perceived as energy, it is easily recognizable that it is composed not of two parts, but of two different types of energy: two different currents of energy, two opposing and at the same time complementary forces that coexist side by side, mirroring, in this fashion, the dual structure of everything in the universe at large.[147]

According to the shamans of ancient Mexico, the left body is under unfair domination of the right body. Accordingly, it is asserted that the right body is responsible for events in the everyday world and is more active in the extent of the dominance of normal life.

On the other hand, the left body is more effective for the ultimate goals of shamanism in terms of energy formation, and they feel it is necessary to free the left body from the yoke of the right.

<u>The dominance of left-part of the brain and the right body</u>:

Although don Juan focuses on the symmetry of the energy body, the physical body also has a perfect symmetry resulting from the dual creation principle of God Almighty. And as a reflection of it, the human brain is also composed of two hemispheres. Just as don Juan said for the symmetry in energy body, they are the same, but their functions are entirely different.

The left brain is the center of analytical thinking, logic and step-by-step procession. And it is also responsible for the conversation. Meanwhile, the right brain is the center of artistic functions. It is synthetic and emotional.

And these two brain hemispheres dominate one half of man. The right brain controls the left side of the human body, while the right brain conducts the left side. And what a coincidence, the conversation and consecutive order that don Juan considers to be the characteristics of the right energy body, are also the functions of the left brain that controls the right side of man. And the liking of the left energy body to silence is also similar to the right brain with the artistic spirit.

---

[147] CASTANEDA, Magical Passes, HarperCollins Publishers Inc., The Fourth Series, The Separation of the Left Body and the Right Body: The Heat Sences

Therefore, just as human beings are made up of two symmetrical parts, both at the body and brain, it is composed of two identical and complementary environments as matter and energy. And these two environments also affect each other directly.

Therefore, as don Juan says, his knowledge is not superior, or, as the science of matter claims, these are not relative nonsense. They are two identical parts of the same whole, two symmetrical parts of the universe. And God Almighty has made them the officers to discover all these things and make them check each other, even if they do not realize it. But, they both rely on the knowledge that God has given them and seek to ignore each other, as they ignore God Almighty.

De-dominating the right energy body:

As for the dominance of the right energy body, this is again parallel to the dominance of the left brain in daily life. Just as there is an obvious hegemony in the analytic thinking of the left brain in our daily lives, so does the right energy body's dominance.

According to don Juan, this leads to permanent crushing of the humans' miraculous left side. Don Juan says the sensation that human beings have of being utterly bored with themselves is due to this predominance of the right body.[148]

Accordingly, in everyday life all factories, companies, and schools apply the methods of the left brain, while the synthesizer right brain is always in the background. The science of matter is again a complete left-brain product. Its job is to analyze, classify and be logical.

The science of seers is the opposite; it is the science of the left body controlled by the right brain. Therefore, being the other side of the polar. And all of their teachings aim to reduce the importance of the right body and activate the left energy body.

In other words, they are pushing the other scale of the balance, thus trying to break the balance in favor of the other side. But God Almighty, who created everything in the universe in pairs, wants us to

---

148 CASTANEDA, Magical Passes, HarperCollins Publishers Inc., The Fourth Series

follow the middle path. He does not want the superiority of one over the other, but wants the balance and creates man in this identity.

Hence, you pray to Him and follow the path of the Prophets, the left body begins to activate, and a balance is formed between the two bodies. However, you're still a member of this world, and you work here, but you never get bored. Because when that right-hand dominance that don Juan mentions goes away, so does the boredom.

Nevertheless, the seers are not contented with this, and they establish their own science through the dominance of the left energy body. And specialize in it as the science of matter does, declaring it as the only truth. However, they are one of the two wings of human beings, and the truth is not revealed without both of them.

THE ASSEMBLAGE POINT

"The hinge of sorcery is the mystery of the assemblage point," says don Juan, and he mentions it as the most important subject of the sorcerers' world. [149]

The reason don Juan attaches so much importance to this is that the seers accomplish everything through the management of the "assemblage point". In other words, their expertise is the assemblage point expertise, and everything they perform during their training is to receive this expertise.

Correspondence of the assemblage point for perception:

Don Juan describes the assemblage that he claims is available in every human being as a luminous point the size of a tennis ball that lies on our energy body.

- In the course of his teachings, don Juan repeatedly discussed and explained what he considered the decisive finding of the sorcerers of antiquity. He called it the crucial feature of human beings as luminous balls: a round spot of intense brilliance, the size of a tennis ball, permanently lodged inside the luminous ball, flush with its

[149] CASTANEDA, The Art of Dreaming, HarperCollins Publishers Inc., The New Area of Exploration

surface, about two feet back from the crest of a person's right shoulder blade.

"What does the assemblage point do?" asks Castaneda, and don Juan answers him saying, "It makes us perceive," and says that it is the decisive finding of the old sorcerers:

- The old sorcerers 'saw' that, in human beings, perception is assembled there, on that point. 'Seeing' that all living beings have such a point of brilliance, the old sorcerers surmised that perception in general must take place on that spot, in whatever pertinent manner.
- First, they 'saw' that out of the millions of the universe's luminous energy filaments passing through the entire luminous ball, only a small number pass directly through the assemblage point, as should be expected since it is small in comparison with the whole.
- Next, they 'saw' that a spherical extra glow, slightly bigger than the assemblage point, always surrounds it, greatly intensifying the luminosity of the filaments passing directly through that glow.
- 'Seeing' that millions of conscious energy filaments pass through the assemblage point, the old sorcerers postulated that in passing through it they come together, amassed by the glow that surrounds it. After 'seeing' that the glow is extremely dim in people who have been rendered unconscious or are about to die, and that it is totally absent from corpses, they were convinced that this glow is awareness.
- Finally, they 'saw' two things. One, that the assemblage points of human beings can dislodge themselves from the spot where they are usually located. And, two, that when the assemblage point is on its habitual position, perception and awareness seem to be normal, judging by the normal behavior of the subjects being observed. But when their assemblage points and surrounding glowing spheres are on a different position than the habitual one, their unusual behavior seems to be the proof that their awareness is different, that they are perceiving in an unfamiliar manner.
- The conclusion the old sorcerers drew from all this was that the greater the displacement of the assemblage point from its customary

> position, the more unusual the consequent behavior and, evidently, the consequent awareness and perception. [150]

The only thing considered by the seers is to move the assemblage point:

Don Juan says that only a small part of the universe's luminous energy filaments passing through the human energy body passes directly through the assemblage point. Thus, this small number of emanations passing through the assemblage point is perceived by us as a steady perception of the world and called reality.

And the seers claim that, if this point is moved to another position within the energy body, since it comes into contact with other filaments there, man begins to perceive different things. And this movement can even make it possible to perceive other realms that are available to his perception.

However, these realms are the permanent ones that exist on their own. So, as Castaneda claims at some parts of his books, the assemblage point does not establish these realms, but the seers join these realms with the assemblage point. Just like the hard-disk on a computer reads the silicon disk with a needle and gives an image to the screen, the assemblage point reads the information about that realm, thanks to the energy filaments passing through it, and enables the seers to be involved in that realm.

The seers have discovered the expertise of moving this point, and all the techniques they have applied are aimed at moving this assemblage point. They look at the world through this window, and what makes it worthwhile is valuable in their world and those who fail to do so seem useless and negligible.

New seers focusing on moving the assemblage point:

"The most important thing the new seers needed was practical steps in

---

[150] CASTANEDA, The Art of Dreaming, HarperCollins Publishers Inc., Sorcerers of Antiquity: An Introduction

order to make their assemblage points shift," says don Juan.[151] According to him, they succeeded in systematically making the assemblage point shift away from its normal position. The old seers had also accomplished that feat, but by means of capricious, idiosyncratic maneuvers:

- The old seers had concentrated exclusively on developing thousands of the most complex techniques of sorcery. What they never realized was that their intricate devices, as bizarre as they were, had no other value than being the means to break the fixation of their assemblage points and make them move.
- I've mentioned to you that sorcery is something like entering a dead-end street. What I meant was that sorcery practices have no intrinsic value. Their worth is indirect, for their real function is to make the assemblage point shift by making the first attention release its control on that point.
- The new seers realized the true role those sorcery practices played and decided to go directly into the process of making their assemblage points shift, avoiding all the other nonsense of rituals and incantations. [152]

Therefore, the new seers examined all the techniques produced by the ancients and discovered that their real goal is to shift the assemblage point. After making this discovery, they only focused on shifting the assemblage point and eliminated everything else.

<u>Power plants</u>:

Power plants are one of the most effective methods of moving the assemblage point. And the use of these plants is the starting point of the seers and their knowledge. However, the side effects of these plants are high, and as a consequence, they put the old seers in a dead end. So, the first thing the new seers do is to reduce the use of these

---

151 CASTANEDA, The Fire From Within, Washington Square Press, Stalking, Intent and the Dreaming Position

152 CASTANEDA, The Fire From Within, Washington Square Press, The Assemblage Point

plants and instead to bring to the forefront techniques such as dreaming and stalking.

In other words, power plants perform their duties historically and lay the foundations of the science of the seers. But after a while, they start to become a millstone around their neck; thus the new seers limit their use.

Don Juan uses these plants on Castaneda, but this is due to Castaneda's logical rigidity. Don Juan is forced to use these plants to shake his worldview and speed things up, but usually, apprentices use them very few. As for Castaneda, he uses them as much as necessary and then completely abandons them.

Stalking:

Don Juan says, stalking is one of the greatest accomplishments of the new seers and has a very humble and fortuitous origin:

- It started from an observation the new seers made that when warriors steadily behave in ways not customary for them, the unused emanations inside their cocoons begin to glow. And their assemblage points shift in a mild, harmonious, barely noticeable fashion.
- Stimulated by this observation, the new seers began to practice the systematic control of their behavior. They called this practice the art of stalking... The new seers, armed with this technique, tackled the known in a sober and fruitful way. By continual practice, they made their assemblage points move steadily. [153]

The most important element of this practice is a "petty tyrant", who is in a position of great authority and power. And the seers who challenged those tyrants had to follow the principles of stalking, which gave them the best opportunity to shift their assemblage point.

- Shifting the assemblage point was the reason why the new seers placed such a high value on the interaction with petty tyrants. Petty

[153] CASTANEDA, The Fire From Within, Washington Square Press, Stalking, Intent and the Dreaming Position

tyrants forced seers to use the principles of stalking and, in doing so, helped seers to move their assemblage points. [154]

For Castaneda, it was thanks to la Catalina[155], who totally frightened him and forced him to practice everything he knew. And of course, it is don Juan himself who cooked up this maneuver:

- In the past, I have arranged bouts between the two of you. I wanted to make your assemblage point shift, and la Catalina, with her sorcery antics, jolted it loose. [156]

Dreaming:

Don Juan explains that dreaming, like stalking, began with a simple observation:

- The old seers became aware that in dreams the assemblage point shifts slightly to the left side in a most natural manner. That point indeed relaxes when man sleeps and all kinds of unused emanations begin to glow.
- They soon realized that the shifting of the assemblage point into the left side is what produces dreams. The farther the movement, the more vivid and bizarre the dream.
- The old seers became immediately intrigued with that observation and began to work with that natural shift until they were able to control it… And they realized that dreaming was in itself the most effective way to move the assemblage point. [157]

The assemblage point was already reportedly shifting during sleep, and the seers aimed to fix it and developed techniques such as finding their hands in their dreams. Then they advanced it and began to dominate

---

154 CASTANEDA, The Fire From Within, Washington Square Press, Stalking, Intent and the Dreaming Position

155 A female member of don Juan's party

156 CASTANEDA, The Fire From Within, Washington Square Press, Stalking, The Shift Below

157 CASTANEDA, The Fire From Within, Washington Square Press, Stalking, Intent and the Dreaming Position

their dreams, and in the end, they started to act as if they were moving in normal life.

The seers have also discovered that dreams are actually given as a window to meet inorganic beings in other realms. Accordingly, the assemblage point is naturally displaced during dreams, which allows to communicate with other realms that the assemblage point can reach. And the seers who discovered all these things turned their dreams into a training field.

After that, they also discovered dreaming as a team; and made use of it to make the most difficult discoveries, such as examining the emanations of Eagle, with the help of this natural effect.

<u>Impeccability</u>:

According to don Juan, dreaming was a useful thing, but as with any sorcery practice, there were pitfalls:

- I'm warning you about the pitfalls of dreaming, which are truly stupendous. In dreaming, there is really no way of directing the movement of the assemblage point; the only thing that dictates that shift is the inner strength or weakness of dreamers.
- At first the new seers were hesitant to use dreaming. It was their belief that dreaming, instead of fortifying, made warriors weak, compulsive, capricious. The old seers were all like that. In order to offset the nefarious effect of dreaming, since they had no other option but to use it, the new seers developed a complex and rich system of behavior called the warriors' way, or the warriors' path.
- With that system, the new seers fortified themselves and acquired the internal strength they needed to guide the shift of the assemblage point in dreams.
- The conviction that the new seers have is that a life of impeccability by itself leads unavoidably to a sense of sobriety, and this in turn leads to the movement of the assemblage point. [158]

---

[158] CASTANEDA, The Fire From Within, Washington Square Press, Stalking, Intent and the Dreaming Position

In addition, impeccability not only provides the inner resistance needed during dreaming, but also increases the energy level of the seers and displaces the assemblage point. According to them, the only thing that could accumulate the energy that a person needs to manage the movement of the assemblage point is "impeccability". So, they try to have impeccable behaviors that will increase their energy.

<u>The assemblage point being mainly driven by increased energy</u>:

- It isn't that as time goes by you're learning sorcery; rather, what you're learning is to save energy. And this energy will enable you to handle some of the energy fields which are inaccessible to you now. And that is sorcery: the ability to use energy fields that are not employed in perceiving the ordinary world we know. Sorcery is a state of awareness. Sorcery is the ability to perceive something which ordinary perception cannot.
- Everything I've put you through, each of the things I've shown you was only a device to convince you that there's more to us than meets the eye. We don't need anyone to teach us sorcery, because there is really nothing to learn. What we need is a teacher to convince us that there is incalculable power at our fingertips. What a strange paradox! Every warrior on the path of knowledge thinks, at one time or another, that he's learning sorcery, but all he's doing is allowing himself to be convinced of the power hidden in his being, and that he can reach it. [159]
- Moving the assemblage point or breaking one's continuity is not the real difficulty. The real difficulty is having energy. If one has energy, once the assemblage point moves, inconceivable things are there for the asking. [160]

"Curtailing self-reflection maximizes the movement of the assemblage point," says don Juan. The reason for this is that when self-importance

---

159 CASTANEDA, The Power of Silence, Washington Square Press, Introduction

160 CASTANEDA, The Power of Silence, Washington Square Press, The Two One-Way Bridges

is limited, the energy emanation it needs stops, and this surplus energy moves the assemblage point.

Similarly, "magical pass movements"[161] that don Juan taught to Castaneda are also believed to help to move the assemblage point, because it mobilizes and puts human energy into use.

In other words, the main point about the assemblage point is the "energy" that the human being possesses, and all the techniques mentioned above to move the assemblage point make sense if there is energy. If there's no energy, there's nothing to do.

For example, don Juan, in the early days, when from an apprentice he become a teacher, thought it would be sufficient to move the assemblage points of his apprentices. However, in time, he saw that it did not work because man was created to balance himself: unless an external intervention to him was internally supported by energy, it did not go beyond temporary effect.

Likewise, the power plants or getting into the heightened awareness by a "nagual blow" has only a temporary effect; and the main thing is the energy level of the apprentice. Even in dreaming, progress cannot be achieved unless supported by impeccability in normal life. Therefore, most of the techniques taught to apprentices by the seers are actually methods of gaining energy, and an impeccable life through the warrior's way provided this energy to man.

<u>Entailment of inner silence for the displacement of assemblage point</u>:

Don Juan says that the internal dialogue is what keeps the assemblage point fixed to its original position. Thus, the internal dialogue is a process that constantly strengthens the position of the assemblage point, because that position is an arbitrary one and needs steady reinforcement. [162]

---

161 See next Chapter: Magical Passes

162 CASTANEDA, The Fire From Within, Washington Square Press, The Position of the Assemblage Point

- The entire human race keeps a determined level of function and efficiency by means of the internal dialogue. The internal dialogue is the key to maintaining the assemblage point stationary at the position shared by the entire human race: at the height of the shoulder blades, an arm's length away from them. By accomplishing the opposite of the internal dialogue, that is to say inner silence, practitioners can break the fixation of their assemblage points, thus acquiring an extraordinary fluidity of perception. [163]
- One of the most mysterious aspects of the seers' knowledge is the incredible effects of inner silence. Once inner silence is attained, the bonds that tie the assemblage point to the particular spot where it is placed begin to break and the assemblage point is free to move. [164]

Don Juan says that seers see that infants have no fixed assemblage point at first, and their assemblage points shift everywhere in the band of man. But due to an endless repetition carried out around them, the worldview of the children is solidified and internalized what was offered to them. The fact of the matter is, many children 'see', but over time they are molded by the elders into a member, and this membership is kept alive through the internal dialogue.

Stopping the internal dialogue is more than not just talking to yourself:

"As you know, the crux of sorcery is the internal dialogue. That is the key to everything. When a warrior learns to stop it, everything becomes possible,"[165] says don Juan, and states that a teacher has begun to teach his apprentices from the very first moment:

- The first act of a teacher is to introduce the idea that the world we think we see is only a view, a description of the world. Every effort of a teacher is geared to prove this point to his apprentice. But accepting it seems to be one of the hardest things one can do; we are

---

163 CASTANEDA, Magical Passes, HarperCollins Publishers Inc., Tensegrity

164 CASTANEDA, The Fire From Within, Washington Square Press, The Position of the Assemblage Point

165 CASTANEDA, Tales of Power, Washington Square Press, The Secret of The Luminous Beings

> complacently caught in our particular view of the world, which compels us to feel and act as if we knew everything about the world. A teacher, from the very first act he performs, aims at stopping that view. Sorcerers call it stopping the internal dialogue, and they are convinced that it is the single most important technique that an apprentice can learn. [166]

So "stopping the internal dialogue" that don Juan is trying to teach is more than just silencing the dialogue within us. While stopping the internal dialogue, the assemblage point starts to move and the world itself actually stops. And the seers become "unbiased witnesses" to this world.[167]

In the absence of the internal dialogue, the universe turns into a state it always is, that is, "can be witnessed, but cannot be talked about", and when that "we-explain-everything" hue and cry dissipates, one is confronted with that tremendous truth.

Displacement of the assemblage point like electrons:

We have already mentioned above that the assemblage point is displaced mainly with increased energy. And this happens when inner silence occurs. So, the assemblage point does not move without energy, but when it does, there's inner silence.

In addition, the movements of the assemblage point, depending on the human energy level, are similar to the movements of electrons around the atoms.

Accordingly, electrons move at seven different energy levels around the atom, and just as enough energy is given to the atom as they go up to an upper level of energy, the assemblage point of the seers also jumps to the next level. And don Juan describes this energy-related jump as follows:

---

[166] CASTANEDA, Tales of Power, Washington Square Press, The Strategy of a Sorcerer

[167] See Chapter 10- Stopping The World

- Any movement of the assemblage point is like dying. Everything in us gets disconnected, then reconnected again to a source of much greater power. That amplification of energy is felt as a killing anxiety.

When this happens in atoms, the electrons rise to a higher energy level, the chemical character of the atom changes and the atom begins to react with respect to this new state. If the energy of the atom is reduced, then the electrons return to their previous energy levels, and the atomic reactions to the previous state are no longer possible.

Likewise, in his books, Castaneda talked about the moments when everything was obvious to him when he was with don Juan but after a while, he experienced that he could hardly remember anything about. These experiences of Castaneda stems from the fact that the assemblage point acts like the same electrons. With don Juan's help, he goes up to a higher energy level, and for a moment, everything seems to be enlightened to him. But after a while, when the external energy supply goes away, the assemblage point returns to its original place and Castaneda cannot remember anything of a higher level. Moreover, this situation goes on like that until he reaches that energy level on his own.

Displacement of the assemblage point by God Almighty:

"What I want you to know is that there really is no procedure involved in making the assemblage point move," says don Juan. "The spirit touches the apprentice and his assemblage point moves. It is as simple as that."[168] And he states, "Intent is the spirit, so it is the spirit which moves the assemblage points." [169]

What don Juan called 'spirit' was actually the intent of God Almighty. And it was also was explained in previous chapters that when he spoke of spirit, he actually spoke of God Almighty. So, when don Juan says, "The spirit moves the assemblage point", it is actually God Almighty

---

[168] CASTANEDA, The Power of Silence, Washington Square Press, Moving the Assemblage Point

[169] CASTANEDA, The Power of Silence, Washington Square Press, Handling Intent: The Third Point

who moves it. In other words, the assemblage point is the manifestation point of God Almighty.

This means that the final decision belongs to God Almighty, whom don Juan calls 'spirit'. In other words, it is God Almighty Himself, who moves the assemblage point, but He does it because of our efforts and the level of energy we have achieved. He almost hits the last seal and the assemblage point shifts. However, it is impossible for it to move without His will.

Don Juan explains this function of God Almighty as follows:

- None of us resolves anything. The spirit either resolves it for us or it doesn't. If it does, a sorcerer finds himself acting in the sorcerers' world, but without knowing how. This is the reason why I have insisted from the day I found you that impeccability is all that counts. A sorcerer lives an impeccable life, and that seems to beckon the solution. Why? No one knows. [170]

The seers are trying to lead an impeccable life, which brings with it the energy, but it is actually God Almighty who gives them that energy and who moves the assemblage point as a result.

Don Juan asks for the reason of it and answers himself: "No one knows it." But this is not the case, and God Almighty gives us the answers that "he does not know".

<u>The assemblage point is given to us to know God Almighty</u>:

Don Juan says that possibly every human being under normal living conditions had, at one time or another, the opportunity to break away from the bindings of convention and moved the assemblage point.

- A moment of elation would suffice to move our assemblage points and break our conventions. So, too, a moment of fright, ill health, anger, or grief. But ordinarily, whenever we had the chance to move our assemblage points, we became frightened. Our religious, academic, social backgrounds would come into play. They would

---

170 CASTANEDA, The Power of Silence, Washington Square Press, The Two One-Way Bridges

assure our safe return to the flock; the return of our assemblage points to the prescribed position of normal living.

- All the mystics and spiritual teachers you knew of had done just that: their assemblage points moved, either through discipline or accident, to a certain point; and then they returned to normalcy carrying a memory that lasted them a lifetime.

According to him, the seers are the only beings crossing these limits:

- You can be a very pious, good boy and forget about the initial movement of your assemblage point. Or you can push beyond your reasonable limits. You are still within those limits. [171]

What don Juan means to say by the term 'pushing beyond the reasonable limits' is that the assemblage point is displaced to the depths of the human energy body, thereby reaching the seven other realms that are accessible to man and more.

And don Juan who succeeded in this, in turn, sees "being a pious boy" as useless. According to him, being a pious boy means being content with a "lateral shift" made by the assemblage point instead of a shift in depth:

- "Lateral shift" means a shift of the point from one side to the other along the width of man's band of emanations[172] instead of a shift in depth.
- On both edges of man's band of emanations there is a strange storage of refuse, an incalculable pile of human junk. It's a very morbid, sinister storehouse. It had great value for the old seers but not for us.
- On the right edge we find endless visions of physical activity, violence, killing, sensuality. On the left edge we find spirituality,

---

[171] CASTANEDA, The Power of Silence, Washington Square Press, Handling Intent: The Third Point

[172] According to the seers, man's band of emanations is a special band in human energy body on which the assemblage point becomes active and groups the emanations meaningfully to create new perceptions.

> religion, God… And any person can reach that storehouse by simply stopping his internal dialogue. [173]

"They are of no value for warriors in search of total freedom," says don Juan. Because their aim is to connect the other realms with their assemblage point expertise, cancel death temporarily and open wings for "freedom". That is why don Juan has seen these lateral shifts dysfunctional, and since they couldn't cross the rational boundaries, he describes religious people as unaware of anything.

But is it really so? Is this assemblage point really given to us to discover the other worlds created by God or to know Him, the Lord of the Worlds? God Almighty tells us that the second choice is true.

Misuse of assemblage point by the seers:

God Almighty says, "We created man from the earth, then we said to him, 'Be!' Then he becomes."[174] So human is an action, and all the equipment that God Almighty has given to him, operate accordingly. And I call it the secret of "Be!" in human nature.

For example, we do not know how we think, but when we want to think, we can. Moreover, we do not know how we see, but when we open our eyes, we do it automatically. The function of the assemblage point for a normal person is the same. It exists and works in the background. We are not consciously aware of it, but inevitably use it.

On the other hand, the seers go one step further and discover its mechanism and use it as they wish. However, God Almighty does not give it to us to use it as the seers do. He gives it so that we can just acknowledge Him, and He teaches us how to do it. Thus, God Almighty gives us human beings "prayer" and "fasting" as the most important worship and gives them to us as a method of natural displacement of the assemblage point.

---

173 CASTANEDA, The Fire From Within, Washington Square Press, The Position of the Assemblage Point

174 Koran/Chapter 3, verse 59

Don Juan, for example, counts the hunger among the natural influences that displace the assemblage point, and fasting works out for this purpose. When man is hungry and thirsty from sunrise to sunset, it displaces their assemblage point and makes them perceive the world differently. In addition, hunger creates a point of reference to man and it turns into a shield that protects them from the evils.

In prayer, man reaches inner silence and thus displaces the assemblage point of the servant who worships their Lord and is filled with human awe. When they repeat this every day, the assemblage point of man regularly enters the area where God is felt, and man establishes a connection with Him. In other words, the parts that don Juan does not care about, are actually the most important parts according to human nature. And what he cares about are the parts that God Almighty put in human nature as a test, but which did not make the main goal.

In other words, God Almighty does not expect us to communicate with the other worlds or to make something uber-super. He wants us to know Him with limited displacement and to continue our lives as a member of this world. But this is not enough for the seers and they surpass the nature that God has created on people, and then they supposedly surpass God Himself. [175]

<u>Conscious displacement of the assemblage point only by man</u>:

Castaneda asks don Juan, whether other organisms are capable of shifting their assemblage points. "Their points can shift," he replies, "but the shift is not a voluntary thing with them." And he continues: "The new seers had observed that only human beings were capable of further clustering the clusters of emanations."[176]

On the other hand, don Juan describes the lack of knowledge regarding the assemblage point through the humanity as "unfortunate"

---

[175] See Chapter 14- Evolution of Awareness

[176] CASTANEDA, The Fire From Within, Washington Square Press, The Position of the Assemblage Point

and says: "The unfortunate truth is that human beings always lose by default. They simply don't know about their possibilities."[177]

The question to be asked here is whether the ants or other animals are also losing by default? What can they do? They don't have that opportunity, but people do. So why is this so? Is it just because a few seers come and use it, or for a universal purpose?

Of course, it is no coincidence that God Almighty, who created humans and jinns as polar twins in this system of worlds, gives these talents only to man on earth. He creates human beings in a nature that will know Him and gives them the necessary equipment. Finally, He sends His revelation and gives us the manuals of these devices. What the seers do is to use these devices outside the intended purpose.

Heart:

In the Koran, God Almighty does not speak directly of the assemblage point. But in the same way, it does not impose a mission on human beings to reach our common ground with the jinns that don Juan calls "unknown". However, He speaks of the "heart" as a reflection of the assemblage point used in this world and defines it as the most important thing that man has.

If you should ask what the "heart" is, this is not the physical heart itself as we understand it, but as an energetic reflection of its vital function, is a manifestation point of human contact with God. In other words, God Almighty reveals His power and judgment over the man with it, and according to what he has done, He almost manages him from there. Therefore, God Almighty, who rules the hearts, also rules the assemblage point, and indeed they are the same thing.

Labelling the heart:

- Oh Turner of the Hearts, keep my heart firm on your religion. (Prophet Muhammad)

---

[177] CASTANEDA, The Fire From Within, Washington Square Press, The Assemblage Point

The verb from which the word "heart" is derived in Arabic means the transformation of something from one shape to another. For example, the word "revolution" in Arabic comes from this root. And in the same way, the heart of the human being gets this name because it changes a lot and changes from state to state. In other words, its direct meaning is "changing thing".

And this denomination is more accurate than the name given to the assemblage point by the seers, who are "unbiased witnesses". Because, although the function of the assemblage point is to unite the emanations of the universe, its main feature is that it often changes. Because it replaces so often that we perceive different things, and we are always moving from state to state.

The assemblage point is already assembling the emanations automatically, and the seers looking at it call it that name, but its main effect is "changing". When it displaces, our perception changes and all the skills of the seers are based on the use of these changes. Therefore, as the real owner of the property, God Almighty, unlike these explorers who discover His property, also tells us its real name.

In addition, God Almighty builds this universe on good and evil, even if the seers deny it. Therefore, He does not call the reflection of the assemblage point in this universe a callous point, and calls it "heart". In other words, this name contains the meaning of change; and also, as the pure, clean ones will enter heaven, there is a conscientious dimension within it.

Hardness of the heart:

13. When Our verses are recited to him, he says, "Legends of the former peoples."
14. No! Rather, the stain has covered their hearts of that which they were earning. (Koran/Chapter 83)

The Almighty God, who has created the universe to determine which of us will do a better job, creates the "heart" as the human feature of it. Accordingly, as a person acts contrary to the will of God, his heart begins to rust and "solidify" in accordance with its nature and eventually leads this person to denial. In other words, the heart loses its ability to move and is no longer able to reach the regions of the acknowledgment of God that the seers mention.

And the "warrior's way", invented by the seers to acquire energy and to move the assemblage point, is in fact, a reflection of what God Almighty wants man to do. Don Juan even says that their path of knowledge resembles a manual for monastic life.[178] And his apprentice La Gorda supports this view:

- There is no difference in terms of life-style between us and true nuns and priests. They are complete as a rule and they do not even weaken themselves with sexual acts.
- I will always cheer for the nuns and priests. We are alike. We have given up the world and yet we are in the midst of it. Priests and nuns would make great flying sorcerers if someone would tell them that they can do it. [179]

Therefore, according to the nature created by God for human beings, the way of not "solidifying" the heart is one, and the seers are also using it. However, they do it by going beyond its purpose and using a device that is given to know God, to discover other realms.

The heart being the manifestation point of faith:

100. It is not possible for a soul to believe except by permission of God. He places defilement upon those who do not use reason. (Koran/ Chapter 10)

The heart, which the seers call the assemblage point, is the manifestation point of God Almighty, and no one except Him has the possession of this. God Almighty uses it like a control panel and makes it possible for people to live according to the order they deserve.

---

178 CASTANEDA, The Power of Silence, Washington Square Press, The Two One-Way Bridges

179 CASTANEDA, The Second Ring of Power, Washington Square Press, The Art of Dreaming

"What a strange feeling to realize that everything we think, everything we say depends on the position of the assemblage point,"[180] says don Juan. In this way, God Almighty determines the current order of man and gives him the flow of energy he deserves at that moment. And the most obvious reflection of it is that God Almighty opens the hearts of whom He wills to faith and seals the heart of whom He wills.

God Almighty commands that, "It is not possible for a soul to believe except for the permission given by Me." So, He is aware of what we all do, and He knows best who is worthy of faith and whose heart must be sealed. And He manifests His judgments through the "heart" after putting us into trials.

God Almighty leaves us free in what we do, but He does not leave the final judgment on the heart to ourselves. In other words, what we do constitutes a base and God Almighty makes its judgment accordingly.

Thus, the "heart" that the Koran introduces to us serves as a manifestation point that is constantly active, transforms from state to state and where everything comes and ends; but it is God Himself, who always has the last word.

But, why do the seers deny God Almighty, even though they are the "professors" of this work of moving the "heart"? Actually, they do not deny Himself, but His prophets and Books. They know Him, but they don't call Him God. What they discover gives them extreme confidence and seduces them. However, what they do is just use the opportunities that God has given them and discover what He has created.

In addition, because they deny good and evil, and the revelations of God, the "heart" actually fulfills its essential function and causes them to deny God despite all their mastery. Therefore, God's laws of nature are still in effect, and their hearts are dragging them into denial.

---

180 CASTANEDA, The Power of Silence, Washington Square Press, The Descent Of The Spirit: Seeing The Spirit

MAGICAL PASSES

In one of his speeches, don Juan complains that Castaneda has begun to become chubby and warns him about that:

- You are way too chubby. You are one step from being fat. Wear and tear is beginning to show in you. Like any other member of our race, you are developing a lump of fat on your neck, like a bull. It's time that you take seriously one of the sorcerers' greatest findings: the magical passes. [181]

Castaneda surprised by these words of don Juan: "What magical passes are you talking about, don Juan? You never mentioned this topic to me before." Don Juan replies: "Not only have I told you a great deal about magical passes, you know a great number of them already. I have been teaching them to you all along."

Accordingly, some of the movements don Juan had made since the very first day, and Castaneda thought "cracking joints" were actually the "magical pass" movements that don Juan was talking about. Don Juan taught them without giving a sign that he was taking advantage of Castaneda's imitation capacity:

- What I meant to say is that you imitate everything I do, so I have been cashing: in on your imitation capacity. I have shown you various

[181] CASTANEDA, Magical Passes, HarperCollins Publishers Inc., Magical Passes

magical passes, all along, and you have always taken them to be my delight in cracking my joints.

- I have shown you ten different ways of cracking my joints. Each one of them is a magical pass that fits to perfection my body and yours. You could say that those ten magical passes are in your line and mine. They belong to us personally and individually, as they belonged to other sorcerers who were just like the two of us in the twenty-five generations that preceded us. [182]

Magical passes, not an invention but a discovery:

Castaneda asks don Juan, "How did the old sorcerers invent those magical passes?" Don Juan replies as follows:

- To think that they were invented implies instantly the intervention of the mind, and this is not the case when it comes to those magical passes. They were, rather, discovered by the old shamans. I was told that it all began with the extraordinary sensation of well-being that those shamans experienced when they were in shamanistic states of heightened awareness. They felt such tremendous, enthralling vigor that they struggled to repeat it in their hours of vigil.
- At first those shamans believed that it was a mood of well-being that heightened awareness created in general. Soon, they found out that not all the states of shamanistic heightened awareness which they entered produced in them the same sensation of well-being. A more careful scrutiny revealed to them that whenever that sensation of well-being occurred, they had always been engaged in some specific kind of bodily movement. They realized that while they were in states of heightened awareness, their bodies moved involuntarily in certain ways, and that those certain ways were indeed the cause of that unusual sensation of physical and mental plenitude. [183]

According to don Juan, the movements that the bodies of those shamans executed automatically in heightened awareness were a sort of

---

[182] CASTANEDA, Magical Passes, HarperCollins Publishers Inc., Magical Passes

[183] CASTANEDA, Magical Passes, HarperCollins Publishers Inc., Magical Passes

hidden heritage of mankind, something that had been put in deep storage, to be revealed only to those who were looking for it. Because of that, he portrayed those sorcerers as deep-sea divers who, without knowing it, reclaimed it.

The "Force" that creates Magical Passes:

After a while, Castaneda decides to ask don Juan about something that has been bothering him for a long time and asks him who might have prepared these magical passes, some sort of hidden treasure, placed in storage for man to find. The only idea that he could come up with was derived from Catholicism. He thought of God doing it, or a guardian angel, or the Holy Spirit. Don Juan answers this by saying:

- It is not the Holy Spirit, which is only holy to you, because you're secretly a Catholic. And certainly it is not God, a benevolent father as you understand God. Nor is it a goddess, a nurturing mother, watching over the affairs of men, as many people believe to be the case. It is rather an impersonal force that has endless things in storage for those who dare to seek them. It is a force in the universe, like light or gravity. [184]

Don Juan gives the responsibility of what the old seers have discovered to some sort of "forces" in the universe. Just like the scientists of matter do. As if God does not exist, and those forces do everything by themselves. However, essentially, the light and the gravity referred to by don Juan belong to God, just as this "force" that don Juan refers to.

17. We have created above you seven layered heavens, and never have We been of creation unaware.
18. And We have sent down rain from the sky in a measured amount and settled it on the earth. And indeed, We are able to take it away. (Koran/Chapter 23)

Don Juan tells about "gravity". However, it is God Almighty who pours water on the earth and settles it on him. The human being discovers the occasion and gives it a name; "the gravitational force."

[184] CASTANEDA, Magical Passes, HarperCollins Publishers Inc., Magical Passes

Then, he pulls out God and thinks that this "curtain of reasons" is real, and accepts unconditionally that these forces will continue forever. On the other hand, God Almighty, as the owner of the property commands, "Indeed, We are able to take it away." Just as the result of the lack of gravity in the moon.

Don Juan says about the magical passes, "It is a force in the universe, like light or gravity". In the same way, the documentaries on television tell us about "nature". In fact, nature is a curtain, and the Almighty God Himself, who rules and reigns over the universe.

As a matter of fact, don Juan knows this too, and he himself says that everything is made out of the "Eagle's emanations" and that "Eagle" rules everything that exists. But what he opposes is the existence of a God, who is actually asking for account in the sense that we understand.

Don Juan is against God introduced to us by the religion. However, his own imagination of God is not very good, as understood from his statements. Because God, presented by Koran, has nothing to do with nurturing goddesses or with benevolent fathers. He is the Lord of the Worlds and the owner of all powers that don Juan speaks of.

Redeployment of the energy with Magical Passes:

"Human beings, perceived as conglomerates of energy fields, are sealed energetic units that have definite boundaries which don't permit the entrance or the exit of energy. Therefore, the energy existing within that conglomerate of energy fields is all that each human individual can count on," says don Juan. [185]

In other words, the seers say, "A person's energy is constant." However, that does not mean that human beings can actively use all of their existing energy. According to the seers, there are five main energy centers in human beings, and the current energy works as long as it is located in these centers:

[185] CASTANEDA, Magical Passes, HarperCollins Publishers Inc., Magical Passes

- The feeling of losing energy, which all of us experience at one time or another, is the result of energy being chased away, dispersed from the five enormous natural centers of life and vitality. Any sense of gaining energy is due to the redeployment of energy previously dispersed from those centers. That is to say, the energy is relocated onto those five centers of life and vitality. [186]

According to don Juan, in the majority of people, most of the energy becomes distant from these centers due to misuse. The first reason is "worrying". The person who succumbed to the stress of daily life is paying a heavy price for this pressure. In addition, the discarded energy is drawn towards the periphery of the human energy body and formed an unusable deposit.

- The magical passes relate to the total human being as a physical body, and as a conglomerate of energy fields. They agitate the energy that has been accumulated in the luminous ball and return it to the physical body itself. The magical passes engage both the body itself as a physical entity that suffers the dispersion of energy, and the body as an energetic entity which is capable of redeploying that dispersed energy.
- Having energy on the periphery of the luminous ball, energy that is not being redeployed, is as useless as not having any energy at all. It is truly a terrifying situation to have a surplus of energy stashed away, inaccessible for all practical purposes. It is like being in the desert, dying of dehydration, while you carry a tank of water that you cannot open, because you don't have any tools. In that desert, you can't even find a rock to bang it with.
- The true magic of the magical passes is the fact that they cause crusted-down energy to enter again into the centers of vitality, hence the feeling of well-being and prowess which is the practitioner's experience. [187]

---

[186] CASTANEDA, Magical Passes, HarperCollins Publishers Inc., The First Group: The Center for Decisions

[187] CASTANEDA, Magical Passes, HarperCollins Publishers Inc., Magical Passes

Briefly, shamans have discovered that human beings possess enormous amounts of unused energy and have tried to find ways to make this inert energy available. And the main purpose of all the techniques and practices available in shamanism is to put this inert energy into use. And "magical passes" are one of these techniques.

Thus, while the teachings relate to daily life, such as "losing self-importance" or "disrupting the routines of life"[188] that prevent the existing energy from becoming useless due to anxiety, practices such as magical passes aim to activate this unused energy.

The medical aspect of the energy body:

Castaneda shows many of the passing movements in his book "Magical Passes" and explains how these affect the human energy body. Accordingly, every physical activity has a counterpart in the energy body of the human being. Although the magical passes seem to be performed with the physical body, they are actually performed on the energy body and affect it.

In other words, the seers are moving the energy in their energy bodies by the movements in the physical body and collecting the energies that are idle on the periphery of the energy body, sending them to the centers of life. In this way, they ensure that the idle energy is absorbed by the existing energy centers.

Therefore, the seers have discovered the "medical of the energy body", thanks to their discoveries. And here lies the secret how don Juan manages to remain younger and more vigorous than Castaneda, despite his age:

- Another example I can give you is the agility of my knees. Haven't you noticed how much more agile I am than you? When it comes to moving my knees, I'm a kid! With my magical passes, I put a dam on the current of behavior and physicality that makes the knees of people, both men and women, stiff with age. [189]

---

[188] See Chapter 7- Stopping the Self and Chapter 9- Stopping the Actions

[189] CASTANEDA, Magical Passes, HarperCollins Publishers Inc., Magical Passes

In addition to this, Castaneda quotes about activating the lodged energy in a tendon center as follows:

- Energy which had become lodged in a tendon center had to be rendered fluid through vibration, and then it had to be pressed, so that it would continue flowing.

And he has noted that the seers even use some simple vibratory and pressure devices to aid in manipulating the flow of energy in the body, which they believed becomes periodically stuck along the tendon track.

In other words, the seers identify the problems in their energy bodies and apply "treatments" accordingly. And just as modern medicine applies angiography into a vein, they release the energy stuck in one place through magical passes. And as practicing a "surgical operation", they regain their energy bodies.

Therefore, God Almighty has put the healing of these troubles both in the physical and energetic realms. Also, in the physical world, just as a plane tree leaf is good for the knees, it is good for the knees to make the appropriate passes in the energy world. And both of these things are the mercy of God and the things that He puts on both sides to be discovered and used. What the seers do is discover them and use them to their advantage.

Prayer:

Yoga and Buddhism, like the magical passes, have fundamental doctrines originating from the energy body. Especially yoga is very similar to magical passes, and its function is almost the same. Although what the seers are doing seems to be more professional, they still do the same thing.

- What the old sorcerers sought avidly and experienced as a sensation of well-being and plenitude when they performed the magical passes was, in essence, the effect of unused energy being reclaimed by the centers of vitality in the body. [190]

---

190 CASTANEDA, Magical Passes, HarperCollins Publishers Inc., Tensegrity

By applying the magical passes, the seers reclaim their energies that have fallen away from their centers of life. And a great "sensation of well-being", the opposite of anxiety, covers themselves. Don Juan calls it "the practical utilization of energy for well-being".[191]

The seers and the other people doing yoga pursue this sensation of well-being that they cannot taste in normal life. On the other hand, those who turn to God live in the same peace with "prayer". And, the main reason why God puts these features in human nature is that He wants to make people love the path leading to Him.

42. And [mention] when the angels said, "O Mary, indeed God has chosen you and purified you and chosen you above the women of the worlds."
43. "O Mary, be devoutly obedient to your Lord and prostrate and bow with those who bow in prayer." (Koran/Chapter 3)

Since the Prophet Adam, God Almighty has made these two fundamental movements an integral part of human worship and commands the human being to do so. Although these do not consist of dozens of different movements, such as magical passes, it is important that the worship and the movement are merging.

In addition, the number and variety of magical passes are already causing problems for the seers. Castaneda, for example, makes a statement about don Juan's method of teaching the passes to his apprentices:

- Don Juan inundated them with a profusion of detail and let their minds be bewildered by the number and variety of magical passes taught to them, and by the implication that each of them individually was a pathway to infinity. His disciples spent years overwhelmed, confused, and above all despondent, because they felt that being inundated in such a manner was an unfair onslaught on them. [192]

There are such side effects of passes created by humans, but there is

---

[191] CASTANEDA, Magical Passes, HarperCollins Publishers Inc., The Fourth Series, The Separation of the Left Body and the Right Body: The Heat Sences

[192] CASTANEDA, Magical Passes, HarperCollins Publishers Inc., Tensegrity

no such thing in prayer. On the contrary, it meets all other needs of man as should be.

For instance, Castaneda says, "One of the aims of the sorcerers of ancient Mexico, was to train their bodies by means of the magical passes, to inhale and exhale deeply," but when you pray, you do so without realizing it. As a natural effect of the awe of the prayer, this breath control automatically takes its place in your body and you do not need to make an additional effort.

Don Juan also says that a person who applies the magical passes reaches inner silence. But passes have nothing to fill this void in man. So, the inner silence is enough for the seers.

In other words, they witness everything, but they do not need to talk about it, because they are already in "silence". Nevertheless, is this really the case? Should this entire universe be met only through silence?

27. O reassured soul!
28. Return to your Lord, well-pleased and pleasing!
29. Enter among My servants!
30. Enter My Paradise! (Koran/Chapter 89)

Certainly, God Almighty gives them the inner silence and the peace of it, but this inner silence is actually an intermediate stop, almost like the summit of the hill. Instead of waiting there, one has to cross that hill and accelerate to the other side. That's what prayer is for.

In the prayer, you leave the whole world behind and come before the Lord of the Worlds. You reach the inner silence and "stop the world" for a moment, but you don't stay there and go forward.

God Almighty commands, "Establish prayer for My remembrance." [193] So, realizing His greatness and that He surrounds everything takes away all the bottlenecks, pride, arrogance from you, and after all these reclamation, you return to this world in a pure and innocent condition.

Your goal is not to gain energy in the prayer, as it is in the magical passes. As the hunter is chasing his prey, you are not pursuing the energy. It already comes as a by-product. Your main aim is to return to

[193] Koran/Chapter 20, verse 14

God, who gives you these energies. And He is already leading you to the shortest route that leads to the energy.

On the other hand, turning the means into an aim gives man more difficulty than convenience, and when it happens, you keep performing challenging things like don Juan's apprentices.

As a result, the prayer that God gives people as a religious duty to be observed is an inartificial, compact and practically applicable version of these passes that don Juan applies to his apprentices. More precisely, gaining energy through the magical passes actually exists for prayer.

God Almighty designs man in such a way that he performs the prayer and that it will be useful for him. But the seers discover and use them for their practical benefits. In other words, the passes are, in fact, a detailed form of prayer that has been deprived of God and made for practical benefit.

Thus, there is no God in the magical passes; but God Almighty gives all those energy-giving movements so that people can grasp His greatness and bow before Him. He gives them as a reward, so they do not fall into the ego, be swept away by arrogance, do not hesitate to confirm Him like don Juan keeps doing. That's the only thing the seers fail to do.

Their situation is the same as that of the modern man who takes advantage of all the blessings on earth and then forgets God. They both practice what God has given them but, it is difficult for them to thank God.

And I feel the same inadequacy here that I felt while I was going to yoga classes during my undergraduate education. The lessons are beautiful, you are full of energy, but at the same time, something is always missing because these functional movements cannot be connected with God and the vastness that surrounds us. All those people are filled with the energy that God has given them, but most of them carry on without knowing this fact. And when that "cornerstone" is missing, they cannot be fully satisfied with this situation.

Tensegrity:

As a reflection of the progressive advance of the science of the seers, Castaneda decides to find new ways to spread this knowledge and begins to reorganize the magical passes under the name of "tensegrity" and start teaching people.

For tensegrity, Castaneda says “the modern version of the magical passes of the shamans of ancient Mexico"[194], but in fact, it's a consolation for Castaneda who is left behind. Because, as Castaneda knows, don Juan is never interested in teaching his knowledge.

"Don Juan was interested in perpetuating his lineage,"[195] says Castaneda, but he also does not really care if his lineage continues. He never cares about the end of the lineage with Castaneda and sees it as a decision of "intent". The only important thing for him is to increase his energy level by the help of the challenging disciples. So, don Juan is teaching his knowledge for his own maturity, and he does not care about teaching his knowledge or his lineage.

In the case of Castaneda, God Almighty finishes this lineage with Castaneda and sends a "scholar" like him to don Juan, and enables the knowledge of the seers to reach out to human beings through the books written by him. But this "intent" of God Almighty is not enough for Castaneda and he goes into other quests.

On the other hand, there is a crucial thing that tensegrity teaches us that it sheds more light on one aspect of the prayer, which is actually the basis of magical passes. Hence, Castaneda speaks of an energetic situation that emerged during tensegrity, which was never reached by don Juan and the shamans of his lineage, and explains this as follows:

- The practice of Tensegrity in very large groups has been more than ideal, because it has given me the unique opportunity of witnessing something which don Juan Matus and all the sorcerers of his lineage never did: the effects of human mass. Don Juan and all the shamans of his lineage, which he considered to be twenty-seven generations

[194] CASTANEDA, Magical Passes, HarperCollins Publishers Inc., Tensegrity

[195] CASTANEDA, Magical Passes, HarperCollins Publishers Inc., Introduction

> long, never were capable of witnessing the effects of human mass. They practiced the magical passes alone, or in groups of up to five practitioners. For them, the magical passes were highly individualistic. If the number of Tensegrity practitioners is in the hundreds, an energetic current is nearly instantaneously formed among them. This energetic current, which a shaman could easily see, creates in the practitioners a sense of urgency. It is like a vibratory wind that sweeps through them, and gives them the primary elements of purpose. [196]

According to Castaneda, don Juan and his friends always implement these movements in an individual way, and therefore cannot witness the enormous contribution of the human mass in the energy context.

On the other hand, God Almighty says that prayer is much more virtuous when performed with a community and encourages people to do so. In other words, the most essential prayer is, in fact, the one performed with a community. Therefore, Castaneda's discovery reveals another aspect of the prayer that we call the pure state of magical passes and confirms in another way that the real reason for the passes is actually prayer itself.

---

[196] CASTANEDA, Magical Passes, HarperCollins Publishers Inc., Tensegrity

7- Stopping the Self

- Self-importance
- Ruthlessness
- Humility of Seers
- Awareness of Death

SELF-IMPORTANCE

Even though the seers obtain energy through magical passes, their main method of gaining energy is "stopping". Accordingly, they stop everything unnecessary in their lives and try to accumulate the energy they spend on them.

Hence, the expertise of the seers is actually a stopping skill. They are accumulating their energies by stopping their selves, their social relationships and all the unnecessary things they do. And at the last point, they use this surplus energy to "stop the world".

The first thing the seers do for this is to stop their self by restricting "self-importance". When they get rid of caring for themselves, they save the energy it wastes.

<u>Self-importance</u>:

Don Juan says, "Self-importance is another thing that must be dropped," and he begins to teach this to Castaneda in the early days of his apprenticeship:

- You take yourself too seriously. You are too damn important in your own mind. That must be changed! You are so goddamn important that you feel justified to be annoyed with everything. You're so damn important that you can afford to leave if things don't go your way. I suppose you think that shows you have character. That's nonsense! You're weak, and conceited!

- As long as you feel that you are the most important thing in the world you cannot really appreciate the world around you. You are like a horse with blinkers, all you see is yourself apart from everything else. [197]

Self-importance causes man to deal only with themselves and prevents them from appreciating this world properly. And that is why the seers declare "self-importance" as their greatest enemy.

- Self-importance is our greatest enemy. Think about it? What weakens us is feeling offended by the deeds and misdeeds of our fellow men. Our self-importance requires that we spend most of our lives offended by someone.
- The new seers recommended that every effort should be made to eradicate self-importance from the lives of warriors. I have followed that recommendation, and much of my endeavors with you has been geared to show you that without self-importance we are invulnerable. [198]

As self-importance is their greatest enemy, the seers are developing a lot of strategies to get rid of this. And the seers, through the ages, have given the highest praise to those who have accomplished to overcome it.

<u>Associating the fight against self-importance with energy but not morality</u>:

18. Do not turn your cheek in contempt toward people and do not walk through the earth proudly. Indeed, God does not like everyone self-deluded and boastful. (Koran/Chapter 31)

Castaneda is disturbed by what don Juan told about "self-importance" and says that it reminded him of Catholic postulates, and after a

---

[197] CASTANEDA, Journey to Ixtlan, Washington Square Press, Losing Self-Importance

[198] CASTANEDA, The Fire From Within, Washington Square Press, Petty Tyrants

lifetime of being told about the evils of sin, he had become callous. Don Juan answers him as follows:

- Warriors fight self-importance as a matter of strategy, not principle. Your mistake is to understand what I say in terms of morality.
- I see you as a highly moral man, don Juan.
- You've noticed my impeccability, that's all... Impeccability is nothing else but the proper use of energy. My statements have no inkling of morality. I've saved energy and that makes me impeccable. To understand this, you have to save enough energy yourself. [199]

Don Juan describes impeccability as the proper use of energy. According to him, all behaviors that save man's energy from an area that consumes it and channel it to the right place are "impeccable". Since self-importance is the most energy-consuming thing, its destruction is at the top of the list of the seers.

So, just like the control of sexual power[200], the seers save the energy that one wastes by dealing with himself and use it for their own benefit. And by doing so, they do not even care about "morality", because all they care about is the energy itself.

<u>Attack on personal self</u>:

According to don Juan, self-importance is not something simple and naive. So he says, "Self-importance can't be fought with niceties."[201] Therefore, the seers use the heaviest methods possible to wipe it off from their lives. And one of these methods is "attack on the person himself."

So the seers harass their apprentices in their narrow groups by using every way possible. Thus, they give a blow to the self-importance of the apprentices. Moreover, outside the group, they find a "petty tyrant",

---

199 CASTANEDA, The Fire From Within, Washington Square Press, Petty Tyrants

200 See Chapter 8- Stopping The Human Relations

201 CASTANEDA, The Fire From Within, Washington Square Press, Petty Tyrants

and this time they, using these tyrants, put pressure on their apprentices in another way.

125. Invite to the way of your Lord with wisdom and good instruction, and argue with them in a way that is best. Indeed, your Lord is most knowing of who has strayed from His way, and He is most knowing of who is rightly guided. (Koran/Chapter 16)

Don Juan tells Castaneda, "The only concrete help you ever get from me is that I attack your self-reflection. If it weren't for that, you would be wasting your time. This is the only real help you've gotten from me."[202]

And the seers make these attacks in humiliating ways, such as laughing at the apprentices, insulting them or making fun of them. But their legitimacy does not matter. The only thing that matters to them is energy, and they see all that is permissible.

For example, don Juan regularly laughs at the things Castaneda and other apprentices are doing and sometimes even rolls on the floor during that time. By doing so, he humiliates them and strikes a blow against their personal importance. And it also has another benefit. In this way, don Juan tears down what they consider normal and makes his agenda dominate.

Don Juan's other attack is to humiliate Castaneda with his words. He often tells him, "You are a fool, obtuse, stupid, etc." And he tries to make him feel worthless and lose his self-importance.

70. We have certainly honored the children of Adam and carried them on the land and sea and provided for them of the good things and made them superior to much of what We have created. (Koran/Chapter 17)

Although the methods of the seers seem to work, they are always unnatural methods. And God Almighty, who makes human dignity

---

[202] CASTANEDA, The Power of Silence, Washington Square Press, The Requirements Of Intent: Breaking The Mirror Of Self-Reflection

worthy of respect, does not allow such methods of insult and humiliation, even if they work.

He loves those who think and behave beautifully and says, "Tell My servants to say that which is best."[203] What the seers do, on the other hand, is more in keeping with the disposition of sinners who always apply these extreme behaviors to the Prophets and believers:

109. Indeed, there was a party of My servants who said, 'Our Lord, we have believed, so forgive us and have mercy upon us, and You are the best of the merciful.'
110. But you took them in mockery to the point that it made you forget My remembrance, and you used to laugh at them.
111. Indeed, I have rewarded them this Day for their patient endurance – that they are the attainers of success." (Koran/ Chapter 23)

Prophets and believers are always subjected to humiliations and insults of those who deny while fighting for the truth. And in this way, they realize the evolution intended by the seers in natural ways.

The seers create an artificial simulation of this within their narrow groups and provide their own personal development. However, if they take a step in the path of God Almighty, they will find what they are looking for.

Petty Tyrants:

6. Mention when Moses said to his people, "Remember the favor of God upon you when He saved you from the people of Pharaoh, who were afflicting you with the worst torment and were slaughtering your newborn sons and keeping your females alive. And in that was a great trial from your Lord." (Koran/Chapter 14)

Another method used by the seers to get rid of personal importance is the "petty tyrant" tactic. Don Juan says, "The perfect ingredient for the making of a superb seer is a petty tyrant with unlimited prerogatives."

---

203 Koran/Chapter 17, verse 53

And he considers the warrior who stumbles on a petty tyrant is a lucky one, because the seers who are dealing with the petty tyrants, are capable of facing anything.

In explaining what the petty tyrant is, don Juan calls him "a tormentor who either holds the power of life and death over warriors or, simply annoys them to distraction." Don Juan says that the warriors should thank them day and night because they help the warriors to destroy their self-importance. And under that kind of pressure, seers reaches sublime states. [204]

Accordingly, the seers either find a real fiend from life and take it as a petty tyrant or use each other as a petty tyrant. Don Juan, for example, has had to work under such a petty tyrant for a long time in his youth. Or in the same way, thanks to Castaneda as an apprentice, he has had more difficulty than ever before.

He also tells Castaneda that "La Gorda is the petty tyrant in your life, but you still haven't caught on to that."[205] And as a matter of fact, la Gorda was later given to Castaneda's protection and was told that he should tolerate whatever she did.

31. And thus have We made for every prophet an enemy from among the criminals. Sufficient is your Lord as a guide and a helper. (Koran/Chapter 25)

In the way of the prophets, such artificial ecosystems are not needed. Because the prophets tell the righteous cause among people, and when this happens, they find their tyrants naturally. Just as He gave Pharaoh to Moses, God Almighty says that He will haunt an enemy on every Prophet.

Therefore, when the prophets tell the righteous cause, their tyrants appear right next to them. And God Almighty reveals this in the Koran as a law of nature. Yet, the seers discover a truth in the universe and form their own tactics, but as they are not on the righteous path, they have to go and find their tyrants by themselves.

---

[204] CASTANEDA, The Fire From Within, Washington Square Press, Petty Tyrants

[205] CASTANEDA, The Fire From Within, Washington Square Press, The New Seers

RUTHLESSNESS

Don Juan explains that seers had unmasked self-importance and found that it is "self-pity" masquerading as something else:

- Self-pity is the real enemy and the source of man's misery. Without a degree of pity for himself, man could not afford to be as self-important as he is. [206]

The formula developed by the seers against it is "ruthlessness". "Ruthlessness is the opposite of self-pity," says don Juan, and for him, it is the first principle of sorcery.[207] Accordingly, the seers do not feel pity for themselves, and they do so through their determination.

Determination:

115. We had already taken a promise from Adam before, but he forgot; and We found not in him determination. (Koran/Chapter 20)

"For a sorcerer, ruthlessness is not cruelty. Ruthlessness is the opposite of self-pity or self-importance. Ruthlessness is sobriety," says don Juan. So, the seers are determined to do what they have before them, and

---

206 CASTANEDA, The Power of Silence, Washington Square Press, The Place Of No Pity

207 CASTANEDA, The Power of Silence, Washington Square Press, Moving the Assemblage Point

this "determination" in them ensures that they do not feel pity for themselves.

Don Juan tells Castaneda at the beginning of his apprenticeship, "You feel that indulging in doubts and tribulations is the sign of a sensitive man. Well, the truth of the matter is that you're the farthest thing from being sensitive."[208] And the seers, after years of struggle, achieve this "determination" and leave doubts and delusions behind.

From the very first moment, don Juan taught Castaneda that "decisions cannot be changed" because of rendering death a guide. For him, the consciousness of death is the antidote to self-pity, and determination is achieved through it:

- In the world of everyday life our word or our decisions could be reversed very easily. The only irrevocable thing in our world was death. In the sorcerers' world, on the other hand, normal death could be countermanded, but not the sorcerers' word. In the sorcerers' world decisions could not be changed or revised. Once they had been made, they stood forever. [209]

Therefore, the rule of not changing the decisions exists in order that there is no self-pity. You decide and do not change your mind; you go all the way. And you do not have any remorse and pity on yourself.

Surrendering to destiny:

50. If good befalls you, it distresses them; but if disaster strikes you, they say, "We took our matter in hand before," and turn away while they are rejoicing.
51. Say, "Never will we be struck except by what God has decreed for us; He is our Friend." And upon God let the believers rely. (Koran/Chapter 9)

The second aspect of ruthlessness is to accept the "fate". Just as warriors are determined in micro-events, so does it require

[208] CASTANEDA, Tales of Power, Washington Square Press, The Dreamer and The Dreamed

[209] CASTANEDA, The Power of Silence, Washington Square Press, Handling Intent: The Third Point

determination in macro-events. But since the touches of "intent" are felt much better here, a warrior needs to do whatever the intent says. Therefore, surrendering to God's will, which the seers call intent, becomes "determination" and it protects man from regrets.

"Power comes only after we accept our fate without recriminations," [210] says don Juan. And as we mentioned before, the main reason for human unhappiness is that he does not accept his fate and feels sorry for himself. And that's why don Juan calls self-pity the "greatest enemy".

La Gorda, for example, says to Castaneda, "The problem with you is that you did not accept your fate."[211] and accuses him of not accepting himself as a "warrior". And says that, only a real warrior can feel that kind of happiness about his fate. But Castaneda refuses to understand that fate wants him to become a warrior by taking him in the way of don Juan and continues to pity himself.

No pity for anyone:

- Warriors are incapable of feeling compassion because they no longer feel sorry for themselves. Without the driving force of self-pity, compassion is meaningless. [212]

What don Juan calls as not feeling sorry for yourself, is actually to surrender to God. You surrender to God Almighty, and you know that everything comes from Him and you do not cry to yourself. You say God is the Knowing, the Wise, and you trust in His wisdom.

This is what the seers do as well. But because they are unaware of God's knowledge, they go to extremes again and reach a point that they do not pity anyone.

---

210 CASTANEDA, The Second Ring of Power, Washington Square Press, The Little Sisters

211 CASTANEDA, The Second Ring of Power, Washington Square Press, The Art of Dreaming

212 CASTANEDA, The Power of Silence, Washington Square Press, The Knock of The Spirit: The Abstract

God Almighty wants us to surrender to His wisdom and destiny, but at the same time, He says, "I am the Most Merciful and the Most Compassionate". Therefore, His destiny proceeds according to this main regime, not ruthlessness.

20. We did not send before you any of the messengers except that they ate food and walked in the markets. And We have made some of you as trial for others – will you have patience? And ever is your Lord, Seeing. (Koran/Chapter 25)

The seers say, "People live their own destiny, so we do not pity anyone, do not interfere with anyone and we do our own business." However, God Almighty makes us a trial for one another to see how we will react to the destiny He gives.

Castaneda, for example, caused a child's collarbone to be broken when he was a child and is still grieved by it. On the other hand, "You made a good gift to him," says don Juan. "There is nothing you can do for that little boy's life. Only he could cancel that act by learning to reduce his wants to nothing."

In fact, it is neither a gift nor a punishment; it is a test of God. Don Juan, on the other hand, thinks that he will get rid of the classic pessimistic view of a person, who sees it as an irreparable shortcoming and calls it a gift.

The seers are making the same extremes for the petty tyrants. They see the "tyrants" that God has plagued as a reward and even thank them. However, that tyrant is, in fact, cruel and not a reward. In addition, if there is someone to thank, it is not the tyrant but God Almighty Himself.

Therefore, the seers cannot "hit the nail on the head", because they don't have a knowledge from God Almighty. They say "gift" and leave the responsibility to others, supposedly staying in a neutral position. Essentially, God Almighty is giving us a test and trying out which one will behave better.

Ruthlessness making the seers frozen cold:

Don Juan talks about the seven female warriors taking care of him while he was at nagual Julian's house and is surprised by the great interest those women have shown to make him happy.

- The seven women were exquisite and they made me feel happy. I liked them and trusted them. They treated me with respect and consideration. But something in their eyes told me that under their facades of charm there existed a terrifying coldness, an aloofness I could never penetrate.
- I was amazed by the profound interest the women took in my well-being. They did everything for me. They seemed to hang on my every word. Never before had people been so kind to me. But also, never before had I felt so solitary. I was always in the company of the beautiful, strange women, and yet I had never been so alone. [213]

According to don Juan, the same coldness was also found in nagual Julian, his own benefactor. And don Juan says, "He was, like all the naguals, as cold as the arctic wind." [214]

Although the seers don't look like that from the outside, they're basically cold people because of their "ruthlessness". Not feeling pity for themselves causes them not to pity others, and as a result, even though they look playful and warm outwardly, their main attitude towards other people is a neutral coldness.

However, the real reason they are so cold is not that they do not feel pity for themselves, but rather they keep God Almighty excluded from their lives. Otherwise, the prophets also do not feel sorry for themselves.

---

213 CASTANEDA, The Power of Silence, Washington Square Press, The Ticket To Impeccability

214 CASTANEDA, The Power of Silence, Washington Square Press, Moving the Assemblage Point

128. There has certainly come to you a Messenger from among yourselves. Grievous to him is what you suffer; he is fond of you and to the believers is kind and merciful.
129. And if they turn away, say, "Sufficient for me is God; there is no deity except Him. On Him I have relied, and He is the Lord of the Great Arsh." (Koran/Chapter 9)

Prophet Muhammad is asked to say, if they leave him alone, "God is enough for me". Therefore, even if everyone goes away and the world around them collapses, believers find God Almighty with them and He is always enough for them.

On the other hand, the seers escape to the twilight of "and yet…" in such a situation:

- However, sorcerers have a peculiar bent. They live exclusively in the twilight of a feeling best described by the words "and yet..." When everything is crumbling down around them, sorcerers accept that the situation is terrible, and then immediately escape to the twilight of "and yet..." [215]

Supposedly this is "not feeling pity for themselves", but in fact, as they do not know God Almighty, they stay all alone and try to cover this deficiency by force.

When the seers are all alone in themselves, they treat other people in the same way and they externalize the loneliness within. Essentially, since they are unaware of God and His warm-heartedness, their heart becomes petrified.

God Almighty says in His Koran, "You have no other friend than God, nor helper". Likewise He adds: "I am closer to you than your jugular vein". On the other hand, since the seers do not accept this close Friend, they do not have friends outside, nor can they become friends with themselves. Their share is no different from coldness.

61. If they incline to peace, then incline to it and rely upon God. Indeed, it is He who is the Hearing, the Knowing.

---

[215] CASTANEDA, The Power of Silence, Washington Square Press, The Ticket To Impeccability

62. But if they intend to deceive you – then sufficient for you is God. It is He who supported you with His help and with the believers
63. And brought together their hearts. If you had spent all that is in the earth, you could not have brought their hearts together; but God brought them together. Indeed, He is Exalted in Might and Wise. (Koran/Chapter 8)

The prophets and believers are compassionate and merciful to one another because they are equipped with the features of God Almighty, but at the same time, they never forget that God is the true Friend.

The Prophet Muhammad is told, "If you had spent all that is in the earth, you could not have brought their hearts together; but God brought them together." Therefore, they can unite in this way because they are united in God and He is the Forgiving and the Merciful. On the other hand, the seers are experiencing a kind of unfortunateness in the name of ruthlessness since they are the deniers of God.

As for today's people, it is experienced as depersonalization with the name of "alienation". We live in cities where millions of people live, but we are all alone, and we live the same coldness almost to a freezing point. Moreover, the reason for that is not so different from that of the seers.

We live without the acknowledgment of God, we do not put Him into the center of our lives, and without His bond, we are scattered like marbles. However, He is the core of everything, and when we take Him out of our lives, we are - like the seers - freezing as hard as a stone.

HUMILITY OF SEERS

Being nothing:

- Be nothing while everyone in this world is trying to be something. May your destination be nothingness. (Mevlana Jalaluddin Rumi)

"Warriors prepare themselves to be aware, and full awareness comes to them only when there is no more self-importance left in them. Only when they are nothing do they become everything,"[216] says don Juan. And he mentions his benefactors as follows:

- Each of the two men had his own flair, but the end result was just the same: emptiness, an emptiness that reflected not the world, but infinity. [217]

In Islamic Sufism, the person who has reached perfection is described with nothingness in the same way as the seers. Therefore, Sufis symbolize human beings with a musical instrument called "ney" - a kind of reed flute used by Sufis. And the main feature of this instrument is that the interior is "empty".

Accordingly, the ney is first removed from the whole, that is, from the

---

216 CASTANEDA, The Fire from Within, Washington Square Press, The Position of the Assemblage Point

217 CASTANEDA, The Active Side of Infinity, HarperCollins Publishers Inc., Who Was Juan Matus, Really?

reed field. Then the inner part is cleaned using a long rasp up to its sound box and its uneven nodes are heated to reshape the cane. After all these processes, the musical instrument that makes the world's most touching sound comes into being.

According to the Sufis, the "perfect human" comes to this world in the same way and falls apart from his origin, God Almighty, and cries like the ney because of this separation. Then, in this world, he is subjected to a test of fire and emptied and becomes nothing. And only after this journey does one deserve to return to God Almighty.

So, both the seers and the Sufis become "nothing" at the end. However, the Sufis fill this gap with God Almighty, that is the source they come from, and are attributed with His beautiful attributes. The seers do not do so and remain empty, which manifests as the ice coldness of the warrior, as we have already mentioned.

36. Does man think that he will be left neglected?
37. Had he not been a sperm from semen emitted?
38. Then he became an attached embryo, and God created him and proportioned him
39. And made of him two mates, the male and the female.
40. Then, He who made all these, cannot give life to the dead? (Koran/Chapter 75)

As a matter of fact, man is already in a state of nothingness, but he needs to discern this. When he is nothing, God creates him from a sperm and makes him an honorable individual. And what is expected of him is to realize his own nothingness and to realize the greatness of God Almighty.

32. It is God who created the heavens and the earth and sent down rain from the sky and produced thereby some fruits as provision for you and subjected for you the ships to sail through the sea by His command and subjected for you the rivers.
33. And He subjected for you the sun and the moon continuously, and subjected for you the night and the day.
34. And He gave you from all you asked of Him. And if you should count the blessings of God, you could not enumerate them. Indeed, mankind is unjust and ungrateful. (Koran/Chapter 14)

All that is in the heavens and the earth belongs to God. Our own body, the car we ride, the water we drink, the food we eat... He gives us all of these things. Normally we don't think so and we think of them as ours; but in fact, they are entrusted to us and the real owner is God Almighty. And to understand this, takes away the self within us and forms the secret-concealed-natural way of getting rid of self-importance.

<u>The humility of the seers</u>:

- Haven't you ever heard of my reputation in this world? I'm nothing, nothing! (Mevlana Jalaluddin Rumi)

The humility of the Sufis stems from the greatness of the Lord of the Worlds and the fact that everything belongs to Him. In fact, their bodies, their knowledge, all their abilities belong to God Almighty. And when there is nothing of their own, there is no situation to be boasted about or to take credit for. They come from God, and in this life, they reflect what belongs to Him and then return to Him.

On the other hand, the humility of the seer results from the fact that they see everything equal to each other. Since they discover other realms that are available to man, they see this universe as only one of the hundreds of possible universes and therefore declare everything in it as insignificant. According to them, everything in this universe is equal, and all human efforts are just an unending lunacy and folly. But the Lord of the Worlds says this is not so:

19. Not equal are the blind and the seeing!
20. Nor are the darknesses and the light!
21. Nor are the shade and the heat!
22. And not equal are the living and the dead. Indeed, God causes to hear whom He wills, but you cannot make hear those in the graves!
23. You are only a warner!
24. Indeed, We have sent you with the truth as a bringer of good tidings and a warner. And there was no nation but that there had passed within it a warner.

25. And if they deny you – then already have those before them denied. Their messengers came to them with clear proofs and written ordinances and with the enlightening Scripture.
26. Then I seized the ones who disbelieved, and they saw what it was to deny Me. (Koran/Chapter 35)

One day don Juan wants to teach Castaneda a lesson that everything is equal, and he kneels in front of a small plant, begins to caress it, and calls it "my little friend".

Don Juan then starts talking to it and tells Castaneda, "It does not matter what you say to a plant. You can just as well make up words; what's important is the feeling of liking it, and treating it as an equal." [218] And in the end, he wants him to thank the plant for being generous to him. Castaneda does not want to do it in his arrogant state, and he can only do so at the insistence of don Juan.

However, even though this behavior of don Juan may seem like a monument of humility, he cannot "hit the nail on the head" as it is not a knowledge coming from God. Don Juan knows quite well that the plant is not his equivalent, but he pretends to be as if it is. He tells something to it but, he says it's okay even if you make them up.

On the other hand, that plant is undoubtedly our friend because of the principle: "We love the created for the sake of Creator". So we love it, but we cannot say meaningless words to show our equivalence. Instead, we look at the great manifestations of God on it, and that plant introduces God Almighty to us in its own language. And we thank it, but we send the true thanks to God Almighty, who gave it to us and showed His great generosity.

<u>They degrade man while trying to fight self-importance</u>:

In order to fight self-importance, the seers sometimes go to the extreme and put themselves even lower than the plants that they see as their equivalents.

---

[218] CASTANEDA, Journey to Ixtlan, Washington Square Press, Losing Self-Importance

Don Juan, for example, says "All of us are fools."[219] Or while describing the people's character types, he describes his oppressive character saying, "I am a fart".[220] Castaneda begins to protest, saying his scheme of classification was demeaning. But don Juan says: "I'll always be a fart, and so will you."

In the Koran, God Almighty commands that He has made man superior to many of the creations. And He creates him with a body as a physical object, but He also makes him a being that can communicate with other realms. The seers know that, and they say that only human beings can enter into the state of heightened awareness, which they call the second attention, and that other living things cannot. So, what is all that discourse - we are equal and everything is equal?

Since the seers are not following a knowledge from God, they are totally missing the balance. On the one hand, they call themselves farts down; but on the other hand, they talk about their success stories, their seeing victories without mentioning God's blessings on them. But God Almighty sends us the truth and places the human being where it should be.

Just as a human being is assembling two different environments, matter and energy, human is also at the intersection point in terms of his personal importance. While he is great enough to make angels prostrate before him, his helplessness against the greatness of God is the source of his nothingness. And the awe against the greatness of God bestows humility upon man, but this does not humiliate him.

<u>Putting the whole universe under man's order</u>:

10. It is He who sends down rain from the sky; from it is drink and from it is foliage in which you pasture your animals.
11. He grows for you with it the crops, olives, palm trees, grapevines, and from all the fruits. Indeed in that is a sign for a people who give thought.

---

[219] CASTANEDA, Journey to Ixtlan, Washington Square Press, The Last Battle on Earth

[220] CASTANEDA, The Power of Silence, Washington Square Press, Intending Appearances

12. And He has subjected for you the night and day and the sun and moon, and the stars are subjected by His command. Indeed in that are signs for a people who reason.
13. And whatever He multiplied for you on the earth of varying colors; indeed in that is a sign for a people who take advice.
14. And it is He who subjected the sea for you to eat from it tender meat and to extract from it ornaments which you wear. And you see the ships plowing through it, and that you may seek of His bounty; and perhaps you will be grateful. (Koran/Chapter 16)

God Almighty gives the whole universe to the command of man and at the same time makes everything in the universe a sign that is conducive to recognize Him.

Since the seers exclude God, they equalize everything in insignificancy, but the Lord of the Worlds says that He has subjected all in the heavens and the earth to us, and He has put them into our service. Therefore, human beings have an exceptional place in this universe and the seers are actually the ones to know this best.

4. We have certainly created man in the best of stature,
5. Then We return him to the lowest of the low,
6. Except for those who believe and do righteous deeds, for they will have a reward uninterrupted.
7. So what yet causes you to deny the religion?
8. Is not God the most just of judges? (Koran/Chapter 95)

Yet, the superiority of the human being mentioned in the Koran is not a means of arrogance, but a submission of the right. Otherwise, one can use all the talent and opportunities offered to him in evil and fall down into a state lower than animals.

However, there are also those who know that these opportunities are given to him by God Almighty and make them conducive to grasp His greatness. In the face of His grandeur, they are transforming into the soil[221], so at the same time, they become both the lord of the earth and

[221] Soil is the symbol of the nothingness of the perfect human in Sufism. Soil absorbs everything and has no arrogance. It is calm and shows us where we had come from.

nothing. And that is the only way for human beings to achieve their purpose of existence.

<u>The humility of the seers being tactical</u>:

> 34. Mention when We said to the angels, "Prostrate before Adam"; so they prostrated, except for Iblees. He refused and was arrogant and became of the disbelievers. (Koran/Chapter 2)

Although don Juan speaks of equality, he calls people outside the seers "ordinary" and places the seers into a different place. Don Juan puts this down to the conclusion that the seers reach areas that other people cannot reach. But the seers are the people that exist within the boundaries set by God and with the life He has given them. Therefore, everyone is small and equal in the face of God's greatness.

The seers make the error where the devil once fell. And just as the devil is rebelling against the command of his Lord, saying 'I am better than Adam', the seers call people "ordinary" and make the same mistake. In their minds, they see themselves as superior to ordinary people, but they also rebel against the Lord of all things, thus resetting everything they do. Despite all their perfection, they forget that it is God Almighty who gave it to them, and they are among the losers.

When don Juan speaks of the old seers, he says that they are the most egocentric people. And despite all their enormous knowledge, they get into a rut because they cannot get over their self-importance. The new seers evaluate the mistakes of the old ones and realize that in order to overcome them, they must destroy self-importance. So, the new ones lose self-importance since it works, and this is an important step in the development of their knowledge.

Therefore, the humility of the seers is tactical as in all other subjects, and they do this because it provides them energy due to human nature. So, their humility is not real but tactical.

Once, don Juan likens himself to the flame of a candle in front of billions of stars and says:

- To seek freedom is the only driving force I know. Freedom to fly off into that infinity out there. Freedom to dissolve; to lift off; to

> be like the flame of a candle, which, in spite of being up against the light of a billion stars, remains intact, because it never pretended to be more than what it is: a mere candle. [222]

Maybe don Juan does not lord it over anything in this universe, but he acts as if he is superior to God, who owns everything in this universe, and ignores His religion and prophets. He says that he is like a candle in front of billions of stars, but speaks of exceeding God, the owner of those stars, and wandering around Him to seek freedom, and he is ungrateful to the power that makes him a "candle". Therefore, they may not be arrogant to people, but they have arrogance against Almighty God.

<u>All praises to God Almighty</u>:

1. Praise is to God, Creator of the heavens and the earth, who made the angels messengers having wings, two or three or four. He increases in creation what He wills. Indeed, God is over all things competent.
2. Whatever God grants to people of mercy – none can withhold it; and whatever He withholds – none can release it thereafter. And He is the Exalted in Might, the Wise.
3. O mankind, remember the favor of God upon you. Is there any creator other than God who provides for you from the heaven and earth? There is no deity except Him, so how are you deluded? (Koran/Chapter 35)

Man is the only living being standing on his two feet on the earth, but God obliges him to prostrate, and he prostrates by his will. His superiority over angels lies here. On the other hand, there are those arrogant who are not doing it, laying claims to their achievements as were theirs.

Don Juan treats a plant as equal, but calls people who are not like them "ordinary people" or speaks of "nagual triumphs", "inadequate praises", "supreme and impeccable stalkers".

---

[222] CASTANEDA, The Art of Dreaming, HarperCollins Publishers Inc., The Fixation of The Assemblage Point

All this is no different from the things an announcer I watched, presenting a documentary on the Swiss Alps, giving praise to the trains, their punctuality and being a marvel of engineering. Both give praise to themselves, not to God. However, the Sufis say, "All praise is to the Lord of the Worlds", and they see themselves only as a mirror.

Therefore, when you remove the Almighty God, who is at the center of everything, you have the teachings whose integrity cannot be ensured. And the main concern of the seers is not humility or losing self-importance, but energy. Losing self-importance matters only if it takes them to energy; otherwise, they have nothing against ego-centrism or self-centeredness. That is why they despise God and consider themselves as successful.

So we have to ask them: How do we become everything when we are nothing? Why are we full of energy when we lose self-importance? And why is there such a thing in human nature? It is because, we are asked to remove the self and replace it with God Almighty, and we are already designed accordingly. That is what the seers discover and use, but they do it by denying God, and fall into error.

AWARENESS OF DEATH

28. How can you disbelieve in God when you were lifeless and He brought you to life; then He will cause you to die, then He will bring you back to life, and then to Him you will be returned. (Koran/Chapter 2)

"The idea of death is of monumental importance in the life of a sorcerer,"[223] says don Juan, and the consciousness of death forms the basis of many things in the knowledge of the seers. That's why don Juan often tells Castaneda about death. But Castaneda is disturbed by this and tells him that he is afraid of death. Don Juan responds to him as follows:

- Focus your attention on the link between you and your death, without remorse or sadness or worrying. Focus your attention on the fact you don't have time and let your acts flow accordingly. Let each of your acts be your last battle on earth. Only under those conditions will your acts have their rightful power. Otherwise they will be, for as long as you live, the acts of a timid man. [224]

---

223 CASTANEDA, The Power of Silence, Washington Square Press, The Somersault Of Thought

224 CASTANEDA, Journey to Ixtlan, Washington Square Press, The Last Battle on Earth

Therefore, the seers see death as an ally, not something to be feared. And they go to death every time they run into trouble:

- Death is the only wise adviser that we have. Whenever you feel, as you always do, that everything is going wrong and you're about to be annihilated, turn to your death and ask if that is so. Your death will tell you that you're wrong; that nothing really matters outside its touch. Your death will tell you, "I haven't touched you yet". [225]

The seers do not lose themselves in despair unless death happens and use the awareness of death as a kind of "antidote" of self-pity. Don Juan always says that "The only deterrent to our despair is the awareness of our death, the key to the sorcerer's scheme of things." [226]

Once, don Juan asks Castaneda, "Do you know anyone who lives happily?" and Castaneda answers, "No. I really don't." With that don Juan says, "I do" and claims that their main feature is nothing but "acting with the full knowledge that they don't have time".

- There are some people who are very careful about the nature of their acts. Their happiness is to act with the full knowledge that they don't have time; therefore, their acts have a peculiar power... Especially when the person acting knows that those acts are his last battle. There is a strange consuming happiness in acting with the full knowledge that whatever one is doing may very well be one's last act on earth. I recommend that you reconsider your life and bring your acts into that light.

And against the objections of Castaneda, don Juan continues in this way:

- You don't have time, my friend. That is the misfortune of human beings. None of us have sufficient time, and your continuity has no meaning in this awesome, mysterious world.
- Your continuity only makes you timid. Your acts cannot possibly have the flair, the power, the compelling force of the acts

---

[225] CASTANEDA, Journey to Ixtlan, Washington Square Press, Death is an Adviser

[226] CASTANEDA, The Second Ring of Power, Washington Square Press, The Art of Dreaming

performed by a man who knows that he is fighting his last battle on earth. In other words, your continuity does not make you happy or powerful. [227]

Death as the source of power:

Don Juan says, "Whatever is touched by death indeed becomes power," and asserts that the idea of death is the source of personal power that the seers have:

- By the time knowledge becomes a frightening affair the man also realizes that death is the irreplaceable partner that sits next to him on the mat. Every bit of knowledge that becomes power has death as its central force. Death lends the ultimate touch, and whatever is touched by death indeed becomes power.
- A man who follows the paths of sorcery is confronted with imminent annihilation every turn of the way, and unavoidably he becomes keenly aware of his death. Without the awareness of death, he would be only an ordinary man involved in ordinary acts. He would lack the necessary potency, the necessary concentration that transforms one's ordinary time on earth into magical power. [228]

That is why the seers accept death as their wise adviser and live every moment effectively, using it as a point of reference. And opposite this, stand ordinary people who do not appreciate the value of their lives:

- Listen to that barking. That is the way my beloved earth is helping me now to bring this last point to you. That barking is the saddest thing one can hear. That dog's barking is the nocturnal voice of a man. It comes from a house in that valley towards the south. A man is shouting through his dog, since they are companion slaves for life, his sadness, his boredom. He's begging his death to come and release him from the dull and dreary chains of his life.

---

227 CASTANEDA, Journey to Ixtlan, Washington Square Press, The Last Battle on Earth

228 CASTANEDA, A Separate Reality, Washington Square Press, Chapter 10

- That barking, and the loneliness it creates, speaks of the feelings of men. Men for whom an entire life was like one Sunday afternoon, an afternoon which was not altogether miserable, but rather hot and dull and uncomfortable. They sweated and fussed a great deal. They didn't know where to go, or what to do. That afternoon left them only with the memory of petty annoyances and tedium, and then suddenly it was over; it was already night. [229]

"Without an awareness of the presence of our death, there is no power, no mystery"[230], says don Juan, and claims that the lives of people who lead their lives without the awareness of death transform into a miserable state.

Awareness of death allowing you to listen to your heart:

We have already said that the three teachings mentioned by Apple's founder Steve Jobs in his famous Stanford speech are related to the teachings of don Juan. Moreover, one of these three teachings is about death, the most fundamental doctrine of the seers. Jobs talks about it this way:

- Remembering that I'll be dead soon is the most important tool I've ever encountered to help me make the big choices in life. Because almost everything — all external expectations, all pride, all fear of embarrassment or failure — these things just fall away in the face of death, leaving only what is truly important. Remembering that you are going to die is the best way I know to avoid the trap of thinking you have something to lose. You are already naked. There is no reason not to follow your heart.

As a second doctrine, Steve Jobs talks about listening to the voice of his heart and doing what he loves. And he uses the thought of death as the catalyst for listening to it:

---

229 CASTANEDA, Tales of Power, Washington Square Press, The Predileciton of Two Warriors

230 CASTANEDA, Tales of Power, Washington Square Press, Having to Believe

- Your time is limited, so don't waste it living someone else's life. Don't be trapped by dogma — which is living with the results of other people's thinking. Don't let the noise of others' opinions drown out your own inner voice. And most important, have the courage to follow your heart and intuition. They somehow already know what you truly want to become. Everything else is secondary.

Here Jobs takes courage that he will hearken to his heart from the notion of death and says, "You are already naked. There is no reason not to follow your heart." On the other hand, don Juan tells these things to Castaneda so that he can give an ear to his heart:

- Years ago, I told you that in his day-to-day life a warrior chooses to follow the path with heart. It is the consistent choice of the path with heart which makes a warrior different from the average man. He knows that a path has heart when he is one with it, when he experiences a great peace and pleasure traversing its length. [231]

Don Juan wants Castaneda to take a "path with heart”. When he talks to him about this, he asks him to relate a subject that surrounds his whole life. Castaneda says "art" and says that he has dreamed of being an artist all his life, but despite some efforts, he has failed. Then don Juan answers him as follows:

- You have never taken the responsibility for being in this unfathomable world. Therefore, you were never an artist, and perhaps you'll never be a hunter. [232]

Elsewhere, don Juan treats Castaneda much harder and asks, "Well, are we equals?" Castaneda answers this question by saying, "Of course we are equals", but in reality, he considers himself superior to don Juan as a university student, a man of the sophisticated Western world. However, don Juan gives him an unexpected answer and says, "No. We are not equals. I'm a hunter and a warrior, and you are a pimp."

---

[231] CASTANEDA, A Separate Reality, Washington Square Press, Chapter 14

[232] CASTANEDA, Journey to Ixtlan, Washington Square Press, The Last Battle on Earth

Castaneda is shocked with his words and does not know what to say. Don Juan continues as follows:

- Don Juan said that I was pimping for someone else. That I was not fighting my own battles but the battles of some unknown people. That I did not want to learn about plants or about hunting or about anything. And that his world of precise acts and feelings and decisions was infinitely more effective than the blundering idiocy I called "my life". [233]

As you can see, don Juan and Steve Jobs both say the same thing. "Follow your heart and do not live someone else's life," they say. And to do that, they say, "Turn to your death and take as advice that you don't have time"

Both the seers and Steve Jobs live on these principles. So, one of them builds the best company in the world, while the others build their own unique science. And as a result, those who obey the divine laws that God Almighty has set are racing to the top both in the material and spiritual worlds.

Awareness of death as being a man-made doctrine:

Unfortunately, Steve Jobs passed away in 2011. And even though the company he founded, using death as an advisor, is one of the best companies in the world today, he is not among us now. So, if death sweeps everything like that, what is the point of achieving success in this world by taking death as a companion? Is there no contradiction here?

Yes, there is. And that's because "using death as an advisor" is a man-made doctrine. It is not holistic because it does not come from God Almighty, and although it contains fragments of truth, it fails at some point.

58. Have you seen that which you emit?
59. Is it you who creates it, or are We the Creator?

[233] CASTANEDA, Journey to Ixtlan, Washington Square Press, Becoming a Hunter

60. We have decreed death among you, and We are not to be outdone.
61. We will change you with alike ones and will generate you in a way which you do not know.
62. You have already known the first creation, so will you not take advice? (Koran/Chapter 56)

"One of the great aids that the shamans of ancient Mexico employed in establishing the concept of the warrior was the idea of taking our death as a companion, a witness to our acts,"[234] says don Juan. In other words, when the seers form the warrior's path, they look around to see what they have in their hands and reach the idea that the notion of death will work, and they begin to use it. So, this is a man-made doctrine created by the seers.

However, for such teaching to exist, something like death must exist in human life. After all, something like death might not have existed. But there is at least for now, and the seers use this notion to develop a teaching for themselves. Yet, it is God Almighty Himself who appreciates death in this way and puts it in human nature.

Since the seers do not have any scriptural knowledge, they say, "Death is our wisest friend". But in the Koran, the Wise God says, "I created life and death", and adds: "You have neither a friend nor a helper but God Himself". In other words, He asserts that it is Himself who even created the thing they consider as their wisest friend and commands them to be friends with nothing other but Him. Then God Almighty Himself declares the true doctrine of death:

99. Finally, when death comes to one of them, he says, "My Lord, send me back
100. That I might do righteousness in that which I left behind." No! It is only a word he is saying; and behind them is a barrier until the Day they are resurrected.
101. So when the Horn is blown, no relationship will there be among them that Day, nor will they ask about one another.

---

[234] CASTANEDA, The Wheel of Time, Washington Square Press, Quotations from a Separate Reality, Commentary

102. And those whose scales are heavy with good deeds – it is they who receive the salvation.
103. But those whose scales are light – those are the ones who are losers, being in Hell, abiding eternally.
104. The Fire will sear their faces, and they therein will have taut smiles. (Koran/Chapter 23)

According to the Koran, death can surely come at any moment. And as soon as death comes, there's judgment and no return. Therefore, everyone has been ensued for winning or losing an eternal life. And everyone will eventually be brought before the Almighty God who created death. In other words, one does not even have a second to waste, and a day spent here is worth millions of years in real life.

Therefore, the awareness of death exists in the Koran much more strongly than it does in the teachings of the seers, but it is in the form that suits best to human nature. It has a start and end, and it is in harmony with all the other things in the universe.

The teachings of the seers, on the other hand, have a significant inconsistency. They say, "death is our best friend", but on the other hand, the ultimate goal of all their teachings is to get rid of death.

So, what the seers embrace as a savior is actually what they ultimately want to defeat. However, God is the One who gives death, and God is the One who gives immortality. And there is no inconsistency in His words. But the seers cannot avoid contradicting themselves since they deny God Almighty, the Creator of all these things.

8- Stopping the Social Relationships

- Erasing Personal History
- Abstaining from Marriage and Sexuality

ERASING PERSONAL HISTORY

We have already said that the general attitude of the seers about the things in this universe is "stopping". And here again, as a reflection of this general state of stopping in their teachings, they end all human relations with ordinary people over time and only deal with people within their narrow groups.

Don Juan, for example, after being a disciple, is getting away from people who know him for years and creates a mist around him. Thus, he sets a barrier between him and his life before he became a warrior. Don Juan calls it "erasing personal history" and says that time began for him after he became a warrior.

Don Juan likewise asks Castaneda to erase his personal story and tells him, "It is best to erase all personal history, because that would make us free from the encumbering thoughts of other people".

- Your father knows everything about you. So he has you all figured out. He knows who you are and what you do, and there is no power on earth that can make him change his mind about you.
- Don't you see? You must renew your personal history by telling your parents, your relatives, and your friends everything you do. On the other hand, if you have no personal history, no explanations are needed; nobody is angry or disillusioned with

your acts. And above all no one pins you down with their thoughts.

- Little by little you must create a fog around yourself; you must erase everything around you until nothing can be taken for granted, until nothing is any longer for sure, or real. Your problem now is that you're too real. Your endeavours are too real; your moods are too real. Don't take things so for granted. You must begin to erase yourself. [235]

The seers use the method of stopping all their relations with normal people as a way of not being accountable to anyone and not being trapped in the thoughts of others. Therefore, they think they have retained their freedom.

With this method, they may be able to avoid accounting to people, but there is no way to run away from God's account.

6. We will surely question those to whom a messenger was sent, and We will surely question the messengers.
7. Then We will relate their deeds to them with knowledge, and We were not far from them. (Koran/Chapter 7)

Because the seers deny God and His account, they find a way to protect themselves from the thoughts of other people by staying away from them. But God Almighty creates us as a human being who lives in society and determines the way of protection from other people to account only to Himself, not to them.

Therefore, the main method is not to cut off ties with people, but to live with them; and not to do what they say, but to do what God says. On the other hand, the seers are forced to resort to artificial methods again since they deny God Almighty.

Balance of Solitude:

1. O you who wraps himself in clothing,
2. Arise the night, except for a little –
3. Half of it – or subtract from it a little

[235] CASTANEDA, Journey to Ixtlan, Washington Square Press, Erasing Personal History

4. Or add to it, and read the Koran with a detailed reading.
5. Indeed, We will cast upon you a heavy word.
6. Indeed, the hours of the night are much more effective for an elaborative comprehension.
7. Indeed, for you by day is prolonged occupation.
8. And remember the name of your Lord and devote yourself to Him with a complete devotion.
9. He is the Lord of the East and the West; there is no deity except Him, so take Him as Disposer of your affairs. (Koran/Chapter 73)

In daily life, people might look a little peaked and confused by the influence of other people. The seers solve this problem by growing away from people. On the other hand, God Almighty sends man His revelation and asks him to use it as a polar star.

This means that when you read a small amount of the Koran at night, the tuning control is fulfilled. The universal perspective of it removes the effects that people have on you and prevents you from being caged in that little world they're trapping you in during the day.

Therefore, there is no absolute seclusion in Islam as applied by the seers; solitude and socializing have balance and harmony. Just as the car stops by the gas station and fills the tank, people fill the tank with the Koran and return to life. And in this way, while living a modern life, at the same time, one can connect his heart to God. The method of the seers, on the other hand, is not suitable for human nature and can only be applied by a handful of people.

<u>The symbolic death of a warrior</u>:

- Die before you die. (Prophet Muhammad)

For years the seers have been practicing "erasing personal history" to isolate themselves from other people. Finally, there comes a moment when they completely put aside their "old continuity" and make a whole new beginning. The seers refer to this rebirth as the "symbolic death of the warrior." And to exemplify this, don Juan tells Castaneda about "his own death":

Don Juan wants to leave nagual Julian's house after spending a few years in apprenticeship training. He says he's tired of their practice and does not want to spend any more time with these stupid things. Nagual Julian does not object to him leaving the house. He lets him go because he knows that don Juan will be devastated in his new life out there and will appreciate the value of his life in this house.

After leaving the house, don Juan starts a new life, gets married and begins to live like an average person, but he cannot be happy in this new life. He loses the discipline and dynamism he acquired unconsciously in Julian's house in a short period. He tries to save his family from poverty but fails. He finally understands he's made a mistake, but it's too late. He eventually suffers a crisis and returns from the brink of death.

"The sorcerers' struggle for assuredness is the most dramatic struggle there is. It's painful and costly. Many, many times it has actually cost sorcerers their lives,"[236] says don Juan. According to him, a warrior has to invalidate the continuity of his old life in order to have absolute certainty about his actions. And the seers of modern times call this process of invalidation the "ticket to impeccability" or the "symbolic death of the warrior".

"We can only really change if we die,"[237] says don Juan's benefactor, nagual Julian. "The seer's ticket to freedom is his death."[238] So, on that day, don Juan dies "symbolically", ends the old continuity of his life. He turns back to nagual Julian's house and starts an entirely new beginning. Moreover, from that day on, he only accepts the friendship of those who have died like him.

In the same way, Prophet Muhammad recommends the believers to "Die before you die". So, a person who decides to believe in God gives up their old bad habits, if any, stays away from the bad friends, repents

---

236 CASTANEDA, The Power of Silence, Washington Square Press, The Ticket To Impeccability

237 CASTANEDA, The Power of Silence, Washington Square Press, Intending Appearances

238 CASTANEDA, The Power of Silence, Washington Square Press, The Ticket To Impeccability

for their past and turns a new leaf. Now they should begin a clean sheet.

However, what Prophet Muhammad meant is somewhat different from that of the seers. What he says is not to deny the old things completely, nor not to meet normal people or have a family, as the seers do. Because the Prophet also says, "I have not been commanded to lead a monastic life."

For example, he acknowledged being right a woman who complained about her husband neglecting her sexually due to his observation of his religious duties. And he said to her husband, "I have not been commanded to lead a monastic life. I marry women. I wake up at night as I sleep. I spend even days without fast, just like I fast. Whoever turns away from this attitude, is not of me." Therefore, it is not right to live in a narrow group as the seers do and to end their social life completely.

The seers isolate themselves to gain success. Because they think that they will achieve "immortality" through their success, and to achieve this, they need an intensive training in such a narrow group. But God Almighty, the Lord of the Worlds, commands that immortality is achieved through forgiveness, not success. And in order to win it, He makes this world a test area for us and asks us to take our place there, not being disconnected from the world.

However, it is not right to think that Prophet Muhammad is constantly with people. For example, he does not stay out late at night and is busy with the Koran and prayer in his house. Or he spends the last ten days of Ramadan month by reading verses and in worship. But these are some kind of breaks and periods to be alone with the Lord. Like gaps between musical notes. At other times, the Prophet is always connected with people. Therefore, there is no such thing as getting away from people, isolating oneself or building walls between them.

As a result, dying before death and making a new beginning is one of the most fundamental truths that God put in human nature. But the seers are again exceeding the limit here, going as far as to follow monasticism.

Though don Juan denies that he is a monastic, the way the seers lead their lives away from other people is a kind of unnamed monachism, and this is not the way of life that God Almighty wants people to live.

ABSTAINING FROM MARRIAGE AND SEXUALITY

Marriage without a marriage:

The seers' opinions about marriage are similar to the clergymen. Though they do not completely reject marriage as the clergy do, they take the useful part of it and leave the other part. And they do so in a purely energy-centered way, not morally.

As an example of this, la Gorda's supervision is given to Castaneda when it comes to the late stages of his apprenticeship. Don Juan tells him that, by this way he can turn his present selfishness into an opportunity:

- Don Juan said that I had to honor la Gorda regardless of what she did to me, and that I had to train my body, through my interaction with her, to feel at ease in the face of the most trying situations. It was much easier to fare well under conditions of maximum stress than to be impeccable under normal circumstances, such as in the interplay with someone like la Gorda. Don Juan added that I could not under any circumstances get angry with la Gorda, because she was indeed my benefactress; only through her would I be capable of harnessing my selfishness. [239]

---

[239] CASTANEDA, The Art of Dreaming, HarperCollins Publishers Inc., Dreaming Together

That's why don Juan asks Castaneda to safeguard la Gorda like the pupil of his eye, and on top of that, he says he can only accomplish his true task by helping La Gorda.

In fact, don Juan coupled Castaneda to la Gorda without marriage, thus providing him with the challenging conditions that would have naturally arisen, even if they were married. Moreover, he's doing it to destroy Castaneda's selfishness and make him learn to behave in the most challenging conditions.

In other words, don Juan makes them do something that is the purpose of marriage without marriage. Also, he says to Casteneda that la Gorda is his benefactress and that he can't accomplish his true task without achieving it.

For this reason, marriage is an important thing, and God gave it to man's nature. Moreover, the normal state of human beings is marriage, and celibacy is an unnatural situation.

On the other hand, the seers again use a mechanism in human nature and remove the responsibility part of it and use it for their own practical benefits. Therefore, their "marriage" is a kind of mutualism: no responsibility, no sexual intercourse, only energy-based exploitation.

<u>Abstaining from sexuality</u>:

Like the clergymen, sexuality is another issue that seers try to restrict. Their general attitude towards sexuality is to accumulate sexual energy and turn it in another direction. And by the word another direction, the seers allude to the "art of dreaming".

Since the seers use dreaming as a gateway to other realms, which constitutes one of the most important parts of their knowledge, it is essential for them. Hence, for the extra work they do, they need extra energy, and they achieve it by cutting down on sex. Don Juan explains it from nagual Elias' perspective:

- The nagual Elias had great respect for sexual energy. He believed it has been given to us so we can use it in dreaming.

- Our sexual energy is what governs dreaming. The nagual Elias taught me - and I taught you - that you either make love with your sexual energy or you dream with it. There is no other way. [240]

So, the seers' attitude towards sexuality is completely energy-centric, and they are abandoning the sexuality that God puts on human nature in order to realize the unnatural dreaming process. Thus, they fall into another non-nature.

For example, La Gorda quotes about don Juan: "He was not a man. He was the Nagual. He had no interest in sex."[241] Therefore, there is only a narrow group for the seer and there is no male-female relationship within that narrow group. They wipe out the relationship between men and women as a result of the teacher-student relationship and therefore, are not interested in each other.

La Gorda says that sexual intercourse weakens the person and that being a warrior requires a disciplined life in full sexual abstinence like Nagual don Juan Matus. According to them, impeccability requires not having sexual intercourse. [242]

This is what the energy calculations of the seers say, but the rules set by God Almighty say the opposite. After all, if our parents had not had sexual intercourse, we would not have been here in this world, nor would there be seers. Therefore, this universe continues itself in accordance with that rule set by God Almighty. For that reason, marriage is the way of God, and although divorce is lawful, it is God's dislike.

---

240 CASTANEDA, The Power of Silence, Washington Square Press, The Knock of The Spirit: The Abstract

241 CASTANEDA, The Eagle's Gift, Washington Square Press, Losing The Human Form

242 The seers are divided into two groups: Stalkers and dreamers. This is true for the dreamers, and sexual intercourse is forbidden for them because of their energy needs for dreaming. But the stalkers are the opposite, and this time everything is free for them without caring about morality. So on this subject, the seers are on the extremities again.

<u>Their abstaining from sex is not moral but energy-based</u>:

At first, Castaneda misunderstands what don Juan has said and thinks that it is a puritanical attitude toward sex, and therefore strongly objects. Don Juan, in turn, laughs to tears since his attitude has nothing to do with morality.

- I have always told you that sexual energy is something of ultimate importance and that it has to be controlled and used with great care. But you have always resented what I said, because you thought I was speaking of control in terms of morality; I always meant it in terms of saving and rechanneling energy. [243]

Although what don Juan says is not moral, Castaneda opposes him because of the value judgments of the modern society in which he lives. On the other hand, don Juan calls it "man's ignorance of and disregard for his magical nature" and explains this magical nature of man from the energy aspect:

- It is the Eagle's command that sexual energy be used for creating life. Through sexual energy, the Eagle bestows awareness. So when sentient beings are engaged in sexual intercourse, the emanations inside their cocoons do their best to bestow awareness to the new sentient being they are creating. During the sexual act, the emanations encased inside the cocoon of both partners undergo a profound agitation, the culminating point of which is a merging, a fusing of two pieces of the glow of awareness, one from each partner, that separate from their cocoons. [244]

Hence, the human being is not a machine, and above all, he "lives". And through sexual intercourse, he contributes to a new "life". However, don Juan says that modern man has turned this noble action into something fun:

- Sexual intercourse is always a bestowal of awareness even though the bestowal may not be consolidated. The emanations inside the

---

243 CASTANEDA, The Fire From Within, Washington Square Press, The Glow of Awareness

244 CASTANEDA, The Fire From Within, Washington Square Press, The Glow of Awareness

> cocoon of human beings don't know of intercourse for fun. The fallacy of man is to act with total disregard for the mystery of existence and to believe that such a sublime act of bestowing life and awareness is merely a physical drive that one can twist at will. [245]

Therefore, sexual intercourse is a mechanism that has been put into human nature by the Almighty God for the continuation of the human generation and the existence of new people in this universe. And in this way, God Almighty donates awareness to people and gives them life.

As don Juan said, the command of God Almighty is that sexual energy is used to create life, so God Almighty does not want it to be used for all the world to see, in an undisciplined way, and establishes certain rules for this sublime thing.

Not banning but restricting sexuality with certain rules:

1. Certainly the believers received the salvation:
2. They who are during their prayer in awe
3. And they who turn away from ill speech
4. And they who work for charity
5. And they who guard their chastity
6. Except from their wives or their dependents for indeed, they will not be blamed –
7. But whoever seeks beyond that, then those are the transgressors (Koran/Chapter 23)

According to the Koran, sexuality is free in a lawful situation, but other than that, it is forbidden to indulge in sexual intercourse outside marriage. In other words, there is a case of "being accessible and inaccessible"[246] that don Juan is talking about. You are not accessible to everyone; you are only accessible to certain people. So, there is a discipline.

---

[245] CASTANEDA, The Fire From Within, Washington Square Press, The Glow of Awareness

[246] CASTANEDA, Journey to Ixtlan, Washington Square Press, Being Inaccessible

The craze for the lack of chastity in today's societies is in fact a slackness and indiscipline. In addition, the people who act in this way are constantly "accessible" and, as don Juan said, it's something that energetically debilitates man.

For example, don Juan says, "It was only when my sexual energy was freed from the world that everything fit into place."[247] Therefore, the uncontrolled sexual energy is returned to man as a spiritual mess.

The seers cut it out completely and transfer the whole energy to another location. But normally, it should be allowed in lawful situations and not outside of them. In this way, discipline that is desired by the seers is provided, and also human beings' needs predetermined by God Almighty are met.

23. And she, in whose house Joseph was, sought to seduce him. She closed the doors and said, "Come, you." He said, "I seek the refuge of God. Indeed, He is my master, who has made good my residence. Indeed, wrongdoers do not succeed."
24. She certainly desired him, and he would have inclined to her had he not seen the proof of his Lord. And thus that We should avert from him evil and immorality. Indeed, he was of Our chosen servants. (Koran/Chapter 12)

In the Koran, Prophet Joseph is given as the symbol of chastity for men. Accordingly, Prophet Joseph opposes the lady host who wants to satisfy her desires with and as a result, he has to spend many years in the dungeon.

91. And mention Mary who guarded her chastity. We blew into her Our Soul, and We made her and her son a sign for the worlds. (Koran/Chapter 21)

In the Koran, Mother Mary is described as the symbol of chaste woman and the role model of believing women. Also, the Koran rejects the unfounded slanders thrown at her at that time.

---

[247] CASTANEDA, The Power of Silence, Washington Square Press, The Knock of The Spirit: The Abstract

On the other hand, the modern societies that have made the "sexual revolution" Castaneda represents are always "accessible", while the seers are permanently "inaccessible" because of their energy-based view. However, what God Almighty commands is in the midst of these two, and invites man to choose the one that sounds plausible. Since it is the Almighty God Himself, who knows the human nature best, His rules are not one-sided like human beings'. And they fully conform to human nature, both morally and energetically.

<u>Love is possible with forbearance</u>:

14. Beautified for people is the love of that which they desire – of women and sons, heaped-up sums of gold and silver, fine branded horses, and cattle and tilled land. That is the enjoyment of worldly life, but God has with Him the best return.
15. Say, "Shall I inform you of something better than that? For those who fear God will be gardens in the presence of their Lord beneath which rivers flow, wherein they abide eternally, and purified spouses and approval from God. And God is Seeing of His servants." (Koran/Chapter 3)

God Almighty commands, "Indeed, the righteous are in Paradise". And He wants us to approach the things He puts before us as tests with forbearance and in obedience to His rules in this temporary world. He does not ask us to abandon these blessings completely, nor to attack them like a parvenu who has suddenly acquired wealth and power. He expects us to find a happy middle between the two.

Today's people are, unfortunately, far from the state of avoiding uncontrolled sexual intercourse. But at the same time, people want to experience the love they watch in movies and are looking for someone who will really love them.

However, for such love, it is necessary to have an "avoidance barrage" behind which emotions will accumulate. Keeping yourself chaste until you get married, being the first person to whom you get married... These are all very special things, and the relationships established without them cannot turn into those desired loves.

Even don Juan says while speaking of an old girlfriend of Castaneda: "You lost her because you were accessible; you were always within her reach and your life was a routine one."

Therefore, when there is no barrage in modern relations, nothing is increased and the marriage is drained because everything is lived and ended before marriage. Since people have already had many relationships before, marriage is no longer something special.

On the other hand, whatever Almighty God commands us in this world, He commands for our happiness. And those true loves that everyone is searching for are only possible with forbearance and avoidance.

9- Stopping the Actions

- Stalking
- Controlled Folly
- Detachment
- Impeccability

STALKING

The seers call the basic discipline that regulates their behavior in everyday life as "stalking". They apply this art from the most menial act in their lives to life and death. And don Juan mentions this art as "the only way to deal with everybody and everything in the world of daily affairs."[248]

The first starting point of this name comes from the fact that the seers stalk their own behaviors. Accordingly, the seers, through a technique called "recapitulation", have been reviewing their lives for years. Thus, they are trying to trace their own behavior and try to "stop" the things they are short of. Don Juan calls it "stalking himself to deliver a jolt to himself".[249] And we have described this in the previous chapters as "stopping the self".

On the other hand, the rules, which are called "stalking" by the seers and regulate their relationship with the outside world, is sort of the external version of stalking themselves. By these rules, the seers are trying to stalk what they are doing in the outside world and turn them into their favor. That means that they "stop" their old powerless actions and replace them with the disciplined actions of the warrior.

---

248 CASTANEDA, The Power of Silence, Washington Square Press, Intending Appearances

249 CASTANEDA, The Power of Silence, Washington Square Press, The Somersault Of Thought

Seven principles of stalking = Warrior's path:

The seers describe the stalking with seven principles that they determined to follow, and Florinda teaches these principles to Castaneda[250] in the late stages of his apprenticeship.

However, Castaneda is no stranger to these rules. Because long before that, don Juan taught him "the path of the warrior", which is nothing more than the practice of unnamed stalking.

Therefore, the seers who apply the principles of stalking actually follow the path of the warrior and thus, care about every action they take and accept it as their last war on earth.

Principle- 1: Choosing the battleground

According to the seers, the first principle of stalking is to choose the battleground. Florinda explains this rule as "a warrior never goes into battle without knowing what the surroundings are". [251]

And the famous war strategist Sun Tzu says similar things in his book The Art of War:

- If you know the enemy and know yourself, you need not fear the result of a hundred battles. If you know yourself but not the enemy, for every victory gained you will also suffer a defeat. If you know neither the enemy nor yourself, you will succumb in every battle.

Therefore, a warrior gets to know everything on the battleground before he goes into battle and thoroughly evaluates the environment. Don Juan calls it "control" and says: "For a warrior, there is nothing out of control."[252]

Principle- 2: Sweeping the battleground

250 A female member of don Juan's party

251 CASTANEDA, The Eagle's Gift, Washington Square Press, Florinda

252 CASTANEDA, A Separate Reality, Washington Square Press, Chapter 12

The second principle of stalking is "to discard everything unnecessary."[253] According to this rule, a warrior who decides to enter a war should not leave anything extra on the battleground and only focus on those necessary.

For example, in Florinda's case, she comes to her benefactor's house with her husband, but her benefactor prevents her husband from coming there again, because he has nothing to do with her husband, but with her. And that's how a warrior cleans up all the unnecessary elements on the battleground, making it a short and clear battle.

Principle- 3: Making a decision and not changing it

The third principle of stalking is to decide whether or not to enter into battle after recognizing the battleground. In this regard, Florinda says:

- Don't complicate things. Aim at being simple. Apply all the concentration you have to decide whether or not to enter into battle, for any battle is a battle for one's life. This is the third principle of the art of stalking. A warrior must be willing and ready to make his last stand here and now. But not in a helter-skelter way. [254]

This is the most critical point for the warriors since there is no turning back for them once they have decided. And it's because of their precise awareness of death.

- Look at me. I (don Juan) have no doubts or remorse. Everything I do is my decision and my responsibility. The simplest thing I do, to take you for a walk in the desert, for instance, may very well mean my death. Death is stalking me. Therefore, I have no room for doubts or remorse. If I have to die as a result of taking you for a walk, then I must die. You, on the other hand, feel that you are immortal, and the decisions of an immortal man can be cancelled or regretted or doubted. In a world where death is the

---

253 CASTANEDA, The Eagle's Gift, Washington Square Press, Florinda

254 CASTANEDA, The Eagle's Gift, Washington Square Press, Florinda

hunter, my friend, there is no time for regrets or doubts. There is only time for decisions. [255]

The seers say that people, with doubts and regrets, actually give up most of the things they can do and can't reach their destiny. So, the seers strictly forbid themselves to change the decisions taken as a precaution. They think a lot before entering the war, but never change their decision after entering it.

- When a man decides to do something, he must go all the way, but he must take responsibility for what he does. No matter what he does, he must know first why he is doing it, and then he must proceed with his actions without having doubts or remorse about them. [256]

As long as your enemy does not give up in a real war, you do not have the chance to leave the war. Parallel to this, the seers consider their decisions as a matter of life and death, and declare their last battles on earth:

- Our death is waiting and this very act we're performing now may well be our last battle on earth. I call it a battle because it is a struggle. Most people move from act to act without any struggle or thought. A hunter, on the contrary, assesses every act; and since he has an intimate knowledge of his death, he proceeds judiciously, as if every act were his last battle. Only a fool would fail to notice the advantage a hunter has over his fellow men. A hunter gives his last battle its due respect. It's only natural that his last act on earth should be the best of himself. It's pleasurable that way. It dulls the edge of his fright. [257]

Principle- 4: Abandoning yourself

The fourth rule of stalking is "abandoning yourself". Accordingly, the warrior who finds the battleground suitable and decides to enter the

[255] CASTANEDA, Journey to Ixtlan, Washington Square Press, Assuming Responsibility

[256] CASTANEDA, Journey to Ixtlan, Washington Square Press, Assuming Responsibility

[257] CASTANEDA, Journey to Ixtlan, Washington Square Press, The Last Battle on Earth

war no longer looks back and surrenders himself to the rhythm of war ahead of him. Don Juan explains this mood as a combination of control and abandon:

- One needs the mood of a warrior for every single act. Otherwise, one becomes distorted and ugly. There is no power in a life that lacks this mood. Look at yourself. Everything offends and upsets you. You whine and complain and feel that everyone is making you dance to their tune. You are a leaf at the mercy of the wind. There is no power in your life. What an ugly feeling that must be!
- A warrior, on the other hand, is a hunter. He calculates everything. That's control. But once his calculations are over, he acts. He lets go. That's abandon. A warrior is not a leaf at the mercy of the wind. No one can push him; no one can make him do things against himself or against his better judgment. A warrior is tuned to survive, and he survives in the best of all possible fashions. [258]

Don Juan calls this "the mood of a warrior" and says that it is always necessary to take action in such a mood. Don Juan also says that the mood of a warrior is the antidote to self-pity, and he explains this as follows:

- The hardest thing in the world is to assume the mood of a warrior. It is of no use to be sad and complain and feel justified in doing so, believing that someone is always doing something to us. Nobody is doing anything to anybody, much less to a warrior. You are here, with me, because you want to be here. You should have assumed full responsibility by now, so the idea that you are at the mercy of the wind would be inadmissible. [259]

Abandoning yourself with God's help:

Don Juan teaches Castaneda a special method of running, which he calls "the gait of power", to give him an example of abandoning

---

[258] CASTANEDA, Journey to Ixtlan, Washington Square Press, The Mood of a Warrior

[259] CASTANEDA, Journey to Ixtlan, Washington Square Press, The Mood of a Warrior

himself. Thus, in this special way of running in which people take very short and steady steps, the person can run very effectively without running into something, even in pitch darkness.

When don Juan teaches this to Castaneda, he first gives him a little practice, and then, in the dark of the night, he sets up a special meeting with "inorganic beings", namely the jinns who are at his service.

We have already talked about the fact that the seers, using the jinns, frighten their apprentices and use it as a catalyst. Here, too, don Juan transforms Castaneda into a marathon runner, who barely applies the gait of power. Thus, he teaches him the practical maneuver of abandoning.

- Don Juan let go of my head and then added in a soft voice that at night the world was different, and that his ability to run in the darkness had nothing to do with his knowledge of those hills. He said that the key to it was to let one's personal power flow out freely, so it could merge with the power of the night, and that once that power took over there was no chance for a slip-up. He added, in a tone of utmost seriousness, that if I doubted it I should consider for a moment what was taking place. For a man of his age to run in those hills at that hour would be suicidal if the power of the night was not guiding him. [260]

Once upon a time, one of my elders similarly told me to don Juan's words: "If you act, God will act."

I am sure you have experienced the same thing in your life: when you act fast and decisively, you have lived moments where everything you do works well, and everything is alright. These are the special moments, as don Juan calls it, when a person abandons himself and the "power" guides him. In those moments, it is as if the whole universe unites and opens your way, and things we thought improbable to solve are easily solved. These are the moments in which God Almighty has helped you to act.

---

[260] CASTANEDA, Journey to Ixtlan, Washington Square Press, The Gait of Power

However, don Juan mentions many times in his words, the "power of the night" or the powers that pave the way for us. But in fact, there are no multiple powers in the universe; there is only God's help, and that help is only with the ones who are determined to take action.

159. So by mercy from God, you were lenient with them. And if you had been rude and harsh in heart, they would have disbanded from about you. So pardon them, ask forgiveness for them and consult them in the matter. And when you have decided, then rely upon God. Indeed, God loves those who rely upon Him.
160. If God should aid you, no one can overcome you; but if He should forsake you, who is there that can aid you after Him? And upon God let the believers rely. (Koran/Chapter 3)

Therefore, if you take action and rely upon God, God Almighty also takes action and supports you along with the whole universe. The seers are well aware that the source of this aid is the Almighty God, whom they call the Eagle, and that there are no multiple powers. But since God Almighty sends His help through His countless servants in the universe, the seers cannot stop using such expressions due to the fact they do not have any scriptural knowledge. Yet, what actually happened is nothing but God's help.

Principle- 5: Retreat

The fifth principle of the art of stalking is the temporary withdrawal of warriors when faced with a difficult situation, and Florinda explains this as follows:

- When faced with odds that cannot be dealt with, warriors retreat for a moment. They let their minds meander. They occupy their time with something else. Anything would do. [261]

In relation to that, don Juan says as follows:

[261] CASTANEDA, The Eagle's Gift, Washington Square Press, Florinda

- It's your duty to put your mind at ease. Warriors do not win victories by beating their heads against walls but by overtaking the walls. Warriors jump over the walls; they don't demolish them. [262]

Therefore, while focusing on realizing their decisions with all their power, the seers are not obsessed with it. If they don't succeed at that moment, they take a step back, calm down and expect the "silent knowledge" to guide them.

On the other hand, God Almighty gives man "worship" as a natural and periodic method of withdrawal and relaxation. So that, one can take a break from this world for a while with worship, and since all his emotions are fulfilled upon return, he can look at things in a completely different way.

I personally have witnessed many times that, when confronted with complex problems or family problems, they are solved easily after worship and I made the right decisions. Therefore, the subject of this withdrawal, which is mentioned by the seers is absolutely correct, and God Almighty has sent us the natural method of this as a mercy again.

Principle- 6: Compress time

"Warriors compress time", says Florinda about the sixth principle of stalking:

- Warriors compress time; even an instant counts. In a battle for your life, a second is an eternity; an eternity that may decide the outcome. Warriors aim at succeeding; therefore they compress time. Warriors don't waste an instant. [263]

So while the warriors are giving their last battle on earth, they focus on every moment of it and compress time without wasting any moment in their life. And this is a natural consequence of taking death as a companion and the awareness of not having enough time.

---

[262] CASTANEDA, Tales of Power, Washington Square Press, The Dreamer and The Dreamed

[263] CASTANEDA, The Eagle's Gift, Washington Square Press, Florinda

Principle- 7: Remaining behind the scenes

Florinda says that this last rule has impressed her the most in the rules of stalking, and she explains this as follows:

- My benefactor was the chief. And yet, looking at him, no one would've ever believed it. He always had one of his female warriors as a front, while he freely mingled with the patients, pretending to be one of them, or he posed as an old fool who was constantly sweeping dry leaves with a handmade broom. [264]

In fact, during Castaneda's training, don Juan does the same thing. He directs all "operations" himself while highlighting don Genaro or other apprentices. And he explains this as follows:

- If one wants to stop our fellow men, one must always be outside the circle that presses them. That way one can always direct the pressure.

In addition, this method of the seers is actually a reflection of God's attributes. As God Almighty rules the whole universe with His might, He is also behind the scene. He is wherever we look at, whereas He is secluded:

1. Whatever is in the heavens and earth exalts God, the Exalted in Might, the Wise.
2. His is the dominion of the heavens and earth. He gives life and causes death, and He is over all things competent.
3. He is the First and the Last, the Apparent and the Intimate, and He is, of all things, Knowing. (Koran/Chapter 57)

The seven rules of stalking are man-made:

While teaching Castaneda the rules of stalking, Florinda says to him as follows:

- Warriors don't have the world to cushion them, so they must have the rule. [265]

---

264 CASTANEDA, The Eagle's Gift, Washington Square Press, Florinda

265 CASTANEDA, The Eagle's Gift, Washington Square Press, Florinda

Therefore, over time, the seers use the available information to form the path of the warrior and teach them to his disciples in a set of rules.

And just like the seven rules of stalking, similar sets of rules are common in today's popular books. The ten rules of a happy marriage or the eight rules of a healthy life, etc. Of course, their content does not compare with don Juan's teachings. But what I mean here is that, the commonness of these rules is that they are man-made and they have emerged over time with people's experiences.

In the Koran of God Almighty, such statements do not appear at all, because the rules that are sequentially arranged in this way, although true, are not actually applicable. They come from the distillery of the centuries and come to us in the most concentrated form. But when people are asked to carry them out, they cannot because they do not include the intermediate stages until they reach those rules. That's why don Juan teaches Castaneda these rules by making him do them. Therefore, although these classified rules that are man-made are true, they are actually things that leave people in the lurch.

As God Almighty is the Creator of man, He knows every subtlety of his emotions; and in the light of this, He makes the Koran compatible with human nature. And unlike books written by human beings, the Koran is a book that teaches through practicing. So, one can use it as a guide on his own without the need for anyone. However, he cannot do so in the seven rules of stalking. For this reason, don Juan's training is needed, but unfortunately, you do not have a don Juan, whom you can reach whenever you wish he be right by your side.

CONTROLLED FOLLY

The seers apply the seven principles of the art of stalking to each of their behaviors. And this constitutes the controlling part of the work, but there is also the "folly" part.

The seers call it folly; because the seers don't actually believe what they do, and they see all kinds of human activity as insignificant in the face of the eternity of the worlds.

Disrupting the routines of life:

Don Juan says that human behavior in daily work is always monotonous. In contrast, any behavior that departed from this monotony is believed to have an unusual effect on our entire being, increasing our energy level. And that effect is thought to be what the seers are looking for.

- The sorcerer seers of ancient times, through their seeing, had first noticed that unusual behavior produced a tremor in the assemblage point. They soon discovered that if unusual behavior was practiced systematically and directed wisely, it eventually forced the assemblage point to move. [266]

---

266 CASTANEDA, The Power of Silence, Washington Square Press, The Four Moods Of Stalking

Since don Juan knew the importance of this, he teaches it to Castaneda in the early years of his apprenticeship, under a different name, "disrupting the routines of life." That in fact, is nothing other than don Juan is teaching Castaneda an unnamed "controlled folly".

- Now I have to teach you the final, and by far the most difficult, part. Perhaps years will pass before you can say that you understand it and that you're a hunter.
- To be a hunter is not just to trap game. A hunter that is worth his salt does not catch game because he sets his traps, or because he knows the routines of his prey, but because he himself has no routines. This is his advantage. He is not at all like the animals he is after, fixed by heavy routines and predictable quirks; he is free, fluid, unpredictable. [267]

Therefore, the seers apply unusual behaviors with great discipline, and they call it controlled folly. Moreover, the main reason for this is that they have discovered that it moves the "assemblage point". In other words, as in all other seeing practices, the work revolves around increasing the personal energy and thus moving the "heart", which they call the assemblage point.

Controlled folly:

The seers who learn the effect of doing unusual behaviors make it an art and apply it to everything like an exercise. In doing so, again they go to the extreme and almost become a theater actor. The situation of dona Soledad and Pablito, two other apprentices of don Juan, is an example to this:

- They carried on as if Soledad were Pablito's mother. To any onlooker, it would seem that they were mother and son pitted against each other, when in reality they were acting out a part. They convinced everybody. Sometimes Pablito would give such a performance that he would even convince himself. [268]

---

[267] CASTANEDA, The Power of Silence, Washington S. P., Disrupting the Routines of Life

[268] CASTANEDA, Eagle's Gift, Washington Square Press, The Intricacies of Dreaming

Don Juan also applies this against Castaneda from time to time. For instance, once he treats Castaneda as an elderly person in order to give a blow on his perception of the normal world, and Castaneda is petrified with astonishment. At another time, nagual Julian, the master of controlled folly, forces don Juan to act like a woman and teaches him "stalking" unnoticed.

- Controlled folly is an art. A very bothersome art, and a difficult one to learn. Many sorcerers don't have the stomach for it, not because there is anything inherently wrong with the art, but because it takes a lot of energy to exercise it. [269]

So controlled folly is an artificial art designed by the seers to gain energy. Since it is very difficult, in order to apply it, the seers have to go to very high energy levels, which forces them to gain energy. Does it work? Yes, it does; but that is not the nature God has created on people.

Natural madness:

Although the seers discover the effects of unusual behavior that disrupts the routine of human nature and use them for their own personal development, there is another reason why God put this feature in human nature. God Almighty gives this to people so that it can work in cases such as fulfilling the right and opposing the oppressors. And here again, the seers discover a feature that God Almighty put in human nature and use it for their own benefit.

135. O you who have believed, be persistently standing firm in justice, witnesses for God, even if it be against yourselves or parents and relatives. Whether one is rich or poor, God is closer to you than those. So follow not personal inclination, lest you not be just. And if you distort your testimony or refuse to give it, then indeed God is ever, with what you do, Acquainted. (Koran/Chapter 4)

God Almighty wants us to do "madness", but He wants us to exhibit it for natural things. For example, one of them is to keep justice alive.

---

[269] CASTANEDA, The Power of Silence, Washington Square Press, Intending Appearances

God Almighty wants us to do this even against our spouse, friends, parents and even ourselves. Is there anyone who does this? Or considering the countries, which country is working for justice on earth, leaving its interests behind? Is there such a fool? No, but God Almighty wants us to do this, and to do this is to row against the tide and to fall into the state of madness. However, this is not an empty, neutral madness like that of the seers, but a madness for the sake of rights.

Calling the Prophets as mad:

52. Similarly, there came not to those before them any messenger except that they said, "A magician or a madman."
53. Did they suggest it to them? Rather, they themselves are a transgressing people. (Koran/Chapter 51)

The prophets sent by God Almighty to proclaim the truth are also accused of being "mad" by their societies, because they bring things that are contrary to the general acceptance of their society.

Hence, they are "disrupting the routines of life" in that society and therefore face resistance. Prophet Noah, the symbolic object of derision and ridicule, is the summit of the Prophets blamed for insanity.

36. It was revealed to Noah that, "No one will believe from your people except those who have already believed, so do not be distressed by what they have been doing.
37. Construct the ship under Our observation and Our inspiration and do not address Me concerning those who have wronged; indeed, they are to be drowned."
38. And he constructed the ship, and whenever an assembly of the eminent of his people passed by him, they ridiculed him. He said, "If you ridicule us, then we will ridicule you just as you ridicule.
39. And you are going to know who will get a punishment that will disgrace him and upon whom will descend an enduring punishment."
40. When Our command came and the oven overflowed, We said, "Load upon the ship of each two mates and your family, except

those about whom the decree has preceded, and whoever has believed." But none had believed with him, except a few.

41. Noah said, "Embark therein; in the name of God is its course and its anchorage. Indeed, my Lord is Forgiving and Merciful."
42. And it sailed with them through waves like mountains, and Noah called to his son who was apart from them, "O my son, come aboard with us and be not with the disbelievers."
43. But he said, "I will take refuge on a mountain to protect me from the water." Noah said, "There is no protector today from the decree of God, except for whom He gives mercy." And the waves came between them, and he was among the drowned.
44. And it was said, "O earth, swallow your water, and O sky, withhold your rain." And the water subsided, and the matter was accomplished, and the ship came to rest on the mountain of Judi. And it was said, "Away with the wrongdoing people." (Koran/ Chapter 11)

Those who disbelieve make fun of Prophet Noah, who built the ship at the top of the hill. But he does not care about it and does what he has to do like an ant.

In terms used by the seers, what Prophet Noah did here is actually "stalking". However, this stalking is not a purposeless one. It has a vector, and it's heading in the same direction as is the whole universe.

Therefore, the Prophets do not need artificial stalking or madness skills. Since they are already tested with an ordeal for their duties, all the instruments that the seers discover and use, are naturally involved in their lives.

Love and Madness:

The Islamic Sufis who follow in the footsteps of the Prophets are likewise endowed with "madness". And Esrefoglu Rumi, the Turkish Sufi living in the 15th century, mentions this in a poem as follows:

Love is to sell the universe to nothing
Love is to pour the wealth and go

Love is to give the sweet in your hand to the others
And to take the poison by yourself

While troubles are raining down on you
Love is to keep your head under it

This world is like a sea of fire
Love is to let yourself dive into it

O Esrefoglu Rumi, there's something true
Love is to make the body mortal

The Islamic Sufis explain the relationship between God Almighty and themselves with the word "ashk", which does not have a one-to-one equivalent in English. Hence, the word "love" is used to replace it in the translation of the poem.

Actually, "ashk" means a very strong love that contains a kind of madness, meaning: being capable of doing anything for his lover. Therefore, this kind of madness is a desirable and acceptable thing for Sufis. So much so, they say, "Without falling into madness, you cannot be a close man to God".

Mevlana Jalaluddin Rumi, the Turkish Sufi who lived in the 13th century, explains this madness of a truth seeker as follows:

> With a mind of their own many people dedicated their lives to blasphemy,
>
> But have you ever seen anyone who became an infidel from madness?
>
> If the trouble has multiplied, walk and be mad; toil falls apart from madness.
>
> Go to the tavern where the madmen go and make a glass of madness.

> O Keykubad and Sencer[270] are so deprived of madness and unlucky.
>
> The horsemen of the army of madness are so joyous and victorious.
>
> If you get a glass of madness, you fly to heaven like Jesus Christ.

Therefore, being a lover and mad is not a monopoly of the seers, and "madness" is the sine qua non of a true friend of God. However, this is not a distorted madness for the self-interest, like that of the seers; but a madness made for the sake of truth. What the seers do is again to discover something that God Almighty put in human nature and use it for his own good.

---

270 Seljuk Anatolian Empire rulers

DETACHMENT

According to the basic principles which the seers call the "Rule", everything surrounding us is an unfathomable mystery. So, whether they are a pebble, an ant, or the person himself, they are all identical. Equally, human decisions are one and the same. To them, our absolute death makes all these things selfsame:

- It doesn't matter what the decision is. Nothing could be more or less serious than anything else. Don't you see? In a world where death is the hunter there are no small or big decisions. There are only decisions that we make in the face of our inevitable death. [271]

The reason why the seers think like this, is their discoveries regarding the Almighty God, which they call the Eagle. Nagual Julian explains that "The Eagle is real and final, and that what people do is utter folly."[272]

The seers discover that everything that is present consists of the emanations of the Eagle. In the face of this supremacy of the Eagle, they arrive to the conclusion that the short life of a human being does not matter.

---

[271] CASTANEDA, Journey to Ixtlan, Washington Square Press, Assuming Responsibility

[272] CASTANEDA, The Eagle's Gift, Washington Square Press, The Nagual's Party of Warriors

Acting just for the hell of it:

Don Juan describes the controlled folly as "a sophisticated, artistic way of being separated from everything, while remaining an integral part of everything".[273] The seers apply this when dealing with people outside their narrow groups. So, it is believed that the seers are always there, but in fact, they do not.

In order to get him used to such manners, don Juan teaches Castaneda a pattern of behavior he calls "acting just for the hell of it" and gives him some meaningless tasks to do on each visit. Moreover, in this way, Castaneda learns to do his actions without believing in them and without expecting rewards:

- A teacher must teach his apprentice another possibility, which is even more subtle: the possibility of acting without believing, without expecting rewards - acting just for the hell of it. I wouldn't be exaggerating if I told you that the success of a teacher's enterprise depends on how well and how harmoniously he guides his apprentice in this specific respect.
- I told don Juan that I did not remember him ever discussing "acting just for the hell of it" as a particular technique; all I could recollect were his constant but loose comments about it.
- He laughed and said that his maneuver had been so subtle that it had bypassed me to that day. He then reminded me of all the nonsensical joking tasks that he used to give me every time I had been at his house. Absurd chores such as arranging firewood in patterns, encircling his house with an unbroken chain of concentric circles drawn in the dirt with my finger, sweeping debris from one place to another, and so forth. The tasks also included acts that I had to perform by myself at home, such as wearing a black cap, or tying my left shoe first, or fastening my belt from right to left. [274]

---

[273] CASTANEDA, The Power of Silence, Washington Square Press, Intending Appearances

[274] CASTANEDA, Tales of Power, Washington Square Press, The Strategy of a Sorcerer

Although the seers are trying to make their actions better than the best person in the world, they do not believe in their actions and do not stick to them like normal people. For this reason, don Juan refers to the controlled folly as "the art of pretending to be thoroughly immersed in the action at hand".[275]

So, as the seers stop their self and the social relations, they also clear out and stop their actions by means of controlled folly. And even though they seem to do their actions in a much-disciplined way, they do not believe them.

Controlled Folly as a result of Detachment:

- I told you once that our lot as men is to learn, for good or bad. I have learned to "see" and I tell you that nothing really matters; now it is your turn; perhaps someday you will "see" and you will know then whether things matter or not. For me nothing matters, but perhaps for you everything will. You should know by now that a man of knowledge lives by acting, not by thinking about acting, nor by thinking about what he will think when he has finished acting. A man of knowledge chooses a path with heart and follows it; and then he looks and rejoices and laughs; and then he sees and knows. He knows that his life will be over altogether too soon; he knows that he, as well as everybody else, is not going anywhere; he knows, because he sees, that nothing is more important than anything else. In other words, a man of knowledge has no honor, no dignity, no family, no name, no country, but only life to be lived, and under these circumstances his only tie to his fellow men is his "controlled folly".
- Thus a man of knowledge endeavors, and sweats, and puffs, and if one looks at him he is just like any ordinary man, except that the folly of his life is under control. Nothing being more important than anything else, a man of knowledge chooses any act, and acts it out as if it matters to him. His "controlled folly" makes him say that what he does matters and makes him act as if

[275] CASTANEDA, The Power of Silence, Washington Square Press, Intending Appearances

> it did, and yet he knows that it doesn't; so when he fulfills his acts he retreats in peace, and whether his acts were good or bad, or worked or didn't, is in no way part of his concern. [276]

"The man of knowledge only has one life to be lived, and death makes everything equal", says don Juan, but in fact, that life does not belong to him. God Almighty gives it to him as a trust and takes it back when He ordains.

And in the same way, everything in this life is not equal as claimed. God Almighty, who gives us that life, says: "I did not give it to you all for nothing, and I will call you to account for what you have done during your life".

20. Know that the life of this world is but amusement and diversion and adornment and boasting to one another and competition in increase of wealth and children – like the example of a rain whose resulting plant growth pleases the tillers; then it dries and you see it turned yellow; then it becomes scattered debris. And in the Hereafter is severe punishment and forgiveness from God and approval. And what is the worldly life except the enjoyment of delusion.
21. Race toward forgiveness from your Lord and a Garden whose width is like the width of the heavens and earth, prepared for those who believed in God and His messengers. That is the bounty of God which He gives to whom He wills, and God is the possessor of great bounty. (Koran/Chapter 57)

According to the Koran, this life is temporary and the Hereafter is the essence. Our stay here is very short with some blessings, but then to God is our final return. Therefore, it is the biggest mistake to engage ourselves and lose our hearts to worldly transient goods in this universe, as the seers state.

But unlike the seers, God Almighty says, "You will be called to account for your deeds" and points out that the life of the Hereafter depends on our performance here. Therefore, He does not create the heavens and the earth in vain and He makes everything out of nothing, just for

---

[276] CASTANEDA, A Separate Reality, Washington Square Press, Chapter 5

the manifestation of the divine truth. It is only the assumption of the deniers to regard them as purposeless. So, there is no place in this universe for nonsense, inanities, and uncertainties.

On the other hand, as usual, the seers manipulate the truth that God Almighty has placed into the human nature, using it to their own advantage and degrade it into something purposeless that they call "controlled folly".

Believers are not full of admiration for temporal concerns in this world like the seers, but they are also devoted to the Owner of everything. On the other hand, the seers are left with nothing other than "controlled folly" for they have removed God Almighty from their knowledge. And when they deny the Owner of everything, they have to deny everything that exists.

Eventually, the seers manage to grope for their rules, and since these rules aren't bestowed upon by the Lord of the Worlds, they miss the target again, driven to extremes. Their rules are disconnected from the whole. They cherry-pick and use a fact, but it is a far cry from other things in the universe. Does it work? Yes, because it is part of the truth, but not the whole picture. God Almighty reveals the whole picture to us, and that's when everything falls into place.

Laughing at oneself:

156. Who, when disaster strikes them, say, "Indeed we belong to God, and indeed to Him we will return."
157. Those are the ones upon whom are blessings from their Lord and mercy. And it is those who are the rightly guided. (Koran/Chapter 2)

"In order to practice controlled folly, since it is not a way to fool or chastise people or feel superior to them, one has to be capable of laughing at oneself"[277], says Florinda. And according to don Juan, "All we can do is practice controlled folly and laugh at ourselves."[278] So the

277 CASTANEDA, The Eagle's Gift, Washington Square Press, Florinda

278 CASTANEDA, The Power of Silence, Washington Square Press, Intending Appearances

seers use "laughing at themselves" as a method of avoiding the unexpected things that have happened to them.

Whenever something bad happens to them, the seers just laugh it off and make themselves believe that it is not so important. However, there is a contradiction here: They say, "Everything you do is your last war and very important", but on the other hand, they laugh at it when they fail. So, when they remove God, who is at the center of everything, their system contradicts itself.

As the Almighty God created all things in the universe, then there is nothing to laugh about here. Whatever we are going through is coming from Him. And whenever believers have been stricken by a calamity, they say "Indeed we belong to God, and indeed to Him we will return."

Therefore, there's no use sitting and waiting, wearing sackcloth and ashes, but also it is no avail to laugh at these things. The only thing to do is accept that it is God's will and humbly follow it. Because it is God Almighty Himself who created the things which the seers can't help laughing at.

<u>Laughing at others</u>:

The seers take "laughing at themselves" one step further, and as a method of attack to personal importance, they are making fun of each other vehemently.

- Stalkers learn never to take themselves seriously; they learn to laugh at themselves. If they're not afraid of being a fool, they can fool anyone. [279]

The seers do not see any problems in this method since they believe that everything is permissible on the road to success. However, for the Koran this is not acceptable. As Prophet Muhammad said, "Whoever speaks, say good things or keep their mouth closed."

Therefore, the seers revoke themselves for the sake of denying God and turn themselves into fools. And they can only wear the "laugh

---

[279] CASTANEDA, The Eagle's Gift, Washington Square Press, Florinda

bandage" on what happens to them, but these are always broken, compulsive doctrines.

Detachment:

Don Juan calls the fact that one does not attach himself to anything as the "detachment" quality of that person and preaches Castaneda a lot in the early stages of his apprenticeship. And for him, detachment is the most "blessed" thing by the seers.

According to don Juan, death equates everything. Oppressors and the oppressed are reaching the same end. Victories and defeats lose their meaning in the face of death. Don Juan calls this state of seeing everything equal as "detachment" and says that the only thing that can provide this detachment is the thought of death.

On the other hand, the Almighty God puts the "detachment" in human nature for human beings to realize this world is temporary, not worthy of being attached to and not preferable when compared to the essential life of the Hereafter. But the seers again cancel the aspect of it that is connected to God and take only the part of detachment. And in the end, they are left alone in this huge universe.

> Neither am I happy about wealth,
>
> Nor do I feel sad over poverty,
>
> I am diverting myself with Your Love,
>
> I need You, only You.

Yunus Emre, the Turkish Sufi living in the 13th century, expresses his own detachment with these verses. But its detachment is not irrelevant, unlike the seers. Yunus Emre says, "I have passed over this universe and I need You God Almighty, the Owner of this universe."

And Yunus Emre also says, "We love the created for the sake of Creator." In other words, the dervishes cross this universe, which is a veil, and reach the Almighty God, the Owner of it. And after being immersed with the names of His Most Compassionate and Most Merciful, they return and treat the whole universe with His mercy. So, their bodies are here, but their selves are bound to God Almighty. And they walk among people with a light from Him.

On the other hand, while describing the warriors, Florinda says the opposite:

- Florinda explained that in the end, those shamans had become extremely cold and detached. Nothing warm existed for them anymore. They were set in their quest their coldness as men was an effort to match the coldness of infinity. They had succeeded in changing their human eyes to match the cold eyes of the unknown. [280]

That's how Florinda describes the coldness of the seers. And the coldness of the seers and the scientists who do not believe in God are in fact similar. Accordingly, both groups are dealing with eternity and are supposedly soaked with its coldness. In essence, they deny God and attempt to compete with Him, so God Almighty keeps them away from His attributes. Since they have nothing to do with the Creator of the universe, they conceive the eternity as absolute cold, as is space.

However, Almighty God introduces Himself as Most Compassionate and Most Merciful. And the believers who are immersed with His attributes, behave to other people by the same attributes. Therefore, coldness is unique to those who do not know God.

The coldness of those who do not know God manifests as detachment, and Castaneda is disturbed when he realized that don Juan's situation is also true of himself:

- Out of the whole conversation with don Juan the only poignant thing in my mind was that he did not care about me; it disturbed me immensely. Over a period of years I had put my trust in him. Had I not had complete confidence in him, I would have been paralyzed with fear at the prospect of learning his knowledge; the premise on which I had based my trust was the idea that he cared about me personally; actually I had always been afraid of him, but I had kept my fear in check because I trusted him. When he

---

280 CASTANEDA, The Wheel of Time, Washington Square Press, Quotations from the Power of Silence, Commentary

> removed that basis, I had nothing to fall back on and I felt helpless. A very strange anxiety possessed me. I became extremely agitated and began pacing up and down in front of the stove. Don Juan was taking a long time. I waited for him impatiently. [281]

Castaneda is very annoyed when he understood that don Juan does not care about him. However, regarding this, don Juan said: "You're being childish". Because according to him, this is a natural result of detachment.

On the other hand, God Almighty does not speak of the Prophets in this way in the Koran and says that they are very compassionate to their fellow believers:

128. There has certainly come to you a Messenger from among yourselves. Grievous to him is what you suffer; he is fond of you and to the believers is kind and merciful.
129. And if they turn away, say, "Sufficient for me is God; there is no deity except Him. On Him I have relied, and He is the Lord of the Great Arsh." (Koran/Chapter 9)

Prophet Muhammad cares about people because he knows that he will be considered for his deeds in this life. Moreover, he knows that what is important in this calculation is his undisguised belief and sincerity in his actions. However, don Juan does not really care what Castaneda does, as he does not believe in the account and fights for his own maturity and success.

Don Juan is disregardful of Castaneda as a result of his supposed detachment, but actually he forgets him because he dismisses God Almighty from his thoughts. On the other hand, Prophet Muhammad is asked to say, "God is sufficient for me if you turn away." And that's the real detachment. Attachment to nothing, but only to the Owner of everything.

[281] CASTANEDA, A Separate Reality, Washington Square Press, Chapter 5

Being reliable:

The seers go so far as to lump detachment, not caring about their apprentices. Also, they fall back on lies and bluffs in order to put them on the right path. As a result, the apprentices lose confidence in their teachers. On the other hand, the most prominent characteristics of the Prophets sent by God Almighty are that they are safe and reliable.

123. Aad people denied the messengers
124. When their brother Hud said to them, "Will you not fear God?
125. Indeed, I am to you a trustworthy messenger.
126. So fear God and obey me.
127. And I do not ask you for it any payment. My payment is only from the Lord of the Worlds." (Koran/Chapter 26)

The word "faith" in Arabic derives from the word "being sure". In other words, the relationship between man and God is a "relationship of certainty and assurance". And the Prophets that act as bridges in this relationship are also the ones who are assured. So, people believe in them because they are "sure".

Prophet Muhammad describes the true believer in the same way as "the one from whom people are safe from the evil of his tongue and hands." In other words, just as the believer is sure of God Almighty, other people are sure of him.

54. And mention in the Book, Ishmael. Indeed, he was true to his promise, and he was a messenger and a prophet. (Koran/Chapter 19)

Another manifestation of being reliable is righteousness, and God Almighty gives it as another truth of the Prophets. The righteousness of the Prophets is the shortest way to bring people to faith by building trust. Therefore, the people admire the honesty and reliability of the Prophets and follow them saying, "There is nothing wrong with this person".

Those who do not believe in Prophets accuse them of lying, and this acts as a litmus paper. Because the Prophets call upon people for consistency and righteousness, while those who do not believe oppose them with inconsistency:

25. We had certainly sent Noah to his people, saying, "Indeed, I am to you a clear warner
26. That you not worship except God. Indeed, I fear for you the punishment of a painful day."
27. So the eminent among those who disbelieved from his people said, "We do not see you but as a man like ourselves, and we do not see you followed except by those who are the lowest of us. And we do not see in you over us any merit; rather, we think you are liars."
28. Noah said, "O my people, have you considered: if I should be upon clear evidence from my Lord while He has given me mercy from Himself but it has been made unapparent to you, should we force it upon you while you are averse to it?
29. And O my people, I ask not of you for it any wealth. My reward is not but from God. And I am not one to drive away those who have believed. Indeed, they will meet their Lord, but I see that you are a people behaving ignorantly.
30. O my people, who would protect me from God if I drove them away? Then will you not take advice?
31. And I do not tell you that I have the treasures of God or that I know the unseen, nor do I tell you that I am an angel, nor do I say of those upon whom your eyes look down that God will never grant them any good. God is most knowing of what is within their souls. Indeed, I would then be among the wrongdoers."
32. They said, "O Noah, you have disputed us and been frequent in dispute of us. So bring us what you threaten us, if you should be of the truthful."
33. He said, "God will only bring it to you if He wills, and you will not cause Him failure.
34. And my advice will not benefit you - although I wished to advise you - If God should intend to put you in error. He is your Lord, and to Him you will be returned." (Koran/Chapter 11)

As it is seen, those who deny Prophet Noah and look down on those who stand beside him accuse them of lying. On the other hand, Noah responds to them in complete consistency, and this consistency is what keeps believers sure. So, they feed on truth and consistency, and thus have a calm heart.

35. No ill speech will they hear therein or any falsehood -
36. A reward from your Lord, a generous gift.
37. He is the Lord of the heavens and the earth and whatever is between them. He is the Most Merciful. They possess not authority from Him for speech.
38. The Day that the Spirit and the angels will stand in rows, they will not speak except for one whom the Most Merciful permits, and he will say what is correct.
39. That is the True Day; so he who wills may take to his Lord a way of return. (Koran/Chapter 78)

Believers, who listen to the truth from the Prophets of God Almighty, also do not hear any nonsense nor lies in Heaven. Likewise, witnesses who are allowed to speak on the Day of Judgement are just telling the truth.

Therefore, there is nothing other than truth in the religion of God, and this coherence and totality makes one's heart satisfied, and allows faith to be easily established. However, the seers do not have this in their path of knowledge, and thus they miss the shortest route.

They lie freely along the way, and the teachers can pull a trick on their apprentices whenever they wish. Therefore, the apprentices cannot be sure of their teachers, they cannot trust their words, and their education becomes a painful process that lasts for years. Adding to this the knockdown when they realized their teachers do not care about them at all; then, one can understand the insecure environment they are actually living in.

On the other hand, God Almighty has put this need for trust in human nature in such a way that even a two-year-old child is in search of it. For this reason, some pedagogues say, "Education to be given to young children consists of trust education".

In fact, since a child growing up in confidence trusts you, he automatically learns what you expect him to learn, and you don't have to teach him anything. Moreover, when you approach them with confidence, their doors open to you.

Thus, God Almighty has planted trust, as the most basic need of human beings, into the nature of humanity. And the faith in God is based entirely on this trusting relationship and offers man the most direct route.

IMPECCABILITY

Don Juan says, "Impeccability is the only thing that counts in the path of knowledge"[282] and accepts this as the true measure of a warrior's spirit. [283]

- For a warrior there is time only for his impeccability; everything else drains his power, impeccability replenishes it.
- The key to all these matters of impeccability is the sense of having or not having time. As a rule of thumb, when you feel and act like an immortal being that has all the time in the world you are not impeccable; at those times you should turn, look around, and then you will realize that your feeling of having time is an idiocy. There are no survivors on this earth! [284]

The seers refer to the behaviors they exhibit by following the path of the warrior as "impeccable behavior" and they try to replace their routine behaviors with "impeccable" ones.

"I have insisted from the day I found you that impeccability is all that counts"[285], says don Juan and explains why he places such emphasis on

---

[282] CASTANEDA, The Fire From Within, Washington Square Press, Petty Tyrants

[283] CASTANEDA, Tales of Power, Washington Square Press, The Strategy of a Sorcerer

[284] CASTANEDA, Tales of Power, Washington Square Press, The Whispering of The Nagual

[285] CASTANEDA, The Power of Silence, Washington S. P., The Two One-Way Bridges

impeccability as follows:

- Everything in a warrior's world depends on personal power and personal power depends on impeccability. [286]

Therefore, it is important for the seers to make something impeccable rather than its identification. Don Juan explains this as "the nature of one's acts are unimportant as long as one acts as a warrior".[287]

Impeccability being related to energy, not religion:

Castaneda complains about don Juan's insistence that his doctrine of impeccability evokes him as "religious morality". Don Juan, on the other hand, says that impeccability has nothing to do with religion, although it looks like that:

- Impeccability, as I have told you so many times, is not morality. It only resembles morality. Impeccability is simply the best use of our energy level. Naturally, it calls for frugality, thoughtfulness, simplicity, innocence; and above all, it calls for lack of self-reflection. All this makes it sound like a manual for monastic life, but it isn't. [288]

In other words, don Juan says, "Tell me about the energy, and never mind the rest", as it is done in controlled folly. But the need for impeccability planted by God Almighty in human nature consists of a quite different purpose in rewarding man with energy in return.

6. That Day, the people will depart separated to be shown their deeds.
7. So whoever does an atom's weight of good will see it,
8. And whoever does an atom's weight of evil will see it. (Koran/ Chapter 99)

---

[286] CASTANEDA, The Second Ring of Power, Washington Square Press, The Genaros

[287] CASTANEDA, Journey to Ixtlan, Washington Square Press, The Mood of a Warrior

[288] CASTANEDA, The Power of Silence, Washington Square Press, The Two One-Way Bridges

God Almighty commands, "I will place before you even the least you did in the world". Therefore, everything that a person does in this world is as precious as gold, and as the seers say, it needs to be done very carefully.

God Almighty bestows the Hereafter upon the ones who use this opportunity in a right way and also gives them an energy reward here as a premise. And thanks to this reward, they count themselves as happy and vigorous in this life.

So, what the seers desire to achieve with impeccability is not a purpose, but a by-product. And God Almighty gives this to mankind as a reward, so that people may love it and feel that they are on the right path. But the seers misuse it, and use their increased energy to break the parameters of normal perception and tries to "stop the world".

10- Stopping the World

- Seeing

SEEING

We have already said that the main skill of the seers is "stopping". Accordingly, they save the energy they need by stopping the self, social relations and actions; and then use this surplus energy to "stop the world".

The reason why the seers intend to stop the world is to reach the "World of Command" beyond the visible world that they call "nagual". So, the seers are trying to break through this visible realm and to go beyond it. And it is their increased energy that enables them to do this.

<u>Seeing</u>:

The seers denote their ability to perceive the flowing energy in the universe "seeing" and explain it as the human's ability to perceive energy directly.

Don Juan describes it as "reaching the realm of pure perception"[289] beyond the visible realm. According to him, the universe is in fact, composed of the energy fields that they call Eagle's emanations, and this energy forms the main fabric of the universe.

Our realm is just one of the millions of possible forms of this tissue. And according to the claims of the seers, human beings have the ability

---

[289] CASTANEDA, Magical Passes, HarperCollins Publishers Inc., The Second Series, The Series for the Womb

of going beyond this visible realm and reach that main tissue. This is what the seers have accomplished and labeled as "seeing":

- Believe me, this sense of finality about the world is a mere illusion. Due to the fact that it has never been challenged, it stands as the only possible view. To "see" energy as it flows in the universe is the tool for challenging it. Through the use of this tool, the sorcerers of my lineage arrived at the conclusion that there are indeed a staggering number of worlds available to man's perception. They described those worlds as being all-inclusive realms, realms where one can act and struggle. In other words, they are worlds where one can live and die, as in this world of everyday life. [290]

So, what is essential for the seers is energy, and the rigidity of this visible realm is nothing but an illusion. And their art is intended to go beyond this visible realm and reach that energy fabric.

Training to "see":

Don Juan asserts that the difference between the seers and ordinary people is that they can "see" the flowing energy in the universe. In other words, the real merit of the seers is their "seeing" activity and all the training of the apprentices aims to teach this to them.

What the seers call seeing makes it come true when the "assemblage point" moves from its usual location to perceive the energy in the universe. Therefore, "seeing" is to use the energy fields that we do not normally use, but which are within our potential. And when the assemblage point moves, it is possible to use these other emanations.

To do this, the assemblage point must first be removed from its usual location, and the seers call it "stopping the world". In order to achieve this, the seers aim to erode and collapse this world, which we see as permanent; and everything they do from the very first moment of apprenticeship is aimed at achieving it.

---

[290] CASTANEDA, Magical Passes, HarperCollins Publishers Inc., Introduction

Therefore, their expertise is aimed at "stopping". Just as they stop the self and the social relations in other parts of their education, at the last point, they "stop the world" and open the door to other worlds.

<u>Power plants</u>:

The seers set off the path of knowledge by eating "power plants" at first, and they learned to "see" after dealing with power plants for centuries.

- The way the Toltecs first started on the path of knowledge was by eating power plants. Whether prompted by curiosity, or hunger, or error, they ate them. Once the power plants had produced their effects on them, it was only a matter of time before some of them began to analyze their experiences. [291]

Therefore, the starting point of "seeing" is composed of power plants, but actually, these are just ancillary tools and their function is to shake up people. And some of the apprentices like Eligio never use them. However, Castaneda, the man of reason, shows more resistance to the teachings of don Juan, so don Juan is forced to give him more power plants.

Don Juan says that the effect of these plants is moving people's "assemblage point", just like sleeping, high fever or hunger. And what the seers long for is that the apprentice can access this ability on his own without any external assistance.

Hence, the function of these power plants is to shake the apprentice's world view and give the habit of breaking the assemblage point from its usual place. But this is only a support and a starting point for the main purpose of the seers.

God Almighty, on the other hand, by giving these plants to human beings, enables the seers to reach these truths. God Almighty gives them this opening, and the seers use it to reach the other realms He has created. Ultimately, what the seers do is to use the tools He gives and to reach the realms that He has created.

---

291 CASTANEDA, The Fire From Within, Washington Square Press, The New Seers

<u>Demonstrations of the nagual</u>:

65. They said, "O Moses, either you throw or we will be the first to throw."
66. He said, "Rather, you throw." And suddenly their ropes and staffs seemed to him from their magic that they were moving.
67. And he sensed within himself apprehension, did Moses.
68. We said, "Fear not. Indeed, it is you who are superior.
69. And throw what is in your right hand; it will swallow up what they have crafted. What they have crafted is but the trick of a magician, and the magician will not succeed wherever he is." (Koran/Chapter 20)

Another method used by the seers to disassemble Castaneda's perception of the normal world is the "demonstrations of the nagual". The task of making these demonstrations belongs to don Genaro, Castaneda's "nagual guide". And with these demonstrations, don Genaro tries to undermine Castaneda's perception of the ordinary world by showing to him the things that cannot be done by a normal human being that are against the "rules of physics":

- Genaro recommended what to do with you from that day on. As your guide into the "nagual", he gave you impeccable demonstrations, and every time he performed an act as a "nagual" you were left with a knowledge that defied and bypassed your reason. He disassembled your view of the world, although you are not aware of that yet.

Don Genaro's job is to "stop" Castaneda's worldview. The things he does for this are such as the act of swimming on the floor, jumping from very high places, impossible acrobatics on trees, etc. Castaneda has described many of these in detail in his books:

- The act of swimming on the floor, which was congruous with other strange and bewildering acts he had performed in front of my very eyes, started as he was lying face down. He was first laughing so hard that his body shook as in a convulsion, then he began kicking, and finally the movement of his legs became coordinated with a paddling movement of his arms, and don

> Genaro started to slide on the ground as if he were lying on a board fitted with ball bearings. He changed directions various times and covered the entire area of the front of don Juan's house, maneuvering around me and don Juan. [292]

Here, don Genaro uses the other "ring of power" possessed by the sorcerers, manipulating Castaneda's awareness, just like the sorcerers who challenged Prophet Moses. By doing this, he pretends to swim on the floor and confronts his reasonableness.

As we mentioned before, don Juan explains this technique through the old Toltec seers:

- The Toltec seers were extraordinary men - powerful sorcerers, somber, driven men who unraveled mysteries and possessed secret knowledge that they used to influence and victimize people by fixating the awareness of their victims on whatever they chose.
- I have to emphasize an important fact that those sorcerers knew how to fixate the awareness of their victims. You didn't pick up on that. When I mentioned it, it didn't mean anything to you. That's not surprising. One of the hardest things to acknowledge is that awareness can be manipulated. [293]

Therefore, the seers are practicing the "art of manipulating awareness" used by the sorcerers who challenged Prophet Moses. Thus, they offer Castaneda nagual demonstrations and try to disassemble his fixed worldview. But unlike the old seers, they use it not for worldly benefit, but only for training their disciples.

Encounters with the allies:

During the apprenticeship period, don Juan keeps applying all methods he knows on Castaneda in order to stop his worldview and tries to teach him to "see" even if the latter is unaware of it. In this process, the "allies" are one of the most important arguments of him.

---

292 CASTANEDA, Journey to Ixtlan, Washington Square Press, The Sorcerer's Ring of Power

293 CASTANEDA, The Fire from Within, Washington Square Press, The New Seers

In addition to the techniques of power plants and nagual demonstrations by don Genaro, don Juan arranges "encounters with the allies" many times and thus tries to enable him to "see".

We have already said that the inorganic beings the seers call allies are actually the jinns that God created. So, the seers are using these beings that do not belong directly to our world and trying to disassemble the worldview of the apprentices.

However, Castaneda does not like these encounters with allies and asks don Juan, "Does the ally have to tackle me?" Don Juan replies, "There is no way to avoid it": In order to "see", one must look at the world as the seers do so, and this cannot be learned without allies. [294]

Side effects of training:

During their trainings, the seers force the human nature and train the apprentices in a way that they are not designed. So, these trainings have side effects, and for example, when something happens to Castaneda like encountering with the allies, it makes him crazy with fear. But as a solution to his fears, don Juan simply asks him not to give up control.

- A warrior is always ready. To be a warrior is not a simple matter of wishing to be one. It is rather an endless struggle that will go on to the very last moment of our lives. Nobody is born a warrior, in exactly the same way that nobody is born a reasonable being. We make ourselves into one or the other. [295]

Another time, Castaneda complains that he's felt uneasy for months owing to his experiences. However, don Juan tells him that the only way to counteract the devastating effects of the sorcerers' world is to laugh at them.[296]

However, these are also not enough sometimes, and Castaneda lives through some experiences which take him to the brink of death during

[294] CASTANEDA, Journey to Ixtlan, Washington Square Press, Stopping The World

[295] CASTANEDA, Tales of Power, Washington Square Press, The Dreamer and The Dreamed

[296] CASTANEDA, Tales of Power, Washington Square Press, The Dreamer and The Dreamed

his exercises on allies and demonstrations of the nagual. In these times, don Juan wants him to make something that belongs to this world, like taking notes or singing a song, so that he can delve into something that belongs to the world. And when that does not work, don Juan even throws him into the cold water, preventing him from dying.

Therefore, these are the side effects of trying to disassemble this world. And when the seers go to extremes, they have to compensate them with other extremes. Although the techniques they apply are a part of human nature, they do not belong to the nature that God has created on people. So, they return to Castaneda as a persecution and make his life unbearable. What don Juan has offered in return, unfortunately, is no more than a band-aid for Castaneda.

Stopping the World:

For the seers, "stopping the world" becomes a touchstone on the road to "see" and constitutes the main goal of everything that don Juan has ever taught. Castaneda, on the other hand, cannot achieve this for years because he is too logical. But by May 1971, he could no longer withstand the attacks of don Genaro and finally managed to stop the world.

When Castaneda stops the world, for the first time, he sees the "lines of the world" and depicts the lines he sees as white fluorescent lights extending in all directions.[297] In other words, when Castaneda stops the world, it is actually the first time he has seen the "Eagle's emanations".

And we have already said that the emanations of the Eagle are actually the emanations of God Almighty, and that this tissue discovered by the seers forms the common tissue of humans and jinns, which are named by the seers as their allies. So, with the help of these allies, the seers go beyond this universe, reach this common tissue with the jinns, and name the first point they succeed in as "stopping the world".

---

[297] CASTANEDA, Journey to Ixtlan, Washington Square Press, Stopping The World

Realization of "seeing" through increased energy:

The seers use the techniques mentioned above to disassemble Castaneda's normal worldview. However, this alone is not enough to "see", and seeing is achieved through increased energy.

Accordingly, the energies that are idle in the internal potential of the human being are put into use by the methods discovered by the seers, and thanks to this increased energy, the energy fields that are not normally handled, can be perceived. That is why the seers try every single way to increase their energy, and all the teachings other than the doctrines of stopping the world actually serve this purpose.

Discipline the daily life, magical passes, stalking, impeccability, self-pitilessness, sexual abstinence, etc., all are a kind of energy-boosting method. And when this surplus energy is combined with the workouts of disassembling the worldview, ultimately "stopping the world" takes place.

Not using eyes in the process of "seeing":

Even though the seers call this perception maneuver "seeing", the eyes do not actually play a role. But they express it in this way because this is the most dominant sense of human being:

- Notice that when I talk about "seeing", I always say "having the appearance of" or "seemed like". Everything one "sees" is so unique that there is no way to talk about it except by comparing it to something known to us.
- The most adequate example of this difficulty is the way sorcerers talk about the assemblage point and the glow that surrounds it. They describe them as brightness, yet it cannot be brightness, because seers "see" them without their eyes. They have to fill out the difference, however, and say that the assemblage point is a spot of light and that around it there is a halo, a glow. [298]

---

[298] CASTANEDA, The Art of Dreaming, HarperCollins Publishers Inc., Sorcerers of Antiquity: An Introduction

Therefore, there is no function of the eyes in the direct perception of energy. So, shamans define it as "having the effect of seeing with their eyes," and this is like the "seeing" of bats. Just as the eyes of the bats are largely blind, and if they "see" their prey with their radar ears, so do the seers using the energy fields that the normal human cannot use.

And just as we can never know firsthand how a bat perceives this universe, likewise are the seers who have a similar difficulty. They find it difficult to pass on to us what they witness, which does not mean that what they see is not real.

Don Juan says that shamans can only describe what they "see" and that syntax is insufficient. However, the shamans' descriptions are as accurate as possible. The difficulty is to translate what is seen into words, or he claims they cannot be mistaken about what they "see". [299]

<u>The fact that every person actually can "see"</u>:

When Castaneda realizes seeing for the first time in his life, he discovers that he had been seeing the energy as it flows in the universe all his life, but he had not been conscious of it. When he told this to don Juan, don Juan replied: "Every person in the world is generally aware of the energy in the flow of the universe. But only the sorcerers are aware of this in a complete and purposeful way".[300]

For example, the seers, observing people traveling along the foot trails, notice that they often rest on the right spot with a positive level of energy. Likewise, when don Juan asks Castaneda to determine the right place to stay at night during his trips in the mountains, he often finds the right place, but thinks it's a "lucky guess". Don Juan tells him that it's not an ordinary choice and says, "You have possibilities you are not yet aware of". [301]

---

[299] CASTANEDA, The Art of Dreaming, HarperCollins Publishers Inc., Sorcerers of Antiquity: An Introduction

[300] CASTANEDA, Magical Passes, HarperCollins Publishers Inc., The Fourth Group: Inner Silence

[301] CASTANEDA, The Power of Silence, Washington Square Press, The Requirements Of Intent: Breaking The Mirror Of Self-Reflection

So, all people perceive the energy in the universe more or less, but they are not aware of it. However, the seers, with their "increased energy, derived from the curtailment of their self-reflection", provide themselves a wider perception capacity and attempt to increase this consciously.

"Seeing" the energy is the limit of mankind:

The seers learn to see through the "jinns", who are created by God Almighty in our system of realms as the polar twins of human beings. The seers call them allies, and what they call "seeing" is the fact that the seers reach the common energy tissue with them.

The seers communicate with these allies, and through them, they learn to perceive this tissue. And eventually they even learn to go back and forth. Castaneda says that anyone who learns to "see" perceives this tissue in the same way:

- For the shamans of ancient Mexico to perceive energy as it flowed in the universe meant that energy adopted nonidiosyncratic, specific configurations that repeated themselves consistently, and that those configurations could be perceived in the same terms by anyone who "saw". [302]

So why is that? Why does someone who "sees" always perceive the same thing?

This is because the energy world is "designed" just like this world of matter. Hence, they bear witness to what God Almighty created and designed, and they do so within the limits set upon them.

- Since perceiving energy as it flows in the universe is not arbitrary or idiosyncratic, seers witness formulations of energy that happen by themselves and are not molded by human interference. Thus, the perception of such formulations is, in itself and by itself, the key that releases the locked-in human potential that ordinarily has never entered into play. In order to elicit the perception of those

---

302 CASTANEDA, Magical Passes, HarperCollins Publishers Inc., The First Series>The Series for Preparing Intent

energetic formulations, the totality of human capabilities to perceive has to be engaged. [303]

The seers discover this hidden potential in man and reach the ecosystem of realms in which God Almighty created humans and jinns together. However, the outside of this ecosystem is closed to human beings and don Juan expresses this limitation as follows:

- Energy is the irreducible residue of everything. As far as we are concerned, to "see" energy directly is the bottom line for a human being. Perhaps there are other things beyond that, but they are not available to us. [304]

So, don Juan says that "seeing" is the limit of mankind, and if there is more beyond it, one cannot know. These limits of human beings originate from his own body, and when don Juan talks about these limits of human perception, he says:

- The limit of man's capability of perceiving is called the band of man, meaning that there is a boundary that marks human capabilities as dictated by the human organism. These boundaries are not merely the traditional boundaries of orderly thought, but the boundaries of the totality of resources locked within the human organism. [305]

In other words, just like the physical body puts limits on human beings and one can never run at 500 mph, the energy body also sets limits on him and there are certain limits within which his perception can reach. And these limits even differ between males and females:

- Shamans maintain that women, because they have a womb, are so versatile, so individualistic in their ability to "see" energy directly that this accomplishment, which should be a triumph of the

---

303 CASTANEDA, Magical Passes, HarperCollins Publishers Inc., The First Series>The Series for Preparing Intent

304 CASTANEDA, The Active Side of Infinity, HarperCollins Publishers Inc., Inorganic Awareness

305 CASTANEDA, Magical Passes, HarperCollins Publishers Inc., The First Series>The Series for Preparing Intent

> human spirit, is taken for granted. Women are never conscious of their ability. In this respect males are more proficient. Since it is more difficult for them to "see" energy directly, when they do accomplish this feat, they don't take it for granted. Therefore male sorcerers were the ones who set up the parameters of perceiving energy directly and the ones who tried to describe the phenomenon. [306]

Therefore, their boundaries arise from their creation and are given to them by God Almighty. And man comes to this world and works within these perceptional limits. The outside of it is closed to him and he does not know the rest.

Why is there such a thing as "seeing"?:

"Seeing" is the research method of the Science of Seers. Thanks to this, the seers discover the energy world created by God Almighty, as the opposite twin of this witnessed realm that we see through our eyes and present it to the knowledge of humanity.

"There is something in all of us that can make us witness with our entire body"[307], says don Juan and expresses the act of seeing as a witnessing act. But to reach this witness, the seers say that the energy level of us needs to be increased. Therefore, in order to perceive the energy universe, we need to increase our energy.

Then, how does this happen? By disciplining yourself, leaving unnecessary routines, having sexual abstinence, rendering every job as if it were the last battle of your life, leaving your personal importance, etc. So, when you put an order in your life and live with great care, you get energy. And this increased energy takes man to "see" by using the methods of stopping the world.

Well, why does one gain energy when putting order in life and leading an impeccable one? Why is there such a mechanism? Alternatively, why

---

306 CASTANEDA, Magical Passes, HarperCollins Publishers Inc., The Second Series, The Series for the Womb

307 CASTANEDA, The Fire from Within, Washington Square Press, The Eagle's Emanations

is this only specific to humans? Why, for example, cannot cows acquire these teachings and go along this path? Why are this talent and a mind to comprehend it be given only to man?

There's no answer that the seers can give. They take it and use it. But God Almighty creates man in such a way that he can ask these questions. And likewise, if he takes care of this life, He creates in a way that will earn the reward.

Therefore, if human beings live in the way that God Almighty wishes, they gain energy, and this energy serves both their world life and the Hereafter. With this increasing energy, they also witness the existence of God Almighty. And in fact, we have come to this universe to "witness".

On the other hand, the seers change the way of human nature created by God Almighty and use it for other purposes. But this is also within the permission and knowledge of God Almighty. And in this way, the seers establish their own science and bring it to us as an anti-thesis of the modern science. God Almighty gets these two opposite sciences to cross-check each other, and in this way, shows us the clues to the truth.

11- Warrior's Training

- Warrior's Training
- Intimidation
- Narrow Group Training

WARRIOR'S TRAINING

All the things the seers do are actually a hands-on training process and they intensively train their disciples from scratch until they become a seer. And in doing so, they also train themselves. Castaneda explains this training process of the seers as follows:

- It takes years of training to teach us to deal intelligently with the world of everyday life. Our schooling - whether in plain reasoning or formal topics - is rigorous, because the knowledge we are trying to impart is very complex. The same criteria apply to the sorcerers' world: their schooling, which relies on oral instruction and the manipulation of awareness, although different from ours, is just as rigorous, because their knowledge is as, or perhaps more, complex. [308]

When don Juan talks about his teacher, nagual Elias, he asserts that he was a great teacher and taught him everything he wanted to in the finest detail. His other teacher Nagual Julian was the opposite and did not believe in transmitting information. That's why he taught don Juan everything he had to teach by practicing.

While teaching Castaneda, don Juan follows a path between these two and says that although he tells Castaneda what to teach, the essential

---

[308] CASTANEDA, The Power of Silence, Washington Square Press, Foreword

knowledge comes forth when he applies them. And to make this knowledge apprehended, he makes him do countless exercises.

Therefore, the seers are practicing like a marathon runner and their benefactors are just trainers who constantly spur them. The only difference between the seers and a marathon runner is that they do "intergalactic" exercises instead of running.

Their teachers sometimes make them practice dreaming, sometimes hang them on a tree for hours. Sometimes they practice looking at dry leaves; sometimes they sit in a crate and recapitulate their past.

So, there are thousands of exercises and techniques like these in the training of the seers. And throughout their training, sessions and exercises follow each other. And the disciples who are applying them almost like a "galactic commando", are trying to achieve success.

Teaching by practicing:

Learning by doing is the primary learning method of human beings and a requirement of the "Be!" secret that God Almighty created the human beings on. Therefore, man has only as much knowledge as he has done, and if he has not done something, he has never actually known it.

Therefore, the seers make their apprentices practice everything they teach by one-to-one, so that it can really be learned and make a place in their apprentices. The reason for this is, although their teachings are understandable, they are not really practicable.

As the seers develop their teachings over time as a product of human experience, they shrink like a funnel and eventually have something very brief and understandable in their hands. But a person can't do them himself when it is demanded.

Take, for example, "losing self-importance". That's the name of the teaching, but how will you do that? There is no answer. That's why the exercises come into play, and their teachers try to teach it by doing so many things. But most of the exercises are artificial ones. Therefore, the seers walk through the path of man-made teachings, again with man-made exercises, and this makes the path difficult to walk.

On the other hand, God Almighty sends the Koran as a book that teaches by practicing, and when people read it, they almost live it. Accordingly, God Almighty sends His prophets to human beings as role models and each sheds light on a different aspect of existence. God Almighty presents their life stories in the Koran in a manner that "will teach by practicing" so that one can use it without the need of anyone else and any artificial methods.

However, books written by a human hand do not have such a feature. Neither Castaneda's books nor this book have such a feature and they will leave you by the wayside in the long run. But the Koran is not so. You read it, then it works, and it never gets old. God Almighty guides you in the same way as He guides His prophets, and by the way, you confirm God Almighty by "practice".

Developing thousands of techniques:

1. E, L, M.
2. This is the Book about which there is no doubt, a guidance for those conscious of God -
3. Who believe in the unseen, establish prayer, and spend for poor from what We have provided for them,
4. And who believe in what has been revealed to you, and what was revealed before you, and of the Hereafter they are certain in faith.
5. Those are upon a guidance from their Lord, and it is those who reaches the salvation. (Koran/Chapter 2)

Don Juan says that old seers have developed thousands of techniques, and that all the exercises Castaneda had made are based on these techniques. However, most of these exercises are unnatural, and they overwhelm Castaneda. That's because what they do always have side effects, and more importantly, it does not make sense to man because they are not one-to-one related to the truth.

For example, don Juan teaches Castaneda a method with the name of the "right way of walking", and in this way, he tries to flood his attention with information and to help him accomplish inner silence:

- In order to stop the view of the world which one has held since the cradle, it is not enough to just wish or make a resolution. One needs a practical task; that practical task's called the right way of walking. It seems harmless and nonsensical. As everything else which has power in itself or by itself, the right way of walking does not attract attention. You understood it and regarded it, at least for several years, as a curious way of behaving. It didn't dawn on you until very recently that that was the most effective way to stop your internal dialogue.
- The right way of walking was a subterfuge. The warrior, first by curling his fingers, drew attention to the arms; and then by looking, without focusing his eyes, at any point directly in front of him on the arc that started at the tip of his feet and ended above the horizon, he literally flooded his tonal with information. The tonal, without its one-to-one relation with the elements of its description, was incapable of talking to itself, and thus one became silent.

Castaneda has been practicing it for years but cannot put it into a place since it is an artificial method. So, does it work? Yes, it does; but it does not make any sense to him, nor does it satisfy his soul. That is why Castaneda describes himself as a "passive subject who could only react to don Juan's maneuvers".[309] Don Juan, in turn, advises him that one could interpret the exercises as being entertainment.

God Almighty, on the other hand, does not give thousands of techniques to mankind. The things He taught him to practice are very limited. Moreover, He does not want people to do them as an exercise. But the seers transform their techniques into exercise and change the things given as a bonus with these techniques into a goal.

For example, don Juan tries to carry Castaneda to inner silence with the right way of walking. And for this, God Almighty gives prayer to man

---

[309] CASTANEDA, The Fire from Within, Washington Square Press, The Earth's Boost

and enables him to reach the inner silence while worshiping Him. The purpose of prayer is not only inner silence, but it also comes as a bonus, and the person who provides inner silence in prayer begins to continue this quietude in his normal life.

Therefore, God Almighty, who created human beings, knows us better than ourselves and offers us the most appropriate recipe. The seers try to copy this recipe with the techniques they developed, yet they succeed to some extent. And most importantly, when they miss the Almighty God, which is the main purpose of all these techniques, what they do becomes useless in the sight of Him.

Their only goal as being success:

> 18. The example of those who disbelieve in their Lord is that their deeds are like ashes which the wind blows forcefully on a stormy day; they are unable to keep from what they earned a single thing. That is what is extreme error. (Koran/Chapter 14)

The seers are doing all the exercises to "succeed", and as they succeed, they face new stages like football teams rising to the upper league.

Since their goal is success, they call what they do as an art or mastery. Don Juan, for example, describes the stalking and intent as mastery, and says that these two are the tremendous success of the new seers.

But in the sight of God, for example, there is no such thing as "being successful in prayer". Or the fact that a person is a Saint does not guarantee that he will go to heaven. Therefore, God Almighty wants us to do our best, but it is in His hands whether to accept it or not. And the most significant factor for this acceptance is sincerity and the fact that the deeds are allotted to Him.

However, this is not what the seers do as they focus on the return of what they do, and they cease to remember the Almighty God who gave them that return. God Almighty, on the other hand, establishes the whole developmental environment and gives them their abilities. And He provides all these to get to know and be aware of Him. Yet, the seers miss out on this and that's why all they do up to the last point become a dead loss.

God Almighty as being the chief instructor:

164. Certainly did God confer a great favor upon the believers when He sent among them a Messenger from themselves, reciting to them His verses and purifying them and teaching them the Scripture and wisdom, although they had been before in manifest error. (Koran/Chapter 3)

On one occasion, Castaneda asks why the seers call their teachers "nagual". Don Juan answers him saying, "As a sign of deference for his lifetime of impeccability, we always prefix 'nagual' to a nagual's name."[310]

Don Juan also says that the expression "benefactor" used for naguals is a gesture their apprentices make, and explains this as follows:

- A nagual creates an overwhelming feeling of gratitude in his disciples. After all, a nagual molds them and guides them through unimaginable areas. [311]

In this way, the seers are grateful and pay homage to their naguals, but they also forget to thank God Almighty, who has evolved everything for them. Because, as in the case of Castaneda, it is the Almighty God who set up the whole educational environment, sent Castaneda to don Juan and made it possible for him to reach maturity and perfection.

83. And that was Our conclusive argument which We gave Abraham against his people. We raise by degrees whom We will. Indeed, your Lord is Wise and Knowing.
84. And We gave to him Isaac and Jacob - all of them We guided. And Noah, We guided before; and among his descendants, David and Solomon and Job and Joseph and Moses and Aaron. Thus do We reward the doers of good.
85. And Zechariah and John and Jesus and Elias - and all were of the righteous.

---

[310] CASTANEDA, The Power of Silence, Washington Square Press, The Descent Of The Spirit: Seeing The Spirit

[311] CASTANEDA, The Power of Silence, Washington Square Press, The Manifestations Of The Spirit: The First Abstract Core

86. And Ishmael and Elisha and Jonah and Lot - and all of them We preferred over the Worlds.
87. And some among their fathers and their descendants and their brothers - and We chose them and We guided them to a straight path.
88. That is the guidance of God by which He guides whomever He wills of His servants. But if they had associated others with God, then worthless for them would be whatever they were doing.
89. Those are the ones to whom We gave the Scripture and authority and prophethood. But if your people deny it, then We have entrusted it to a people who are not therein disbelievers.
90. Those are the ones whom God has guided, so follow their guidance and say: "I ask of you for this message no payment. It is not but a reminder for the Worlds." (Koran/Chapter 6)

God Almighty sends the Prophets chosen and guided by Him to people in order to ensure their evolvement. The seers do the same thing through their naguals and make their apprentices reach maturity and perfection. However, the seers are only grateful to the naguals because they cannot establish the connection with God Almighty and put Him out of their mind. Yet, those naguals are able to accomplish what they have done through a guidance from God.

Therefore, it is not the naguals, but the Almighty God that the apprentices should be grateful for. But since the seers are ignorant of God's message, they lose out on this truth and fall from grace.

INTIMIDATION

39. God praises those who convey the messages of God and fear Him and do not fear anyone but God. And sufficient is God as Accountant. (Koran/Chapter 33)

"One of the greatest forces in the lives of warriors is fear. It spurs them to learn,"[312] says don Juan. Therefore, the seers often drive their apprentices into a corner by frightening them and by this means teach them what they want.

"The best of us always comes out when we are against the wall, when we feel the sword dangling overhead. Personally, I wouldn't have it any other way,"[313] says don Juan. Therefore, the seers frighten their apprentices, sometimes with death, sometimes with the help of inorganic beings, thus pushing their limits.

Castaneda tells about one of those frightening moments as follows:

- But are they (inorganic beings) real, don Juan?
- Of course! They are so real that ordinarily they kill people, especially those who stray into the wilderness and have no personal power.

---

312 CASTANEDA, The Fire from Within, Washington Square Press, The Eagle's Emanations

313 CASTANEDA, Tales of Power, Washington Square Press, The Island of The Tonal

- If you knew they were so dangerous, why did you leave me alone there?
- There is only one way to learn, and that way is to get down to business. To only talk about power is useless. If you want to know what power is, and if you want to store it, you must tackle everything yourself...
- Even you would agree with me if you could remember what you did last night. You ran as fast as any sorcerer only when your opponent became unbearable. We both know that and I believe I have already found a worthy opponent for you. [314]

Castaneda frequently describes such events in his books. He even refuses to obey in sometimes, but don Juan does not care much about it and says to him, "There is nothing wrong with being afraid. When you fear, you see things in a different way."[315] And by using this impulse, the seers force their disciples to live an impeccable life:

- The only reason we need a teacher is to spur us on mercilessly. Otherwise, our natural reaction is to stop to congratulate ourselves for having covered so much ground. [316]

However, these intimidations also have a side effect, and Castaneda says, "Being with don Juan for thirteen years had conditioned me, above everything else, to conceive of panic as something that was just around the corner at all times, ready to be released."[317] Therefore, even though he loves don Juan, he can never trust him and never be sure of him.

---

[314] CASTANEDA, Journey to Ixtlan, Washington Square Press, The Gait of Power

[315] CASTANEDA, The Teachings of Don Juan, Washington Square Press, Chapter 2

[316] CASTANEDA, The Power of Silence, Washington Square Press, Intending Appearances

[317] CASTANEDA, The Art of Dreaming, HarperCollins Publishers Inc., The Tenant

Fear of God:

36. Is not God sufficient for His servant? They threaten you with those other than Him. And whoever God leaves astray - for him there is no guide.
37. And whoever God guides - for him there is no misleader. Is not God Exalted in Might and Owner of Retribution? (Koran/ Chapter 39)

God Almighty puts fear as a fundamental power in the nature of human beings. The seers discover this mechanism and use it in their teachings as a source of discipline.

However, don Juan constantly frightens Castaneda with other things than God; therefore, panic is always at hand in Castaneda's life. But in the Koran, God Almighty describes his believing servants as "They fear Him and do not fear anyone but God."

Therefore, it is necessary to fear only God Almighty in this universe. And a person who is afraid of God, the Owner of everything, will be afraid of nothing else on earth.

On the other hand, the seers frighten their apprentices with almost everything except God and try to keep them in the direction. But what they actually do is to use a virtue that God Almighty has exclusively dedicated to Himself, and the things they use to frighten them are already created by God Almighty.

48. We send not the messengers except as bringers of good tidings and warners. So whoever believes and reforms - there will be no fear concerning them, nor will they grieve. (Koran/Chapter 6)

Moreover, God does not give the fear to man alone and sends his Prophets as "bringers of good tidings and warners". Therefore, what is essential in the sight of God is the balance of fear and hope, and His gospel is always ahead of His warning.

So, the fear of God is a blessing for human beings and enables them to "stop" themselves. And it does its job without the side effects of the way of the seers.

Balance of fear and hope:

15. Only those believe in Our verses who, when they are reminded by them, fall down in prostration and exalt God with praise of their Lord, and they are not arrogant.
16. Their sides part from their beds; they supplicate their Lord in fear and hope, and from what We have provided them, they spend for poor. (Koran/Chapter 32)

Because God creates everything in the universe as polar twins, He creates "fear" as the opposite twin of "hope" and wants a believer to have both actively.

Therefore, as in don Juan's methods, an unrestrained and excessive intimidation is not correct. There must be fear on the one hand and hope on the other. And one is asked to walk along with the sparks that the interaction of these two produce.

23. God has sent down the best statement: a consistent Book containing similar duals. The skins shiver therefrom of those who fear their Lord; then their skins and their hearts relax at the remembrance of God. That is the guidance of God by which He guides whom He wills. And one whom God leaves astray - for him there is no guide. (Koran/Chapter 39)

God Almighty puts fear into the human nature as an active force and, as the seers do, guides the human beings through the right way with it. However, at the same time, one does not panic because He balances it with hope. The awe, which occurs from the combination of these two, enables the feelings of the heart to fall into place. And God Almighty guides people through this sense of awe.

156. "Decree for us in this world that which is good and also in the Hereafter; indeed, we have turned back to You." God said, "My punishment - I afflict with it whom I will, but My mercy encompasses all things." So I will decree it for those who fear Me and give charity and those who believe in Our verses - (Koran/Chapter 7)

God Almighty says, "With My punishment, I visit whom I will." So the punishment is deserved, and this is a clear threat to human beings. But at the same time, God Almighty introduces himself above all, as Compassionate and Merciful, and says: "My mercy encompasses all things".

Therefore, human beings do not have the luxury of neglecting what they do; but there is also a Lord in front of them responding in ten steps to each step taken by themselves. And His mercy always precedes His punishment, which is not far for the righteous.

NARROW GROUP TRAINING

The seers perform their "symbolic death" with the method of erasing the personal history we mentioned before, and thus they stay alone with their own narrow group and continue their training in this way.

During this training, those outside the group do not interest them at all. Amongst themselves, they take advantage of each other and ensure their own personal development.

- The shamans of my lineage are not teachers or gurus. They don't give a fig about teaching their knowledge. They want heirs to their knowledge, not people vaguely interested in their knowledge for intellectual reasons. [318]

The seers are not looking for someone to teach their knowledge. They acquire a small number of apprentices within their narrow group, and in fact, train themselves as they pass on their knowledge to them. Then, those apprentices develop and come to a position to educate an apprentice themselves; thus, the cycle goes on and on.

Therefore, what they call "looking for an heir to their knowledge" is actually a situation that aims their own maturity. That is why they teach their knowledge to a limited number of apprentices, rise in a narrow group, and show no interest to those outside the group.

---

318 CASTANEDA, The Wheel of Time, Washington Square Press, Quotations from the Teachings of Don Juan, Commentary

<u>Keeping their information to themselves</u>:

13. And present to them an example: the people of the city, when the messengers came to it -
14. When We sent to them two but they denied them, so We strengthened them with a third, and they said, "Indeed, we are messengers to you."
15. They said, "You are not but human beings like us, and the Most Merciful has not revealed a thing. You are only telling lies."
16. They said, "Our Lord knows that we are messengers to you,
17. And we are not responsible except for clear notification." (Koran/Chapter 36)

In one of her conversations, la Gorda tells Castaneda, "You don't think that you can go around picking people up off the street to help them, do you?" and adds: "The impeccability of a warrior is to let them be and to support them in what they are."[319] Therefore, the seers keep their information to themselves, ignore other people, and completely negate the warning.

On the other hand, God Almighty sends His prophets as "bringers of good tidings and warners". That's why they wander from street to street, as la Gorda says, and spread the word of God to every person they meet. And this being their only duty to fulfill.

67. O Messenger, announce that which has been revealed to you from your Lord, and if you do not, then you have not conveyed His message. And God will protect you from the people. Indeed, God does not guide the disbelieving people. (Koran/Chapter 5)

In one of their conversations, Castaneda feels sorry for the plight of humanity and asks if there is anything that can be done against it. Don Juan says in answer to him:

- There's nothing that you and I can do about it. All we can do is discipline ourselves to the point where they will not touch us. How can you ask your fellow men to go through those rigors of

---

[319] CASTANEDA, The Second Ring of Power, Washington Square Press, The Second Attention

> discipline? They'll laugh and make fun of you, and the more aggressive ones will beat the shit out of you. [320]

Don Juan says, "There is nothing we can do for them," but that is why God sends His prophets and asks them to convey His messages.

Don Juan says in return, "If you warn them, they'll make fun of you, and the more aggressive ones will beat you." And these are exactly what the prophets encountered. But despite that, God Almighty sends His prophets as the light from Himself and commands, "Do your duty, I will protect you from the people."

So the seers are working for themselves, and the Prophets are working for us. That's why God helps them in their duty and protects them from aggression.

<u>No free training</u>:

20. And there came from the farthest end of the city a man, running. He said, "O my people, follow the messengers.
21. Follow those who do not ask of you any payment, and they are rightly guided." (Koran/Chapter 36)

The seers are not interested in people outside their narrow groups, and as a result, there is an unhealthy relationship within the group, which is evident in Castaneda's words.

Accordingly, Castaneda was greatly influenced by don Juan's interest in him in the early days of his apprenticeship. On the other hand, he cannot understand the reason for this and feels discomfort:

- Years before, I had been both very moved and very confused by don Juan's tremendous dedication to helping me. I could not imagine why he should show me such kindness. It was evident that he did not need me in any way in his life. He was obviously not investing in me. But I had learned, through life's painful experiences, that nothing was free; and being unable to foresee

---

[320] CASTANEDA, The Active Side of Infinity, HarperCollins Publishers Inc., Mud Shadows

what don Juan's reward would be made me tremendously uneasy. [321]

Castaneda realizes that nothing is actually free as time goes by, and he decides to ask don Juan what he is getting out of their association. Don Juan replies as follows:

- Nothing you would understand... Well, let me just say that, although you could understand it, you are certainly not going to like it.

This answer annoys Castaneda and insists don Juan to tell what he meant.

- Sometimes we should not poke the truth at the bottom. If we look carefully at the deepest stone, we may not like the consequences. I prefer to stay away from it.

Don Juan tries to stay away from the truth at the bottom, but Castaneda continues to insist, and don Juan replies to him as follows:

- If you judge me by my actions with you, you would have to admit that I have been a paragon of patience and consistency. But what you don't know is that to accomplish this I have had to fight for impeccability as I have never fought before. In order to spend time with you, I have had to transform myself daily, restraining myself with the most excruciating effort. [322]

While teaching his knowledge, don Juan is using Castaneda as a training tool for himself, and with this help, he pushes the limits and reaches the impeccability. As don Juan said, Castaneda does not like it at all, tries not to lose face and makes a sarcastic comeback, saying "I'm not that bad, don Juan".

---

[321] CASTANEDA, The Power of Silence, Washington Square Press, Moving the Assemblage Point

[322] CASTANEDA, The Power of Silence, Washington Square Press, Moving the Assemblage Point

The prophets not asking for any payment:

104. You do not ask of them for it any payment. It is not except a reminder to the Worlds. (Koran/Chapter 12)

In the Koran, God Almighty states the most fundamental characteristic of the Prophets as not asking for any payment. Whereas in this world, everyone wants payment for his work. Even don Juan wants to get the "impeccability award" in the end, but the Prophets are not like him.

As a requirement of sincere commitment, the Prophets do their duty only for the sake of God and do not ask for anything from people. They expect their wages only from God, in whom they put their faith. Therefore, they can receive their rewards only if whom they believe exists; and far from it, if He does not exist, the reward will be pointless.

Impeccability reward:

51. O my people, I do not ask you for my notification any reward. My reward is only from the One who created me. Then will you not reason? (Koran/Chapter 11)

Since the aim of the seers is to reach maturity and increase their energy, they live in their narrow groups, use each other as a means of training and develop themselves. However, in the way of God, there is no such use, because the main criterion along this road is not the maturity, but the sincerity.

God Almighty says, "We have made you a test tool for each other". And He tries us, one with the other, in a natural process. But the seers confine it to a narrow space, turn it into an accelerated course, and use it for their own maturity. However, this has no value in the cause of God, because in the end, they do it for their own benefit.

Don Juan says that his own profit is "impeccability" at the end of this process. However, there is no such thing as impeccability in the sight of God. Impeccability only belongs to Him. According to the verse, "If God were to impose blame on the people for what they have earned, He would not leave upon the earth any creature,"[323] impeccability is not enough to enter the Heaven. Therefore, what is essential is God's forgiveness, and what will enable us to gain it is not impeccability, but the sincere and righteous deeds dedicated to God.

Already Castaneda is disturbed by the fact that don Juan's behavior towards him is not sincere, that he is running after his own benefit and interest. Therefore, what don Juan says is the "deepest stone" is actually the most fundamental law of human nature imposed by God, but the seers ignore it and construct their knowledge on the wrong stone.

[323] Koran/Chapter 35, verse 45

12- The Science of Seers

- Witnessing
- Naming
- Laws of Physics
- Using Your Mind
- Polar Twins
- Claim to Explain Everything
- Developmental Progress

WITNESSING

While explaining the truths about the mastery of awareness, don Juan describes the universe for Castaneda as follows:

- The first truth was that our familiarity with the world we perceive compels us to believe that we are surrounded by objects, existing by themselves and as themselves, just as we perceive them, whereas, in fact, there is no world of objects, but a universe of the Eagle's emanations.

After explaining this, a conversation takes place between them as quoted here:

- I told him that I was not following his teachings, for I had become obsessed with his description of the Eagle and what it does. I remarked over and over about the awesomeness of such an idea.
- It is not just an idea. It is a fact. And a damn scary one if you ask me. The new seers were not simply playing with ideas.
- But what kind of a force would the Eagle be?
- I wouldn't know how to answer that. The Eagle is as real for the seers as gravity and time are for you, and just as abstract and incomprehensible.

- Wait a minute, don Juan. Those are abstract concepts, but they do refer to real phenomena that can be corroborated. There are whole disciplines dedicated to that.
- The Eagle and its emanations are equally corroboratable. And the discipline of the new seers is dedicated to doing just that. [324]

Don Juan describes his knowledge as a "discipline of science", and says that, like the science of matter, it is dedicated to verifying the truths in the universe. The difference between them is that these two sciences have different starting points. One examines the universe based on matter, and the other based on energy. But the things they do are the same.

They both "unbiasedly witness" the universe and uncover its mechanisms. However, they do not have an answer to the question "What is that?" about the enormous picture they put before us.

Don Juan knows this, and answers Castaneda's above question saying, "I wouldn't know how to answer that", and he defines them as corroboratable, but not comprehensible truths, just like gravity and time. Because according to him, human reason can only witness an external order and has nothing to say about it.

And the place where the science of matter comes from is not so different. The human brain, which is said to have been formed as a result of evolution, has been born as a child of this universe. And since it evolves through the action-reaction relationships within it, it develops only on the basis of this universe, but it does not have the ability to think about another universe or different dimensions. What it can think of them is always the product of the syntax of this universe, and all it can do is nothing but the endless repetition of its allegations as a cat vainly turns around to catch its tail. So, even the scientists, when they go deeper into the matter and cross the threshold of quantum mechanics, begin to assert, "Leave your mind outside the door and come in". Because "Newton mechanics" in which the human brain develops comes to a standstill respectively.

---

[324] CASTANEDA, The Fire from Within, Washington Square Press, The Eagle's Emanations

Don Juan explains this situation as follows:

- To make reason feel safe is always the task of the teacher. I've tricked your reason into believing that the "tonal" was accountable and predictable. Genaro and I have labored to give you the impression that only the "nagual" was beyond the scope of explanation; the proof that the tricking was successful is that at this moment it seems to you that in spite of everything you have gone through, there is still a core that you can claim as your own, your reason. That's a mirage. Your precious reason is only a center of assemblage, a mirror that reflects something which is outside of it. Last night you witnessed not only the indescribable nagual but also the indescribable tonal.
- The last piece of the sorcerers' explanation says that reason is merely reflecting an outside order, and that reason knows nothing about that order; it cannot explain it, in the same way it cannot explain the nagual. Reason can only witness the effects of the tonal, but never ever could it understand it, or unravel it. The very fact that we are thinking and talking points out an order that we follow without ever knowing how we do that, or what the order is. [325]

On the other hand, Castaneda objects to this and says, "Scientists' research into the workings of the brain reveals some clues as to what this order might be". Don Juan, in turn, says, "No matter what we do with reason, or how we do it, we are merely witnessing the effects of the tonal," and describes the reason as a mirror that reflects something outside of it.

The reason, namely our brain, reflects the outside to the "living us". That's why don Juan says that man is, above all, a "perceiver". Therefore, first you "live", and your brain reflects an existing order to "you". But according to some scientists, there is no "you" who lives like that. Hubert Reeves, for example, says in his book The First Second: "Millions of brain cells that evolved over time in the evolution of the universe are now investigating their own history."

---

325 CASTANEDA, Tales of Power, Washington Square Press, The Bubble of Perception

Just as scientists ascribe all what is happening in the universe to some self-existent forces and not to God, they also reduce you to several brain cells to wipe you out. On the other hand, don Juan says, "The essence is you; the reason is a mirror that reflects only one of many possible external orders and allows you to witness it".

As a result, both sciences are witnesses to this universe. The seers know it, but scientists do not. Moreover, they tell us, "Wait a while, we'll explain everything." The seers show us how close they are.

Scientists think that when they find the equation of something and give it a name, they explain everything. For example, the force of gravity is a "fait accompli" for them, something explained, but is it really so?

The force of gravity is happening in every corner of the universe, at every moment. So, what do the equations explaining gravity do? Does it explain everything about gravity, or is it just witnessing that there is an order for it, as don Juan said?

Actually, what the Science of Matter does is nothing but witness to the order that existed, just as the Science of Seers does. So, human beings are in a "tabula rasa" in the face of the universe and have nothing to say in the matter. For this reason, Almighty God, the owner of all this order, sends his revelation by saying, "He taught man that he does not know" and reports to the human being the talisman of the universe.

<u>Witnessing the truth</u>:

50. They say, "Why are not signs sent down to him from his Lord?" Say, "The signs are only with God, and I am only a clear warner."
51. Is it not sufficient for them that We revealed to you the Book which is recited to them? Indeed in that is a mercy and reminder for a people who believe.
52. Say, "Sufficient is God between me and you as Witness. He knows what is in the heavens and earth. And they who have believed in falsehood and disbelieved in God - it is those who are the losers." (Koran/Chapter 29)

The concept of "witnessing" which don Juan frequently mentions, is one of the crucial concepts of the Koran. Therefore, God Almighty commands, "God is, over all things, Witness".

6. On the Day when God will resurrect them all and inform them of what they did. God had enumerated it, while they forgot it; and God is, over all things, Witness. (Koran/Chapter 58)

One of the several names of God Almighty mentioned in the Koran is "Witness". So, the witnessing shows the status of God in the face of the universe, and this concept is also true for Prophets and believers:

83. When they hear what has been revealed to the Messenger, you see their eyes overflowing with tears because of what they have recognized of the truth. They say, "Our Lord, we have believed, so register us among the witnesses. (Koran/Chapter 5)

God Almighty says that He is a Witness over everything, and that those who follow His path witness the "truth". Therefore, while the human being is a mere witness who cannot explain anything in this universe, thanks to the revelation sent by God, he becomes a "real witness" and begins to look at the universe with the comprehensive knowledge of its essential nature.

Thus, people have a single duty in this universe: to witness the existence and unity of God Almighty, and the magnificent manifestations of Him all around the universe. Human beings do not have a second task and we are here to witness this fact.

NAMING

30. [Mention] when your Lord said to the angels, "Indeed, I will make upon the earth a successive authority." They said, "Will You place upon it one who causes corruption therein and sheds blood, while we declare Your praise and sanctify You?" He said, "Indeed, I know that which you do not know."
31. And He taught Adam the names - all of them. Then He showed them to the angels and said, "Inform Me of the names of these, if you are truthful."
32. They said, "Exalted are You; we have no knowledge except what You have taught us. Indeed, it is You who is the Knowing, the Wise."
33. He said, "O Adam, inform them of their names." And when he had informed them of their names, He said, "Did I not tell you that I know the unseen of the heavens and the earth? And I know what you reveal and what you have concealed." (Koran/Chapter 2)

We have already said that the Prophet Adam's story is one of the most critical stories in the Koran and that as the representative of mankind, information about the most basic tendencies of human beings is transmitted through Prophet Adam.

One of them was the desire for eternity, and we explained that this was the most basic motivation of man. Here we talk about the tendency of mankind to discover the existence and to name what it has discovered.

Accordingly, while the angels tell God Almighty, "Will You place upon earth one who causes corruption therein and sheds blood?", God Almighty takes sides with the human beings and replies, "Indeed, I know that which you do not know". After that, Prophet Adam informs the angels of the names of "things" they witness but do not know what.

God Almighty says, "We taught all the names" to Prophet Adam, the prototype of mankind. However, just as Prophet Adam's eating of the tree of eternity is the embodiment of man's desire for eternity, this is also an embodiment of man's desire for naming and not a « fait accompli ». Since the Prophet Adam, God has been teaching names to human beings.

Accordingly, both seers and scientists inquire into the entire universe and name everything they discover. And in this way, God Almighty teaches all names to mankind.

However, as the verse says, both sciences are taught only with "names". When we say water for water or when we say that its formula is H_2O, we discover and name something that actually exists. Yet, the water is existing at any moment by the command of God Almighty, the waves in the seas hit the shore for millions of years, the rivers flow, the rains are raining, etc. and we are only witnesses of them. We discover and give names to them. And in fact, the whole adventure of both sciences consists of this naming process.

What is the real nature of these things that we named? Why is there all this? Both the Science of Seers and the Science of Matter cannot answer these questions, but they can only witness the existence. On the other hand, God Almighty Himself gives the answer to these questions. He sends his revelation by saying, "He taught man that he does not know" and tells us the essential nature of the things, the names of which had been taught to us by Him.

Naming by the two sciences:

Both sciences name things they have discovered, but people's weaknesses are reflected in these names. Don Juan, for example, uses a lot of different terms to explain "intent" to Castaneda:

- Sorcerers call intent the indescribable, the spirit, the abstract, the nagual. I would prefer to call it nagual, but it overlaps with the name for the leader, the benefactor, who is also called nagual, so I have opted for calling it the spirit, intent, the abstract. [326]

In other words, the seers cannot give a full name to their knowledge even in the most basic subject, and the names they offer cannot explain the exact nature of them. Because they do not come from God and they are discovered as a result of developed progress. In accordance with the verse saying, "Man has ever been, most of anything, prone to dispute"[327]; every seer looks at each incident from another aspect and comes up with new definitions.

On the other hand, the naming of God Almighty in the Koran finds the exact target. For example, the Koran calls the entities that the seers call "inorganic beings" as "jinn". And the root meaning of the word jinn means that something is hidden to the sense organs. For instance, the baby in the womb is called the "jenin", which derives from this word in Arabic because it is hidden in the womb. Therefore, the name is given to the jinn because they are hidden to the sense organs.

About jinns, don Juan says, "They're always with us, but we do not notice". Therefore, this word in the Koran gives exactly what the genre of "jinn" is, but the "inorganic beings" that the seers call them do not fully meet it. It's not wrong, but it does not give an idea of its existential role and cannot hit the nail on the head.

1. By the sky and the Tariq -
2. And what can make you know what is the Tariq?
3. It is the piercing star. (Koran/Chapter 86)

---

[326] CASTANEDA, The Power of Silence, Washington Square Press, The Manifestations Of The Spirit: The First Abstract Core

[327] Koran/Chapter 18, verse 54

The same goes for the science of matter. For instance, the science of matter sees this name appropriate for black holes, the most important celestial body in the universe. It's dark because even light can't escape it; it also swallows everything around it like a hole. As in naming the inorganic being, the depiction is precisely true, but it can't give a satisfactory answer for the essential nature of this "hole".

In the Koran, the word "Tariq", which means "star", is used for black holes and it is asked, "What can make you know what is the Tariq?" This phrase is transcribed in very few places in the Koran to emphasize that what is mentioned is very important. And in the next verse, its nature is reported as a "piercing star". So, this is a star that forms a "hole".

As you know, black holes are actually stars having completed their life. Under some special conditions, stars gradually collapse inward, concentrate, and have an incredible gravitational force. Even that light can't escape, and they look like black holes to the observer. But the name given by science gives no mention about the star. God Almighty says in the section of the Koran that He describes black holes as a "piercing star". In other words, it's like a black hole that pierces the space-time where it locates, and everything flows into it, but it's actually a star.

And it is also worth remembering here that black hole theories say they might be some kind of "wormhole" and that they can open up to other universes or elsewhere in this universe. If that is true, then the expression used in the Koran for this star, which pierces space and time, would make even more sense.

Beautiful names of God:

22. He is God, other than whom there is no deity, Knower of the unseen and the witnessed. He is the Most Compassionate, the Most Merciful
23. He is God, other than whom there is no deity. The Sovereign, the Pure, the Perfection, the Bestower of Faith, the Overseer, the Exalted in Might, the Compeller, the Superior. Exalted is God above whatever they associate with Him.

24. He is God, the Creator, the Inventor, the Fashioner; to Him belong the most beautiful names. Whatever is in the heavens and earth is exalting Him. And He is the Exalted in Might, the Wise. (Koran/Chapter 59)

God Almighty, who teaches mankind all the names, says in the Koran, "The most beautiful names belong to Me". In the Koran, there are close to one hundred names of God Almighty, and each of which sheds light on an aspect of His. If we think of these names as "waves", this universe is actually the refraction of these names. Moreover, we actually come to this world only to know and learn the manifestations of these names in the universe.

36. Exalted is He who created all pairs - from what the earth grows and from themselves and from that which they do not know.
37. And a sign for them is the night. We remove from it the light of day, so they are left in darkness.
38. And the sun runs toward its stopping point. That is the determination of the Exalted in Might, the Knowing.
39. And the moon - We have determined for it phases, and its route returns like the old date stalk.
40. It is not possible for the sun to reach the moon, nor does the night overtake the day, but each, in an orbit, is swimming. (Koran/Chapter 36)

There is a group of verses where the two important names of God, Exalted in Might and the Knowing, are mentioned above. And according to these verses, all the movements of the sun and moon form at the sole discretion of God Almighty, and this becomes a manifestation of His names Exalted in Might and the Knowing.

In other words, God the Exalted in Might establishes this order with his superior power. At the same time, He is the Knowing and connects the whole universe with His infallible mathematical rules. And in this way, the entire universe comes into being as a manifestation of the names of God Almighty, and we are asked to witness them and realize His greatness.

In the above verses, God Almighty also says, "the sun runs toward its stopping point", and even declares that the sun keeps moving towards a halt. Koran says this in the seventh century, which is to say about a thousand years before Copernicus and Galileo. Moreover, according to these two scientists, as the world moves, the sun remains steady.

In addition, the Koran says that this movement of the sun is not endless and is moving towards a stopping point. In other words, it supports the words of scientists who claim the expansion that started with the Big Bang will slow down and stop one day. Moreover, the expression here is interesting. It does not say that it will stop but says it will come to a halting point. Therefore, there is no final stop. It's going to stop there for a while and maybe come back for the "Big Crunch".

As a result, the science of matter witnesses these infallible rules set by the Almighty God and reveals their order in a developmental progress. Yet, their original source is God Almighty and the whole universe is a manifestation of His beautiful names. And what both sciences witness in this universe belongs to Him.

LAWS OF PHYSICS

Continuity:

As we have already mentioned, the main argument of the science of the seers is to "stop". Their aim is to stop everything that belongs to this universe and to reach the system of realms beyond it. For this reason, they stop social relations, their selves and ultimately the world. They dispose of all the connections of this universe to become a free awareness that can go to the other realms.

On the other hand, the basic argument of the science of matter is "continuity". It continues its existence by studying the "law of physics" which assumedly will never lose its continuity. Although there is no guarantee that these rules will continue to exist a second later, the science of matter takes it as an unquestionable presumption and begins as such. Therefore, while the science of matter drives profit from continuity, the science of the seers says that continuity is a mirage and tries to destroy it.

41. Indeed, God holds the heavens and the earth, lest they cease. And if they should cease, no one could hold them after Him. Indeed, He is Forbearing and Forgiving. (Koran/Chapter 35)

Don Juan says this continuity in the universe is a result of the Eagle's emanations, namely its commands. Yet, the science of matter rejects

"Eagle", but the only material in its possession is the continuity of these emanations.

Therefore, the science of matter is in a difficult situation. Since it does not know the other realms, it does not know the awareness, nor the God Almighty the source of this continuity. All it takes is a few millimeters thick surface of the water. Below it, there is a huge ocean that holds it in place, so that God Almighty provides continuity in the universe.

The merit of the seers is to break this continuity on the surface and dive into the ocean. In doing so, all they have is their awareness and all the rules they are subject to belong to God Almighty.

So they know as much as He allows, and they can dive as deep as He allows. Their difference from the scientists is that they know the God Almighty, namely the Eagle, and that He rules the whole universe. Hence, they behave accordingly, whereas the scientists do not know even that.

Laws of Physics:

> 31. Say, "Who provides for you from the heaven and the earth? Or who controls hearing and sight and who brings the living out of the dead and brings the dead out of the living and who arranges every matter?" They will say, "God," so say, "Then will you not fear Him?" (Koran/Chapter 10)

The science of matter explores the laws of physics that continue infallibly, but does not actually know what they are. It unquestionably acknowledges that these rules will always continue existing this way, and all that it is doing is merely witnessing their "continuity".

The science of matter names the continuities it discovers, such as gravitational force, electromagnetic force, etc. And then it describes them as if they exist on their own, doing all the job by themselves. In other words, for the sake of denying God, they invent almost unlimited "gods" and give all the powers to them.

On the other hand, God Almighty says, "The clouds, I have assigned them a mission; the rain, I make it pour; and the wind, I blow it." That is to say; there are no movable forces on their own. Moreover, God Almighty proves Himself with this order and says, "Of course there should be a Ruler of them." And asks: Will you still not use your mind?

The seers say that the "laws of physics" consist of the commands of the Eagle that the continuity of these rules is provided by God Almighty, whom they call Eagle. According to them, this seeming continuity is a thin shell, and they pass it to the great ocean behind it by using their awareness. So these rules and awareness are not disconnected, but things that interact with each other.

The seers are also talking about a power called "intent" in the universe. Don Juan calls it the intent of the Eagle's emanations and he even says that this is the motive behind the biological evolution. In other words, while some aspects of commands of the Eagle establish the universe, others decide the direction it will expand towards.

Moreover, at the same time, this power is closely related to human beings and governs everything as well as their destiny. Therefore, the human and the universe are not disconnected and they are both reflections of universal consciousness.

However, the science of matter is not far from Aristotle, which considers the universe a static one. Only, the static laws of physics were born from the static universe idea: that the laws of physics exist on their own, independent of everything. However, there is no such thing. They are the commandments of God, therefore the product of a consciousness.

> 73. It is He who created the heavens and earth in truth. Whenever He says, "Be," and it is, His word is the truth. And His is the dominion on the Day the Horn is blown. He is the Knower of the unseen and the witnessed; and He is the Wise, the Acquainted. (Koran/Chapter 6)

In fact, the solution is very simple. As the Prophet Muhammad said, our bodies are our bearers; God Almighty governs the universe in the same way as we govern ourselves. So, your proportion to your own body is like God's proportion to this universe.

You do not know how you think or how you walk, but you can do these things by virtue of the secret "Be" when you wish to. In the same way, God Almighty creates and governs the whole universe by virtue of the secret "Be". Therefore, to deny God Almighty is to deny yourself. Perish the thought! Claiming that there is no God means, you do not exist.

And as a result, we come full circle. Science of Matter offers us a dead universe and a dead "human", whereas the Science of Seers shows that we live. Moreover, it shows that this universe is the product of consciousness. And it rejects the notion of the dead universe made by the science of matter and cross-checks it for us.

However, the seers also cannot make the final statement, because they say that we can only witness what we see, and there is nothing to say about this. On the other hand, God Almighty reveals the nature of these truths that they can only witness. By doing so, He introduces the true nature of this universe to us.

USING YOUR MIND

The seers want to demolish rationality:

- Whenever you are in the world of the "tonal", you should be an impeccable tonal; no time for irrational crap. But whenever you are in the world of the "nagual", you should also be impeccable; no time for rational crap. For the warrior, intent is the gate in between. It closes completely behind him when he goes either way. [328]

Rationality is an extension of continuity in the universe. And for this reason, the science of matter is actually in pursuit of it. The seers, on the other hand, are in pursuit of the ocean they call "nagual", which maintains this continuity witnessed by the science of matter.

Don Juan says, "In the world of nagual there is no time for rationality". Because the human brain has been developed to be functional in this universe and does not work beyond this limit. Hence, logic no longer works. However, that does not mean that the so-called ocean does not exist, but it shows that the human mind has reached its limits.

For example, it is claimed, "If the universe is constantly expanding, it must have an end". Well, what is there where it ends? The science of matter can't answer this question. They say, "Where it ends, there's nothing left to talk about since continuum or space-time reaches its

---

[328] CASTANEDA, Tales of Power, Washington Square Press, In Nagual's Time

end". In fact, where the universe ends, the human brain ends and reaches its limits. Which is why they can't find anything to say.

- I've told you over and over that being too rational is a handicap. Human beings have a very deep sense of magic. We are part of the mysterious. Rationality is only a veneer with us. If we scratch that surface, we find a sorcerer underneath. [329]

The science of matter builds everything on the continuity of the laws of physics and calls the things that conform to this as "rational". On the other hand, the seers build their training on breaking down the logic of the apprentices and showing that these laws may not continue. So they can use their "intent" as a door and become "rational" in dealing with tonal and "irrational" with nagual.

- We can better explain this by saying that the task of the teacher is to wipe clean one half of the bubble and to reorder everything on the other half. The benefactor's task then is to open the bubble on the side that has been cleaned. Once the seal is broken, the warrior is never the same. He has then the command of his totality. Half of the bubble is the ultimate center of reason, the "tonal". The other half is the ultimate center of will, the "nagual". That is the order that should prevail; any other arrangement is nonsensical and petty, because it goes against our nature; it robs us of our magical heritage and reduces us to nothing. [330]

Don Juan says the seer who reaches this ability has reached the "totality". Also, he declares any other arrangement nonsensical and contrary to our nature. According to him, this integrity is the triumph of the "man of knowledge". So he criticizes Castaneda many times for being too rational.

Quantum mechanics as the "nagual" of the science of matter:

Don Juan calls this realm the tonal island we have witnessed and

---

329 CASTANEDA, The Power of Silence, Washington Square Press, The Requirements Of Intent: Breaking The Mirror Of Self-Reflection

330 CASTANEDA, Tales of Power, Washington Square Press, The Strategy of a Sorcerer

describes the nagual as the endless ocean that holds and surrounds it. What is essential to him is nagual and this visible realm is only one of its millions of forms. And the human brain is a mirror that only works within the tonal and reflects it to the "living us".

The final point reached by the science of matter, the opposite twin of the science of the seers, is not much different. Moreover, as they descended into the subatomic world, in fact they have reached their own "nagual".

Accordingly, the human brain, which was functionalized to operate in the Newtonian mechanics scale entered into quantum mechanics with difficulties, and things considered "irrational" for the normal world became a commonplace for scientists.

For example, a scientist talks about the quantum entanglement, the most interesting subject of quantum physics, as follows:

- This is the most bizarre thing of quantum mechanics. It is impossible even to comprehend. Don't even ask me why, don't ask me how it works, because these are illegal questions. All we can say is that is apparently the way the world takes. [331]

As you see, he talks just like don Juan and confirms his words, "Human mind can only witness this universe, but it can't talk about it." Because the human brain is a child of this universe, and works only in it. He can only witness what is going on in front of him, but he has nothing to do with it.

Quantum entanglement:

In quantum entanglement, the two particles generated by quantum entanglement communicate with each other no matter where they are, and this communication is faster than the speed of light. Rather, it happens at the same time, and a change in one causes an immediate change in the other. What is happening here is not the teleportation of the distant molecule, but the loading of that information in that space-time tissue.

---

[331] Beyond the Cosmos, Quantum Leap Documentary with Brian Greene

Being motivated by the theorem, scientific documentaries make many teleportation fantasies: If a photon's information can be loaded, so can the one for human one day. Yet that is something that can be already achieved by the seers. In all reason, it seems impossible in everyday life, but as you can see, this is already happening in the universe.

The mistake of science is to regard the universe as matter. He examines them as independent photons, quarks, etc., whereas matter is a consequence and a sub-tissue causes it. Also, this tissue is not entirely separate from consciousness as it is supposed. Therefore, when the scientists consider those quarks and mesons an officer of God, then they will relax and everything will be in order.

Double-slit experiment:

Another example about the quantum mechanics is the double-slit experiment. In double-slit experiment, electrons are sent to the experimental apparatus and act interferingly like waves, but when they are sent one by one, unlike expected, they again create interference. After which, when scientists try to measure it, they behave like particles! This means that when you don't observe, there are waves of probability; when you observe it, there are particles of experience. Moreover, the particles we know as solids are actually the scattered wave of possible positions and all of these at any moment. But when you try to measure them, they take on only one of these positions…

How though? It's explained exactly like in Castaneda's books, isn't it?

This means that the universe does not have a form unless you observe it, and it is made up of millions of waves of probability, yet it appears to you as matter when you observe it. So the "universe" shows us the face it wants to show, but there are millions of other possible faces. Don Juan explains it as we quoted before:

- Something out there is affecting our senses. This is the part that is real. The unreal part is what our senses tell us is there. Take a mountain, for instance. Our senses tell us that it is an object. It has size, color, form. We even have categories of mountains, and they are downright accurate. Nothing wrong with that; the flaw is simply that it has never occurred to us that our senses play only a superficial role. Our senses perceive the way they do because a specific feature of our awareness forces them to do so.

- Seers say that we think there is a world of objects out there only because of our awareness. But what's really out there are the Eagle's emanations, fluid, forever in motion, and yet unchanged, eternal. [332]

"Our senses perceive the way they do because a specific feature of our awareness forces them to do so", says don Juan about which "face" of the universe we're going to see. In other words, everything revolves around "observer". Science of matter also says that when there is no "observer", particles are probability waves, but when an observer is present, they behave like particles. Thus, two sciences actually say the same thing.

However, it is not the "universe" that shows us what it wants, but God Almighty. While don Juan says, "A specific feature of our awareness forces them to do so", he explains the same idea in a different way as "the compelling power of the Eagle's emanations":

- The new seers, being pragmatically oriented, became immediately cognizant of the compelling power of the emanations. They realized that all living creatures are forced to employ the Eagle's emanations without ever knowing what they are. They also realized that organisms are constructed to grasp a certain range of those emanations and that every species has a definite range. The emanations exert great pressure on organisms, and through that pressure organisms construct their perceivable world.
- In our case, as human beings, we employ those emanations and interpret them as reality. But what man senses is such a small portion of the Eagle's emanations that it's ridiculous to put much stock in our perceptions, and yet it isn't possible for us to disregard our perceptions. The new seers found this out the hard way - after courting tremendous dangers. [333]

---

[332] CASTANEDA, The Fire from Within, Washington Square Press, The Eagle's Emanations

[333] CASTANEDA, The Fire from Within, Washington Square Press, The Eagle's Emanations

Elsewhere, don Juan says, "Intent is the pervasive force that causes us to perceive. We do not become aware because we perceive; rather, we perceive as a result of the pressure and intrusion of intent." [334] And as we said before, what he calls "intent" is the intent of God Almighty.

So, there is a conversion of nagual into the tonal, but this conversion is not nondirectional and takes place at the command of God Almighty, who the seers call the Eagle. And God Almighty shows us what He wants to in this universe.

Using your mind:

A scientist says, "After learning the quantum mechanics, you can never see the world in the same way again". That is also true for the teachings of don Juan. Because they both pass behind this description and start touching the "nagual", and plain logic no longer works there.

In fact, those who deny God use this plain logic, the logic of the Newtonian universe, and deny Him. For example, a scientist calls it "allergy of nonsense". However, what quantum mechanics brings is also "nonsense", but at the same time, they are the truths.

Therefore, God Almighty gives us our minds to make use of all the existing data and not leave any of them out of use. But if you only use your mind to guard Newtonian mechanics, quantum mechanics sounds ridiculous, also don Juan's sayings sound ridiculous; but that does not mean they're not true!

However, the scientists, although they have discovered the quantum mechanics and met the limits of human logic, "rationality" is their stronghold, and they have no intention of quitting.

On the other hand, in the Koran, there is no static concept of "logic" or "rationality" merely, "using your mind" instead. Interestingly, this word always comes in the verb form wherever used in the Koran and is not mentioned as a name anywhere. This means that reasoning is a dynamic thing, not a static concept like logic. So in the universe, there

---

334 CASTANEDA, The Power of Silence, Washington Square Press, Introduction

is a state for man whether or not to use the mind, rather than the rational or irrational separation.

For example, while Castaneda is explaining to don Juan what the wind is, he is making a science-based explanation of it. On the other hand, don Juan bursts into laughter to break his plain logic, because although Castaneda's statement is true, it actually reflects his own syntax and literally expresses one aspect of the truth. Don Juan knows that this is just a description.

- "What is the wind then?" he asked in a challenging tone.
- I patiently explained to him that masses of hot and cold air produced different pressures and that the pressure made the masses of air move vertically and horizontally. It took me a long while to explain all the details of basic meteorology.
- "You mean that all there is to the wind is hot and cold air?" he asked in a tone of bafflement.
- "I'm afraid so," I said and silently enjoyed my triumph.
- Don Juan seemed to be dumbfounded. But then he looked at me and began to laugh uproariously. "Your opinions are final opinions," he said with a note of sarcasm. "They are the last word, aren't they? For a hunter, however, your opinions are pure crap. It makes no difference whether the pressure is one or two or ten; if you would live out here in the wilderness you would know that during the twilight the wind becomes 'power'. A hunter that is worth his salt knows that, and acts accordingly."

The science of matter witnesses this truth and reveals its order, yet cannot answer the question of why. Therefore, his description is not enough for the human mind. On the other hand, God Almighty says, "If you use your mind, you will find many signs that will lead you to Me in the blowing of the winds", and the order that the science of matter finds is actually a sign that reveals Himself.

164. Indeed, in the creation of the heavens and the earth, and the alternation of the night and the day, and the ships which sail through the sea with that which benefits people, and what God has sent down from the heavens of rain, giving life thereby to the

> earth after its lifelessness and dispersing therein every kind of moving creature, and His directing of the winds and the clouds controlled between the heaven and earth are signs for a people who use reason. (Koran/Chapter 2)

In other words, God Almighty says, "I created this universe in the form of a magnificent palace and created everything in order. Will you not still use your mind to see my signs surrounding you?"

God Almighty wants us to use the mind He has given us with its all capacity and evaluate everything. While all that the science of matter does is to say, "These things are irrational" and then not to use some of the mind. Therefore, what God Almighty means by reasoning is really to use the mind, and what the science of matter does is to adapt the mind to its own patterns.

Although the science of matter does not officially accept it, its main purpose is to explain the whole universe in a way that does not require God. And for this reason, instead of using the full capacity of the human mind and the all available data, it neglects the things that are not measurable, like the discoveries of the seers. Therefore, it chains the human mind and limits its use. The great creation of the universe, the existence of everything in pairs, or the teachings that don Juan tells us do not matter to it, because they are not formulated. However, they are also within the limits of the human mind's comprehension, and one can evaluate them and come to accurate conclusions.

OPPOSITE TWINS

49. And of all things We created two counterparts; perhaps you take advice. (Koran/Chapter 51)

We have already stated that God Almighty has created the whole universe from pairs that are opposite to each other, but at the same time complementary to each other. And both the science of the seers and the science of matter have discovered and confirmed this.

As a reflection of this universal principle of creation in pairs, God Almighty creates the Science of Seers as the opposite twin of the Science of Matter and thus makes these two sciences cross-check each other.

The two sciences verifying each other:

God Almighty creates this universe with the Big Bang from a matter zero and brings it up to this day by developing it over time. He puts His own signature on every corner of it, making it an example for people who use their minds. The science of matter studies this universe created by God and finds the current order in it.

The seers, on the other hand, develop the science of "energy" behind this visible face examined by the science of matter and reveal the order in it for us.

However, the seers say, "The world we all know is only a description" and they trivialize all the patterns revealed by the science of matter. The science of matter, in the same way, sees what the seers describe as fantasy.

In other words, they both state that the knowledge they operate with is absolutely true. However, God Almighty creates them as opposite twins to complete one another, and even though they do not know it themselves, they cross-check each other.

Therefore, all this reality is not for nothing. Neither the creation of the universe in billions of years nor all the rules and order that the seers have discovered are in vain. God Almighty creates these two sciences as a matter of fact, and He collides these two dimensions of being with each other giving us the opportunity to cross-check.

The science of the seers shows us that mankind is not a robot, that we are alive. The science of matter, on the other hand, is discovering the pattern of this universe that can't be just a description. In the end, they're both telling the truth, but the conclusions they make from what they discover are not totally true. They only make comments by looking at one part of the reality, and they make mistakes by doing so.

They find mechanisms, but they can't answer the question, "What is this in essence?" Moreover, what they find cancels each other's answers without any outside interference. God Almighty, on the other hand, as the Owner of all things, opens the talisman of the universe and reveals to us the true nature of what they have discovered with the secret of "Taught man what he did not know".[335]

Being anti-thesis of each other:

Castaneda complains that the knowledge of the seers is ignored by the Western world and explains it this way:

- The perceptual claims of sorcerers, when examined in terms of the linear concepts of our Western world, make no sense whatsoever. Western civilization has been in contact with the

[335] Koran/Chapter 96, verse 5

> shamans of the New World for five hundred years, and there has never been a genuine attempt on the part of scholars to formulate a serious philosophical discourse based on statements made by those shamans. [336]

This is actually a consistent attitude for scientists and it's not surprising. Because these two sciences are anti-thesis of each other and there is no set of intersections between them, at least at the beginning. But they're also like soul mates with different bodies. The methods, the things they do, their final destination, they're always the same.

God Almighty has made these two sciences polar twins of each other, just as humans and jinn have made polar twins of each other in this universe. Humans and jinn live, but they don't have a body of common ground. They're both alive, but they're in different capsules. Furthermore, they exist to show us that life is the truth and matter is its occasion.

That also goes for the two sciences we're talking about. They are in different bodies, but what they do is the same, and they bear witness to the signs of God. And just as the human-jinn polarity shows us life, they show us God Almighty.

These two sciences, which generally reject God, also reject each other. Even though they don't know it, they are the servants of God. God collides them with each other and makes them cross-check, and the combination of these two sciences shows us God Almighty.

Therefore, the Science of Seers and the Science of Matter do not actually have to reject each other. On the contrary, God has created them to complement each other, and when they do not reject each other, they also do not reject God Almighty.

Therefore, the fact that these two sciences deny their own polar pair is an illusion. And in this case, the ones in the wrong are none other than the ones who are in denial, which leads them to nothingness. When everyone accepts and approves of each other, everyone wins.

---

336 CASTANEDA, Magical Passes, HarperCollins Publishers Inc., The Second Group: The Recapitulation

Every science illuminates a piece:

Since God is the Owner of all things and mankind is a part being, people can only shed light on one side of the truth and no one can afford to light them all.

God Almighty gives an angle illumination task to the seers, while he gives another angle illumination task to the scientists. But He keeps to Himself the explanation of the whole truth in the way of revelation. Even in this way, He sends His prophets only in a way that sheds light on a certain angle.

For example, He sends a tough but good-tempered prophet, like Prophet Moses, against a figure of power like Pharaoh, to show how to fight the tyrants of the age; but on the other hand, He also gives body to a prophet like Abraham with a soft heart. Or through Prophet Joseph, He teaches how He leads people with His guidance, which the seers call "intent".

In the same way, God Almighty develops the Science of Matter in the known part of the continents, while He provides the development of the Science of Seers in Central America where people live isolated from the "known world".

In fact, this may be the reason why God Almighty has divided the world into two main parts. Because of this, the development of these two sciences, which are both opposite and complementary to each other, is achieved on the same planet, thus shedding light on two complementary dimensions of existence.

The science of energy:

"We are energetic probes created by the universe,"[337] says don Juan. This is the definition of the "scientist" in the language of the seers. Accordingly, they discover the universe as the scientists of matter do and what they find is again the laws of this universe.

---

[337] CASTANEDA, The Active Side of Infinity, HarperCollins Publishers Inc., Mud Shadows

In other words, the seers are not much different from the scientists who find the atom, and they also observe the universe with their own methods.

- It was through "seeing" that the new seers discovered certain undeniable facts, which they used to arrive at certain conclusions, revolutionary to them, about the nature of man and the world. [338]
- To "see" energy as it flowed in the universe was, for them, an essential tool that they employed in making their classificatory schemes. Because of this capacity, for instance, they conceived the total universe available to the perception of human beings as an onion-like affair, consisting of thousands of layers. The daily world of human beings, they believed, is but one such layer. Consequently, they also believed that other layers are not only accessible to human perception, but are part of man's natural heritage. [339]

Don Juan describes energy, that is nagual, as a vast ocean surrounding the island of tonal, that is matter, and making it stand. In his view, the main thing is energy and matter is one of the millions of forms it can take, and this universe is one of the millions of universes it can create.

The case for the science of matter is similar. Although our daily lives run through matter, the main thing is energy and matter is a "condensed" form of it, according to the $E=mc^2$ formula. So, energy is also the main base for the science of matter.

Although their methods and results are totally different, when the seers and the scientists get behind this witnessed universe, they get to the "energy". One looks at the event on one hand and the other on the other, and they see the same thing. In other words, what they are trying to explain is actually the same thing and they are calling it "energy". So, both of these sciences are actually energy science.

---

338 CASTANEDA, The Fire from Within, Washington Square Press, The Eagle's Emanations

339 CASTANEDA, Magical Passes, HarperCollins Publishers Inc., Introduction

And this is also a reflection of God's name, the "One". These two sciences, the polar twins, unite in energy as researchers of this universe and thus witness the unity of God Almighty.

CLAIM TO EXPLAIN EVERYTHING

Castaneda says the following in relation to the energetic realities the seers discovered in the universe:

- Those shamans had derived their construct by means of their ability to see energy as it flows freely in the universe. Therefore, the warriors' way was a most harmonious conglomerate of energetic facts, irreducible truths determined exclusively by the direction of the flow of energy in the universe. Don Juan categorically stated that there was nothing about the warriors' way that could be argued, nothing that could be changed. It was in itself and by itself a perfect structure, and whoever followed it was corralled by energetic facts that admitted no argument, no speculation about their function and their value. [340]

Castaneda says that these seer shamans have reached the ultimate and irreducible truths, and it is a perfect structure in itself. According to him, what they are witnessing is a truth, and there is no way to deny it.

The same goes for the scientists. They also witness the laws of physics in the universe and call their immutable continuity "reality". They also think their own "science structure" is perfect. However, there is a difference between seers and scientists.

---

340 CASTANEDA, The Wheel of Time, Washington Square Press, Quotations from the Journey to Ixtlan, Commentary

The seers claim that "This world can be witnessed, but it cannot be talked about", while scientists aspire to explain everything. Actually, what they do is only witness the signs of God, as the seers do. However, this is not enough for them and they say, "we will explain everything". But will they really be able to explain it all?

The human mind as a mirror:

"Our mistake is to believe that the only perception worthy of acknowledgment is what goes through our reason,"[341] says don Juan. Therefore the human being, above all, is a perceiver and the brain, a mirror reflecting the outside order.

In other words, the human brain and the universe are in fact a means for the human being to live. If we were to exist in a different universe, then we would have a brain that would fit there, and we would perceive that universe in the way it reflects; but the only thing that did not change was the fact that we perceived it.

Therefore, mankind "lives" first and foremost, and the brain given to him is a "tool" that allows him to work in this universe. What's more, this device has no ability to know outside the universe. That is why don Juan says, "Reason is merely reflecting an outside order, and that reason knows nothing about that order and cannot explain it."[342]

The human brain as a child of this universe:

According to the science of matter, since the human brain is formed as a result of biological evolution, it develops as a result of the effects and reactions in this universe. So the human brain is a child of this universe and only capable of understanding the space-time of it. So, the human brain has limits, and is not limitless as science hopes. More importantly, this is not a matter of philosophical debate, it is an objective phenomenon.

That's why scientists, whenever they try to talk about another universe

341 CASTANEDA, Tales of Power, Washington Square Press, The Strategy of a Sorcerer

342 CASTANEDA, Tales of Power, Washington Square Press, The Bubble of Perception

in their books or documentaries, can only say, like the five-dimensional universe, the seven-dimensional universe, things that are actually the product of the syntax of this universe. Because the limits of the human brain do not allow them to think beyond it. And every time they try to define it, they are forced to use the syntax of this universe again.

That's why don Juan says as for the human mind, "It can only witness this universe, but cannot talk about it." Because the human brain is a child of this universe, and it only works in this universe. And other than that, it does not work.

Since it does not know the outside of the universe and cannot establish a reference point, it can't provide an objective answer to the question of why this universe exists. And that is why God Almighty sends his revelation and teaches man what he does not know.

Therefore, the human mind is trapped by this universe in terms of the science of matter's claim to explain everything. And in the same way, it is a natural consequence of reason to find that reason is limited. So, the claim of modern science to explain everything with reason is a carrot put before itself. And the science of the seers already shows us how close they are.

The human mind, limited but sufficient:

"Every species has a definite range set by the Eagle,"[343] says don Juan. According to this, the perception abilities and physical characteristics of a human being are not the same as other creatures. For example, caterpillars cannot establish the "science of seers," or crocodiles cannot open universities for the "science of matter". Only people can do that.

However, God Almighty, like every living thing, places limits on human beings. He says, "We made human beings superior to much of what We have created,"[344] but He does not say, "We made them superior to all of them."

---

343 CASTANEDA, The Fire from Within, Washington Square Press, The Eagle's Emanations

344 Koran/Chapter 17, verse 70

The science of matter, by contrast, claims: "I will explain everything." But caterpillars or pigeons have no science. They can't do philosophy like we do or produce new compounds. They can only think to some extent. Then how do we know a human being can think to the last point?

There are quadrillions of stars up there, and there are also quadrillions of star-like atoms inside our bodies. Yet, in the midst of these two incomprehensible magnitudes, we are barely able to get to the Moon. So what's out of space? What do the other realms look like? There's no answer to that, because the human brain is a child of this universe, and the human mind does not function beyond.

So how do we make sure our mind understands everything? We cannot, because it does not exist. Therefore, the human mind is not unlimited. Just as the caterpillars are limited, so are we. But while ours is sufficient, theirs is insufficient.

Since God Almighty created mankind with a special mission and with the appropriate equipment, mankind is able to establish both the science of seers and the science of matter. Even so, God Almighty still keeps the last word to himself, and where they are stuck, He teaches mankind "what he does not know" by His revelation.

Although the human brain is limited, it is in sufficient condition to evaluate the products of these sciences with the revelation and reach a satisfactory conclusion. Therefore, the limitation of the human brain is complemented by the revelation sent by God Almighty, and the integrity of the human being in this universe is thus ensured.

<u>The human mind has no answer for the question of why</u>:

Don Juan describes the new seers as "terribly practical men" and says they only do whatever is necessary energetically. Hence, the seers look only at the practical benefit of what they're doing, without caring why.

The main reason for don Juan's attitude is that he has no answer to the "why" question. And what's more, he knows it. Don Juan knows what he does not know, and he's taking a position on it. Scientists, on the other hand, don't know what they don't.

- You are dealing with that immensity out there. To turn that magnificence out there into reasonableness doesn't do anything for you. Here, surrounding us, is eternity itself. To engage in reducing it to a manageable nonsense is petty and outright disastrous. [345]

"They didn't know why, but they knew how it happened," don Juan says about the old seers. Therefore, although the seers may regard their knowledge as superior, they do not have the slightest idea of its cause, and what they do is to discover and use what God Almighty puts before them.

For example, the seers know the "intent" and adjust their entire lives to that power. So why is there such a thing in the universe as "intent"? They cannot respond to this, but they continue to acknowledge and use its existence.

And the same goes for the science of matter. They know that hydrogen and oxygen combine to form water. They lay out all the equations about it, but they do not know why it occurred.

Why are these two substances turning into the water? Why is the water colorless or freezing at 0 degrees Celsius? They don't know, but unlike the seers, they always pretend to explain it with hope. It's not enough for them to be witnesses.

Therefore, the science of matter puts a success it will never achieve ahead of humanity and leaves mankind at dusk in the hope of achieving it. But there is no certainty in such a life.

<u>Leaving mankind in the twilight zone</u>:

The science of matter does not offer certainty to mankind, rather it offers ambiguity and says, "Please wait a few thousand years, then we'll explain everything." The seers, on the other hand, reach a much larger area than scientists, so they know there will be no explanation. Therefore, they accept everything as it is and choose to explore rather

---

345 CASTANEDA, Tales of Power, Washington Square Press, An Appointment With Knowledge

than think about the reasons:

- Man's possibilities are so vast and mysterious that sorcerers, rather than thinking about them, had chosen to explore them, with no hope of ever understanding them. [346]

Even though scientists seem to follow "why" questions, it always stays in the macro dimension and when they go home in the evening, they forget all about it and live a practical life. Yet because there is no certainty in their lives, their daily lives are not as disciplined as those of the seers, and the ambiguity they have keeps their normal lives in the twilight mode.

For the seers, on the other hand, certainty is the most important thing. Don Juan says, "Modern-day practitioners, if they were honest with themselves, would pay whatever price to live under the umbrella of such an intent."[347] So certainty is something that human beings need more than just the weather, and it is a reflection of that the universe is a "truth".

However, the certainty that the seers have stems from knowing what they don't know. They accept the current situation, don't care anymore and they mind their business. But the problem actually still stands.

Yet there is one reality, and it is "certain". So there is no mystery in the universe, but only certainty. However, you can't find it in your own way. For this reason, God Almighty, who teaches people what they do not know, tells us this and teaches us the reasons for what these two sciences have witnessed. And what the sciences are doing is using this "certain" order established by God in practice.

Kingdom of Boredom:

Don Juan tells Castaneda the extraordinary nature of mankind as follows:

---

[346] CASTANEDA, The Power of Silence, Washington Square Press, Moving the Assemblage Point

[347] CASTANEDA, The Wheel of Time, Washington Square Press, Quotations from a Separate Reality, Commentary

- Let your eyes be free; let them be true windows. The eyes can be the windows to peer into boredom or to peek into that infinity. [348]

The science of matter, which denies this mysterious nature of mankind, offers a dull and static life, just like itself really is. Don Juan tells this dull nature of modern science through the classifications it makes:

- I'm not interested in classifications. You have been classifying everything all your life. Now you are going to be forced to stay away from classifications. The other day, when I asked you if you knew anything about clouds, you gave me the names of all the clouds and the percentage of moisture that one should expect from each one of them. You were a veritable weatherman. But when I asked you if you knew what you could do with the clouds personally, you had no idea what I was talking about.
- Classifications have a world of their own. After you begin to classify anything, the classification becomes alive, and it rules you. But since classifications never started as energy-giving affairs, they always remain like dead logs. They are not trees; they are merely logs. [349]

The science of matter is not a living tree, but a dead log. In the same way, the human explanation it presents to us is not a living, but a dead human being. And it's not just a case that's on paper or on a philosophical basis, because it sees the human beings as very complex robots and it is not possible for it to offer us a lively life.

Don Juan describes it as follows:

- Modern man has left the realm of the unknown and the mysterious, and has settled down in the realm of the functional. He has turned his back to the world of the foreboding and the exulting and has welcomed the world of boredom. [350]

---

348 CASTANEDA, Tales of Power, Washington Square Press, In Nagual's Time

349 CASTANEDA, The Active Side of Infinity, HarperCollins Publishers Inc., Beyond Syntax: The Usher

350 CASTANEDA, The Fire from Within, Washington Square Press, The Shift Below

That's why at the end of Hubert Reeves's book about the first second of the universe, after all the scientific explanations, all he can talk about is a barbecue party:

- As the colorful clouds slowly faded away, we were discussing the future of the world billions of years from now, even though our hopes for life were limited to decades. What's the point? But does not that the beautiful day, the hot date around delicious food, answer that question already?
- This meal, eaten among friends, was a blessed moment in the history of the universe. Soon the lives of each of us would end, like the sun, like the stars, maybe even like the universe. Still, aren't moments like this enough to justify the adventure of the universe? What is wisdom but to believe it?

Indeed, what Reeves is saying is nothing but cold comfort. He knows that we spend a short life next to millions of years and everything is going to disappear shortly. But he says, aren't these blessed moments like this beautiful meeting enough to justify the adventure of the universe which is 96 billion light-years in size?

That, unfortunately, is the depth of scientists' worldviews outside of those scientific equations. Don Juan describes these scientists as the "scholars, after arranging the world in a most beautiful and enlightened manner, who go home at five o'clock in order to forget their beautiful arrangements."[351] Because they do not treat mankind and the universe as universal, they are not experienced in the relationship between mankind and the universe, in exchange for all their knowledge of matter. They can't even get near the vast wisdom of the science of the seers and instead, seek out the wisdom at barbecue parties.

We can see better here that they're not actually using their minds, because using the mind is not just dealing with equations or solving mechanisms. Actually, that's the easy and effortless part. The brain is already doing that automatically. The real reasoning comes into play after that, and what matters is what they do with what they find. Thus, that's all the connection Reeves can make with the information he has.

[351] CASTANEDA, The Second Ring of Power, Washington Square Press, La Gorda

He has a vast knowledge of the horizontal, but its depth does not exceed two inches.

In addition, it's similar to how Castaneda explained all the cloud types and their expected moisture percentages to don Juan. But when don Juan asks him what he can do personally with these clouds, he does not even understand what he's saying.

All the clouds, however, are flowing at any time by God's leave, and they are always holding a parade and making us introduce God Almighty in their own language. Some of us look at them and think, "My God, you did not create these beauties in vain," and some of us are content with the cold comfort and enjoy their food in their shadow.

DEVELOPMENTAL PROGRESS

Don Juan says that the old seers explained everything that can be explained. However, he does not like them and keeps telling about their mistakes. Then, how do we know the new seers have reached their final destination?

And the same goes for the science of matter. For example, when scientists first discovered the atom, they thought everything would be solved rapidly, but it never happened. Even more so, quantum mechanics came about, and things got more complicated.

So both sciences are evolving, and the previous one is advancing. Each one adds something new and complements the previous one. And that "end point" keeps going and going.

Moreover, the end points reached by the two sciences are completely different from each other and completely rejecting each other's claims that "I am the only truth".

Development of Sciences:

Castaneda says, "For the American Indian, perhaps for thousands of years, the vague phenomenon we call sorcery has been a serious bona fide practice, comparable to that of our science."[352] So, the science of

---

[352] CASTANEDA, A Separate Reality, Washington Square Press, Introduction

the seers becomes what it is today with a thousand years of effort, just like the science of matter.

Don Juan, for example, calls his generation the new seers and tells Castaneda about their development as follows:

- Don Juan explained that the new seers had had formidable barriers of tradition to overcome. At the time when the new cycle began, none of them knew for certain which procedures of their immense tradition were the right ones and which were not. Obviously, something had gone wrong with the ancient seers, but the new seers did not know what. They began by assuming that everything their predecessors had done was erroneous. [353]

So the followers of the old seers, when their methods are at an impasse, pull themselves back to see what's going on. Then they determine what works and return to work. Thus begins a new era with a new paradigm, made even better with additions over time. For example, don Juan speaks of his benefactor, Nagual Elias, as an "innovator" and says he threw away all the rituals practiced.

The science of matter also works similarly. Over the years, many scientists have been doing studies, increasing the level of knowledge, and then a genius comes along and combines all this raw material into a new paradigm.

For example, at the beginning of the last century, Einstein came to give Newtonian physics an entirely new dimension with his Theory of Relativity. However, in the light of discoveries, new situations arose that it could not explain. And this time, quantum physics was developed.

Hence, the science of matter and the science of the seers are both evolving, and each comer breaks down the previous one and builds the new one. On the basis of this, the social sciences claim that religions are also like this, and they supposedly claim that polytheistic religions predominate at first, and monotheistic religions emerge later.

---

353 CASTANEDA, The Fire from Within, Washington Square Press, The Eagle's Emanations

God Almighty, on the other hand, says in the Koran that this is not true. Because the prophets who have come since Prophet Adam are the ones sent by the same God and all preach the same religion. Therefore, the basic things in the religion they conveyed are the same, and there is no change in them.

83. So is it other than the religion of God they desire? To Him all those within the heavens and earth have submitted, willingly or by compulsion. And to Him they will be returned.
84. Say, "We have believed in God and in what was revealed to us and what was revealed to Abraham, Ishmael, Isaac, Jacob, and the Descendants, and in what was given to Moses and Jesus and to the other prophets from their Lord. We make no distinction between any of them, and we are submitting to Him." (Koran/ Chapter 3)

Therefore, all Prophets are brothers of each other and convey the same truths. In addition, as in the sciences, there is no denying the previous one or finding its wrongs. Even if the details of the revelation change according to the social conditions at that time, there is no change in the basic truths. The Prophets all affirm each other and convey the existence and unity of God Almighty.

Therefore, since religion comes from God Almighty and He is the Eternal and the Everlasting, there is no change in it. However, since mankind is a captive of time, what they discover becomes as such and is always revised.

13- Biological Evolution

- Two Evolution
- Biological Evolution
- Vasat-ı Camia

TWO EVOLUTION

Although some of the scientists think they have finished everything with Darwin's theory of evolution and that there is not much left to solve, the science of the seers does not say so. Accordingly, just like the science of matter, the science of the seers has its own "evolution theory", and it seems that God Almighty creates their "evolution of awareness" as a continuation and complement of the evolution of matter in this universe.

"The sorcerers of my lineage were convinced that man could not evolve biologically any further; therefore, they considered man's awareness to be the only medium for evolution,"[354] says don Juan. In other words, according to the seers, the human being who developed and came to these days in the aspect of matter, continues its evolution from this moment on, not in terms of matter, but in terms of awareness.

Therefore, while the human body within the scope of the science of matter is the subject of "biological evolution", the awareness within the scope of the science of seers is the subject of the "evolution of awareness". By the rule of God, that everything in this universe is created as opposite twins, these two evolutions form the opposite twins and crosscheck each other simultaneously.

---

[354] CASTANEDA, Magical Passes, HarperCollins Publishers Inc., The Second Group: The Recapitulation

One is starting us from a matter zero and bringing us to today, while the other is losing back within the system of realms. They both complement each other, but their views are diametrically opposed. The only place they meet is to ignore God Almighty and not answer the question of why.

BIOLOGICAL EVOLUTION

Life as an essence, our bodies as a medium:

- Your bodies are your bearers. (Prophet Muhammad)

"The basic premise of sorcery is that we are perceivers," says don Juan, explaining its relationship to the evolution of awareness as follows:

- The totality of the human body is an instrument of perception.
- And the first step of evolution is the acceptance of the premise that human beings are perceivers. [355]

Castaneda resents don Juan's intense insistence on this issue and opposes him saying, "We already know that we are perceivers. What else can we be?"

Don Juan, on the other hand, says to him: "Think about it! Perception plays only a minute role in our lives, and yet, the only thing we are for a fact is perceivers."

Don Juan keeps repeating this because it's an incredibly important thing, and it's the epitome of the whole story. So, he says, we live first and foremost, and this body that we have is a means to exist in this universe. And we could have existed in another universe, with another body, just as there were inorganic beings. Therefore, life is essential and

---

[355] CASTANEDA, Magical Passes, HarperCollins Publishers Inc., The Second Series, The Series for the Womb

our bodies are just carriers.

- We are perceivers. We are an awareness; we are not objects; we have no solidity. We are boundless. The world of objects and solidity is a way of making our passage on earth convenient. It is only a description that was created to help us. We, or rather our reason, forget that the description is only a description and thus we entrap the totality of ourselves in a vicious circle from which we rarely emerge in our lifetime. [356]

So, we are perceivers and we are ALIVE. Yes, I'm alive. So, are you?... Is the answer "Yes"?... Are you really sure?

Don Juan says we live first, but we need an environment, an interface to live. And our interface is this universe. Likewise, inorganic beings, the polar twin of mankind, have their own universes.

In addition, everyone has a body fit for inclusion in their universe. As Prophet Muhammad said, "our bodies are our bearers," and through them, we exist in this universe for a while, and then we leave.

For me, the most important thing the seers have shown us is to have made it clear that we are ALIVE. You may say, "So, what, I'm not already alive?" If you accept the evolution, as Darwinists understand it, yes, you are not. Because in their books, in their documentaries, behind all the gilded and proud words, they look you in the eyes and say, you don't actually live.

Richard Dawkins says in his book The Selfish Gene that we are "survival machines". According to them, the human brain is encoded by cause-and-effect relationships in the process of evolution, and by which response we will react to which effect was determined in this process. In this point of view, we are no different from the refrigerator or the washing machine in the house. Just as they start working when we push the button, according to Darwinists, we are much more complex robots that do all of our work in this way, and whose response to which effect is determined by the process of evolution.

---

356 CASTANEDA, Tales of Power, Washington Square Press, The Secret of The Luminous Beings

In other words, as the seers called this universe an illusion, Darwinists call "life" an illusion. However, if you look at their documentaries, they explain how "life" on Earth began. But they actually tell us there is no such thing as life. More importantly, they tell us, "Actually, you do not exist", but unfortunately, we do not notice.

On the other hand, Prophet Muhammad says, "Who knows himself, knows his Lord". So if you know you are living, you know God. And if you exist, then so does God. However, the science of matter, for the sake of denying God, also denies you.

<u>Darwinists call evolution a coincidence</u>:

> 67. It is He who created you from earth, then from a sperm-drop, then from an attached embryo; then He brings you out as a child; then He develops you that you reach your time of maturity, then further that you become elders. And some you are taken in death before that. All this is for you to reach a specified term; and perhaps you use your mind. (Koran/Chapter 40)

We all come into the world as babies, and then we grow up. In the stars, hydrogen becomes helium, and helium becomes other elements. And the universe continues to expand...

Everything in the universe is moving, and at every moment, turning into something else. Therefore, "evolution" is one of the most fundamental rules of this universe. However, what Darwinists are really advocating is not the existence of evolution, but the fact that evolution is the result of coincidences. They have no proof of that, but that's what they really want.

I personally studied engineering at University. And I've seen a lot of industrial products discontinued, because they haven't been sold in time. Likewise, I have witnessed many products that have "evolved" over the years to become market leaders. This was a natural result of the competition in the universe, which Darwinists call "natural selection". However, I haven't seen any products that engineers haven't worked on in their design to date. On the contrary, thousands of engineers have worked on each product, and they were the ones doing the real work. The competition was just about who would remain.

Darwinists, in their own theories, claim that these "lost engineers" are random mutations: but they had to be unconscious, because that's what they wanted. Moreover, Dawkins accuses those who say these could be conscious mutations of dealing with "idealistic nonsense".

However, the paths that evolution must take simultaneously with mutations are so great in terms of engineering. Let alone making a simple product, it's perhaps like building a space shuttle. In other words, evolution is a process that has actually happened, but is not possible on its own. Therefore, God Almighty, as the universal mind that governs the evolution, has signed his own signature on every point of it.

In other words, contrary to Darwinists' claims, evolution does nothing but show the existence of God. And, in order for mankind to say there is no mind behind the evolution, they must deny both the universal mind and their own.

So, it is not a coincidence that both the Seers and Darwinists, who claim to have worked in the name of rationality, disregard the human mind when they reach the final point. Because, when they deny God Almighty, the owner of the universal mind, they eventually have to ignore the human mind, which is a reflection of it. And at the final point, they both miss the target.

Chemical evolution:

Contrary to popular belief, evolution in the universe is not just biological evolution. Starting with the Big Bang, the universe has been evolving since its first second. The energy first turns into hydrogen, then into other elements. And the stars that host this process serve as matter factories of the universe.

So, evolution is a whole, but there is no "mutation" involved in the transformation of energy into matter or the transformation of hydrogen into helium. These are the "hard facts" in the universe, and the science of matter accepts them without any question while they are actually carried out by God Almighty.

So why does energy turn into hydrogen? Or how are the properties of the new substance changed when hydrogen turns into another substance? Why does the water always freeze at zero degrees? What keeps them stable? There's no answer that science of matter can give. They only witness the existence.

Therefore, those who refer biological evolution to random mutations do not have any mutations that can refer to chemical evolution. In fact, both are happening by the leave of God, and they are unbiasedly witnessing what exists.

<u>God as the Lord of Evolution</u>:

> 55. From the earth We created you, and into it We will return you, and from it We will extract you one more time. (Koran/Chapter 20)

Lord is the second most commonly used name after God among the hundred names mentioned in the Koran. Therefore, after the divinity of God Almighty, His Lordship is the first angle in His relationship with this universe.

In the Arabic language, Lord means "educator". He is the one who builds something in stages until it reaches maturity. Moreover, this is not only a word used for God Almighty, but also for human beings in normal life. For example, the Lord of the horse becomes the one who trains it, or the Lord of the house becomes its Lord because he can shape it as he pleases. Therefore, God Almighty, as the Lord of the Worlds, is the One who creates the system of worlds and matures them as He wills.

Indeed, God Almighty introduces himself as the Lord of the Worlds at the beginning of the Koran, and it is said that all praise belongs to God. In other words, the emergence of this universe, which is so great as to be praised, is the result of His Lordship and His decency. Therefore, God's relationship with the universe and with mankind is a first-degree consummation relationship.

All things in the universe are His servants. God Almighty uses them and builds the universe in His own way. In doing so, He uses evolution, one of the most fundamental rules He has set in the universe. And by the secret of "God is in a new business at any moment"[357], everything evolves and does so without stopping.

The science of matter shows us that evolution exists, but it cannot explain how it happens. Or rather, the way it explains shows us God Almighty, contrary to their claims. On the other hand, the seers know how it happens, but they can't answer why such an evolution exists or why this universe was created due to this evolution.

Therefore, while these two sciences check each other and cover each other's shortcomings, they actually show us God Almighty. That's why, while they both think they are against God, they are indeed the servants of God.

<u>The guidance of God to evolution</u>:

13. What is the matter with you that you do not respect God,
14. While He has created you in stages?
15. Do you not consider how God has created seven heavens in layers,
16. And made the moon therein a reflected light and made the sun a burning lamp?
17. And God growed you from the earth like a plant.
18. Then He will return you into it and will extract you with another extraction. (Koran/Chapter 71)

We've mentioned before that the power that don Juan calls "intent" is the motive behind everything and every event in this universe. Therefore, this universe is first and foremost a "universe of intent". And don Juan says that evolution, like all other things, is a product of that intent.

In addition to his views, Castaneda says intent is also responsible for all the possible mutations in the universe, so they don't occur because of

---

[357] Koran/Chapter 55, verse 29

arbitrary, blind circumstances.

- Another of such masses of filaments, besides the dark sea of awareness which the shamans observed and liked because of its vibration, was something they called intent, and the act of individual shamans focusing their attention on such a mass, they called intending. They saw that the entire universe was a universe of intent, and intent, for them, was the equivalent of intelligence. The universe, therefore, was, for them, a universe of supreme intelligence. Their conclusion, which became part of their cognitive world, was that vibratory energy, aware of itself, was intelligent in the extreme. They saw that the mass of intent in the cosmos was responsible for all the possible mutations, all the possible variations which happened in the universe, not because of arbitrary, blind circumstances, but because of the intending done by the vibratory energy, at the level of the flux of energy itself. [358]

Don Juan gives dinosaurs as an example to this. According to him, dinosaurs started flying because they actually "intended" to fly. In other words, the "mutations" that lead to their evolution do not occur in a random way, but as a reflection of the intent of a living being. Therefore, what don Juan is saying here is that evolution is not a matter of randomness, but of intent.

And as we explained in the intent issue, the main thing about intent is the "universal intent". As the verse says, "You cannot will except that God wills"[359], the intentions of living beings come true after they have been accepted by the universal intent of God Almighty. Don Juan calls it, "Our command can become the Eagle's command." Therefore, the essential is what God Almighty says. He owns the master plan, and is the One who decides what dinosaurs are going to be.

In other words, what don Juan is saying, in fact, not the dinosaurs but the universal intent carried out the evolution. And God Almighty uses

---

[358] CASTANEDA, The Teachings of Don Juan, Washington Square Press, Author's Commentaries on the Occasion of the Thirtieth Year of Publication

[359] Koran/Chapter 76, verse 30

all his officials in the universe to achieve His desired result.

For this reason, throughout the history, Islamic scholars have called this evolution issue as "maturation" instead of evolution. The difference between them is that, maturation has a direction, and there is an intelligence in it.

Therefore, there is evolution, but this matter is not something Darwinists claim as unclear in its direction. There is a direction, and it is the intent of God Almighty that determines that direction.

On the other hand, the red line of Darwinists is that evolution is "mindless". It was Charles Darwin who first came up with this and formulated it that way. However, centuries before that, Islamic scholars have been expressing his ideas one-on-one. But they did this without denying God, and therefore were of no value to the science of matter.

- The world of creation started out from the minerals and progressed, in an ingenious, gradual manner, to plants and animals. The last stage of minerals is connected with the first stage of plants, such as herbs and seedless plants. The last stage of plants, such as palms and vines, is connected with the first stage of animals, such as snails and shellfish which have only the power of touch. The animal world then widens, its species become numerous, and, in a gradual process of creation, it finally leads to man, who is able to think and to reflect.

This is what Tunisian scientist Ibn Khaldun says in the 14th century in his book "The Introduction". Also before him, many Islamic scholars wrote about evolution. For example, Al-Jahiz is the first scholar in history to speak of evolution in his "Book of Animals" in the 10th century. In addition, his successor Ibn Miskawayh takes his thoughts forward in the 11th century, and even says in his book "The Smallest Achievement" that monkeys are the closest animals to human beings. I can also add to these scientists a Turkish scholar, Erzurumlu Ibrahim Hakki and his book "Marifetname" written in the 18th century.

So, it is not Darwin who owns this idea, but it is he who developed it in accordance with the norms of the Science of Matter. As Dawkins put it: "Darwin made it possible to be an intellectually fulfilled atheist." So, the main concern of the Darwinists is not evolution but atheism. On the other hand, Islamic scholars say evolution exists, but they also say it is an evolution guided by God. So they do not deny the "Universal Mind" behind it, as they use their mind.

VASAT-I CAMIA

71. Mention when your Lord said to the angels, "Indeed, I am going to create a human being from clay.
72. So when I have proportioned him and breathed into him of My Soul, then fall down to him in prostration."
73. So the angels prostrated - all of them entirely.
74. Except Iblees; he was arrogant and became among the disbelievers. (Koran/Chapter 38)

In Islamic Sufism, the human is called "vasat-ı camia", the entity that unites environments. And at the intersection of matter and energy, there is mankind.

Therefore, on one hand human beings eat and drink like animals, but on the other hand they have a door to other worlds. And while the science of seers examines this aspect of awareness, the science of matter examines the animal side.

When God Almighty makes the Angels prostrate to Adam, Iblis gets trapped to his animal side and underestimates him saying, "Never would I prostrate to a human whom You created out of clay."[360] Just like Freud said, "Biological research robbed man of his peculiar privilege of having been specially created, and relegated him to a descent from the animal world, implying an ineradicable animal nature

360 Koran/Chapter 15, verse 33

in him." However, the main characteristic of mankind is not in their creation from clay, but in their ability to transcend it. Animals can't get beyond this, but human beings can, because God blows His own Soul into them.

Similarly, the Angels say to God, "Will You place upon earth one who causes corruption therein and sheds blood, while we declare Your praise and sanctify You?" God Almighty's answer to them is very meaningful: "Indeed, I know that which you do not know."[361]

Therefore, in spite of all the animal nature of mankind, they also have the ability to open up to other realms don Juan told us about. The evolution of matter, on the other hand, applies to the material body of mankind and gives rise to the "capsule" that allows them to exist in this world. And God Almighty, who created everything for a reason in this "realm of reasons", makes evolution the cause of this capsule thus enabling the formation of the body of mankind.

But that's not what human beings are all about. Mankind is nothing but an animal in this state, and the Koran calls it "beser", not human.[362] When God Almighty blows His soul into him, then he becomes a human, and a human being can do all the things that the seers have accomplished:

- You are a creature of awareness, a perceived like the rest of us. Human beings are on a journey of awareness, which has been momentarily interrupted by extraneous forces. Believe me, we are magical creatures of awareness. If we don't have this conviction, we have nothing. [363]

---

[361] Koran/Chapter 2, verse 30

[362] The word "beser" does not have one to one translation in English. It is the name of the body-based animal side of humans. It is the biological part of human beings which the science of matter and Freud are interested in, so we can say that it is homo sapiens. And in the verses above #71 and # 30, the word which had to be translated as human being is actually "beser", to whom Iblees and the Angels opposed. And after God Almighty blows His soul into him, then Adam is called as human. So, these two words are used like that in the Koran very consciously and you can see the same usage all over the Koran.

[363] CASTANEDA, Magical Passes, HarperCollins Publishers Inc., Tensegrity

That is why God Almighty makes Angels prostrate to mankind. He breathes His own soul into him; thus he becomes a "magical being" put into a material body. Today's Darwinists, like The Iblees, look at the earthly side of mankind, underestimate him and say, "this is an animal," but that's not how it works.

God Almighty creates man from the earth, but at the same time breathes into him His own soul, giving him a bond with eternity. And so, while man is a matter among the matter in this universe, he also has the ability to get behind this visible world. In other words, even though human beings live in this universe, they do not actually belong here and have been placed here temporarily.

That's why, despite all its greatness, this universe is too narrow for him. And he's always trying to get over it. The matter side of him is establishing the science of matter and thus trying to unravel the secrets of the universe in terms of matter. The "life" side of him that God breathes into human beings is establishing the science of awareness and trying to transcend this universe in terms of awareness. The fact is, they're like two wings of a bird. Without one, the other has no meaning. And since human is a being that unites the environments, they have to have both in themselves.

14- Evolution of Awareness

- Aim: Immortality
- Death
- Evolution of Awareness
- The Nature of Immortality
- Immortality by Disobeying God
- Immortality by Achievement
- World and Hereafter
- Carrots for Two Sciences

AIM: IMMORTALITY

19. "O Adam, dwell, you and your wife, in Paradise and eat from wherever you will but do not approach this tree, lest you be among the wrongdoers."
20. But Satan whispered to them to make apparent to them that which was concealed from them of their private parts. He said, "Your Lord did not forbid you this tree except that you become angels or become of the immortal." (Koran/Chapter 7)

When his benefactor explains the "Rule" to don Juan in his youth and tells him about the possibility of achieving freedom for the first time, don Juan gets very excited and stunned by joy. Then, like every new seer, the opportunity to reach that "freedom" becomes the sole purpose of his life.

Therefore, the ultimate goal of all the teachings of new seers, all the things they do, is to defeat death and achieve freedom. That's the only goal this entire vast collection of information is headed for. And that's the same as achieving immortality as the aim of the first human being, Prophet Adam.

This endless adventure of the seers begins in the time of the old seers. These ancient seers that have interacted with inorganic beings are struck by the length of their lives and begin to develop a variety of methods to live as long as they can. These methods do not bring them immortality, but they manage to maintain their consciousness for a very long time.

The new seers, on the other hand, take the methods of the old ones one step further and reach the ultimate that humans can within this system of realms. However, this last point is not to reach immortality, but they are getting very close to it.

<u>Seeing death as the end</u>:

29. They said, "There is none but our worldly life, and we will not be resurrected."
30. If you could but see when they were made to stand before their Lord. He said, "Is this not the truth?" They said, "Yes, by our Lord." Then He said, "So taste the punishment because you used to disbelieve." (Koran/Chapter 6)

All the aim the seers have is about not to die. They want to be free of death because they see it as an end. As they have no belief in the hereafter, they try to be free of death in this world.

Speaking of the first members of the new generation of seers, don Juan says they died stupid deaths, just as the average man does. He finds it intolerable after a life full of discipline and danger.

While describing the stages of death, he says, "Death smashes against us with quiet fury and power until it dissolves our lives into nothing. "[364] According to him, at the moment of death, God Almighty, whom he calls the Eagle, oppresses us so much that even the smallest crumb of consciousness we have is being wiped away.

This is what don Juan says, but this journey that mankind takes after death towards God is described many times in the Koran, by saying "to God is the return". Therefore, this journey, as don Juan claims, does not mean mankind will disappear into nothingness. It's just a short stop, like when you sleep and wake up. Then He will wake us up and tell us what we have done.

---

[364] CASTANEDA, A Separate Reality, Washington Square Press, Chapter 13

<u>Seeing death as our opponent</u>:

Don Juan sees death as our opponent and explains it this way:

- Sorcerers say death is the only worthy opponent we have. Death is our challenger. We are born to take that challenge, average men or sorcerers. Sorcerers know about it; average men do not.
- I personally would say, don Juan, life, not death, is the challenge.
- Life is the process by means of which death challenges us. Death is the active force. Life is the arena. And in that arena there are only two contenders at any time: oneself and death.

So, don Juan puts himself in front of death as the opposite pair of this. God Almighty, on the other hand, gives life and death as opposite pairs and says, "I created them both". Of course, you may ask what the difference is between these two. Yet there is a difference, a very subtle and important difference.

1. Blessed is He in whose hand is dominion, and He is over all things competent -
2. He is the One who created death and life to test you which of you is best in deed - and He is the Exalted in Might, the Forgiving - (Koran/Chapter 67)

Don Juan says death is our opposite. According to him, when life is over, we are also over. However, according to the Koran, when life is over, we are not over. So, while the Koran puts life against death, don Juan puts himself.

The purpose of the seers is to defeat death, so they see it as our opponent. God Almighty says, on the other hand, "I am the One who created death and life to test which of you is best in deed," and says; "I will give you life again after your death."

The truth is that we exist from now, and death is nothing but a sleep procedure that we shall soon wake up from. The seers seek immortality, but we are already immortal. We were born once, and now we exist forever.

Death as a temporary thing:

The seers are constantly trying to save themselves from death, but death is explained in the Koran as a temporary thing and is referred to as a kind of intoxication:

19. The intoxication of death came as a truth; that is what you are trying to avoid.
20. And the Horn was blown. That is the promised Day.
21. Every soul come, with it a driver and a witness.
22. Indeed, you were unaware of this, but We have removed from you your cover, so your sight is sharp today. (Koran/Chapter 50)

In the same way, sleep is called a kind of death in the Koran:

42. God takes the souls at the time of their death, and those that do not die during their sleep. Then He keeps those for which He has decreed death and releases the others for a specified term. Indeed in that are signs for a people who give thought. (Koran/Chapter 39)

Therefore, death is not an end and extinction; it is a break and recess. And people will awaken from slumber when the day of resurrection comes.

51. The Horn was blown; and at once from the graves to their Lord they hasten.
52. They will say, "O woe to us! Who has raised us up from our sleeping place? This is what the Most Merciful had promised, and the messengers have told the truth."
53. It is not be but one blast, and at once they are all brought present before Us. (Koran/Chapter 36)

Just as a man who sleeps for hours thinks he has only slept for a few minutes, people will find themselves before their Lord without even understanding what happened after death, and no man will ever taste death again.

So there is no life that goes into nothingness as the seers think. We come from God and return to God. Then He gives us another life, after which there is no death. However, the seers deny it and strive to find other ways out.

Exaggeration of life by seers:

26. Say, "God causes you to live, then causes you to die; then He will assemble you for the Day of Resurrection, about which there is no doubt. But most of the people do not know." (Koran/Chapter 45)

In the Koran, God Almighty says, "We have made you a people who follow a moderate path"[365]. Therefore, it is essential to be reasonable; but Darwinists go to one end by saying "there is no life," while the Seers go to the other end by making "fetishism of life".

"As you sit here now, you have nothing except the force of your life that binds that cluster of feelings,"[366] don Juan says to Castaneda. In other words, their lives are all that the seers have and all their efforts are aimed at protecting the life given to them.

However, as they well know, this life has been given to them. Don Juan calls it "bestowing awareness by the Eagle". They know this, but because they do not accept religion, they think that God Almighty created us for nothing.

56. I did not create the jinn and mankind except to worship Me. (Koran/Chapter 51)

God Almighty sends us here to know Him. However, when the seers find life in their hands, they cradle it and do their best not to lose it. In other words, they cling to life instead of God, who gave them life and try to be immortal in this world.

However, they are still not completely distanced from the reality of mankind and are struggling to make maximum use of human being's current potential. Their lives are peppy and powerful, but the life that Darwinists offer is dull and boring.

---

365 Koran/Chapter 2, verse 143

366 CASTANEDA, Tales of Power, Washington Square Press, The Bubble of Perception

As the seers know life, they also know death and make every moment of their lives alive with the awareness that it can catch us at any moment. "Without an awareness of the presence of our death, there is no power, no mystery."[367] says don Juan. And they use death as a springboard to fill the life they live with energy.

Darwinists, on the other hand, have no prescription for human beings. They don't know life, they don't know death, and they think that microorganisms will eat us up, and that's it. However, the seers show us that this is not the case.

[367] CASTANEDA, Tales of Power, Washington Square Press, Having to Believe

DEATH

185. Every soul will taste death, and you will be given your full compensation on the Day of Resurrection. So he who is drawn away from the fire and admitted to Paradise has attained the salvation. And what is the life of this world except the enjoyment of delusion. (Koran/Chapter 3)

Before he passed away at the age of 56, the last words of Steve Jobs were, "Oh, wow! Oh, wow! Oh, wow!"

For don Juan, this reaction from Steve Jobs is something to be expected. Because according to him, death has two stages, and he explains it like this:

- Death has two stages. The first is a blackout. It is a meaningless stage, very similar to the first effect of Mescalito, in which one experiences a lightness that makes one feel happy, complete, and that everything in the world is at ease. But that is only a shallow state; it soon vanishes and one enters a new realm, a realm of harshness and power. [368]

Don Juan depicts this second stage of death as something of a horror and describes it as:

---

368 CASTANEDA, A Separate Reality, Washington Square Press, Chapter 13

- There is nothing gorgeous or peaceful about death. Because the real terror begins upon dying. With that incalculable force you felt in there, the Eagle will squeeze out of you every flicker of awareness you have ever had. [369]

God Almighty explains this situation by using an interesting phrase in the Koran: "Every soul will taste death." Hence, there is a situation here that every person will necessarily experience and feel one-on-one. And that is expressed as "tasting".

This is how God Almighty has sealed the life of mankind at the end of a lifetime. And most likely, at that moment, mankind passes away from this universe by fully understanding what they and this universe really are. Don Juan calls it "the revelation of total mystery during the death." [370]

When the seers witness this, they see death as a horror, and they see it as an end. However, God Almighty repeats in the Koran "to God is the return" many times. So the person who tastes death understands that this was not a joke, and then goes back to his Lord, and He informs him of what he has done.

<u>The tumbler</u>:

"I want you to try 'seeing' the Eagle's emanations," says don Juan in one of his exercises. When Castaneda "sees" the emanations, something like a "ball of fire" arises and hits him.

Castaneda is alarmed, but fails to roll out of its way. Then he asks don Juan, "What is all this?" Don Juan describes these balls of fire as "a force from the Eagle's emanations. A ceaseless force that strikes us every instant of our lives."

He explains that those balls of fire are of crucial importance to human beings because they are the expression of a force that pertains to all details of life and death, something that the new seers call the "rolling force":

---

[369] CASTANEDA, Eagle's Gift, Washington Square Press, The Not-Doings of Silvio Manuel

[370] CASTANEDA, Tales of Power, Washington Square Press, The Strategy of a Sorcerer

- The rolling force is the means through which the Eagle distributes life and awareness for safekeeping. But it also is the force that, let's say, collects the rent. It makes all living beings die. What you saw today was called by the ancient seers the tumbler. [371]

Don Juan tells Castaneda, "No sooner had you begun to 'see' than the tumbler stopped you. If you had remained a moment longer it would have blasted you." Then he describes how we are protected from this tumbler in normal times:

- It is a force from the Eagle's emanations. A ceaseless force that strikes us every instant of our lives, it is lethal when "seen", but otherwise we are oblivious to it, in our ordinary lives, because we have protective shields. We have consuming interests that engage all our awareness. We are permanently worried about our station, our possessions. These shields, however, do not keep the tumbler away, they simply keep us from "seeing" it directly, protecting us in this way from getting hurt by the fright of "seeing" the balls of fire hitting us. Shields are a great help and a great hindrance to us. They pacify us and at the same time fool us. They give us a false sense of security. [372]

Don Juan tells Castaneda he had successfully endured his first brief encounter with the Eagle's emanations, but that a couple of shoves from the tumbler had dangerously opened up his "gap". Elsewhere, don Juan explains this gap as follows:

- I've talked many times about a gap that man has below his navel. It's not really below the navel itself, but in the cocoon[373], at the height of the navel. The gap is more like a dent, a natural flaw in the otherwise smooth cocoon. It is there where the tumbler hits us ceaselessly and where the cocoon cracks.

---

[371] CASTANEDA, The Fire From Within, Washington Square Press, The Rolling Force

[372] CASTANEDA, The Fire From Within, Washington Square Press, The Rolling Force

[373] Energy body, energy cocoon

- As the tumbler hits us over and over, death comes to us through the gap. Death is the rolling force. When it finds a weakness in the gap of a luminous being it automatically cracks it open and makes it collapse. [374]

Don Juan says that every living being has a gap and remarks: "If it didn't have one, it wouldn't die."

According to him, the gap of inorganic beings is very different from ours and therefore, more resistant to death. Thus, the ancient seers were attracted to the long lives of inorganic beings, and all the knowledge that the seers have today is a product of efforts to find ways to enable the ancients to live as long as the inorganic ones do.

<u>The rolling force</u>:

60. It is He who takes your souls by night and knows what you have committed by day. Then He revives you by day that a specified term may be fulfilled. Then to Him will be your return; then He will inform you about what you used to do.
61. He is the subjugator over His servants, and He sends over you guardians until, when death comes to one of you, Our messengers take him, and they do not fail in their duties.
62. Then they are returned to God, their true Friend. Unquestionably, His is the judgement, and He is the swiftest of accountants. (Koran/Chapter 6)

In the above verses, God Almighty says He sends over human beings "guardians" until the death prevails. However, when time is over, His messengers come to him and carry out their duty. Don Juan explains the mechanism of this process as follows:

The "rolling force" discovered by the ancient seers as a force that originates from the Eagle's emanations, giving mankind both life and awareness for safekeeping, whilst at the same time killing him. Therefore, the same force produces two effects that are diametrically opposed.

---

[374] CASTANEDA, The Fire From Within, Washington Square Press, The Rolling Force

The old seers have focused on the destructive side of the force and thought they could survive death if they understood it. The new seers, with their usual thoroughness in refusing tradition, have gone to the other extreme. They were at first totally averse to focusing their "seeing" on the tumbler; they argued that they needed to understand the force of the emanations at large in its aspect of life-giver and enhancer of awareness and called it "circular aspect".

"The new seers were wrong on this count, but in due course they corrected their mistake," says don Juan.

- At the beginning, the new seers did exactly the opposite from what their predecessors did. They focused with equal attention on the other side of the tumbler. What happened to them was as terrible as, if not worse than, what happened to the old seers. They died stupid deaths, just as the average man does.
- These new seers realized, after they had readopted their tradition, that the old seers' knowledge of the rolling force had been complete and concluded that there were, in effect, two different aspects of the same force. The tumbling aspect relates exclusively to destruction and death. The circular aspect, on the other hand, is what maintains life and awareness, fulfillment and purpose. [375]

According to don Juan, the rolling force constantly hits living creatures. With the life-giver aspect, the Eagle offers us awareness and life, while the destructive side causes our destruction, that is, our death. However, until death comes, its awareness and life-giver side dominates and becomes our "guardian".

- What the new seers discovered is that the balance of the two forces in every living being is a very delicate one. If at any given time an individual feels that the tumbling force strikes harder than the circular one, that means the balance is upset; the tumbling force strikes harder and harder from then on, until it cracks the living being's gap and makes it die. [376]

---

[375] CASTANEDA, The Fire From Within, Washington Square Press, The Rolling Force

[376] CASTANEDA, The Fire From Within, Washington Square Press, The Rolling Force

According to don Juan, the ancient seers have focused on the destructive side of the rolling force, because they hoped that if they uncovered its secret, they would be invulnerable and immortal. Therefore, they tried to make their "gaps" as durable as those of inorganic beings. They developed the strangest techniques for it, and thus managed to take their lives up to a thousand years.

They have taken the allies as an example and buried themselves to use the "earth's boost". The ancient seers were thus able to keep their assemblage points fixed in one of the other seven bands of inorganic awareness, thus surviving as allies, if not as normal people.

However, in spite of their tremendous knowledge, the old seers couldn't reach the natural end of the mastery of awareness. Don Juan explains this situation as follows:

- The new seers changed it all by realizing that there is no way to aspire to immortality as long as man has a cocoon. The old seers apparently never realized that the human cocoon is a receptacle and cannot sustain the onslaught of the rolling force forever. In spite of all the knowledge that they had accumulated, they were in the end certainly no better, and perhaps much worse, off than the average man.
- The old seers were imprisoned by the rolling force, and the new seers are rewarded for their toils with the gift of freedom. By becoming familiar with the rolling force through the mastery of intent, the new seers, at a given moment, open their own cocoons and the force floods them rather than rolling them up like a curled-up sow bug. The final result is their total and instantaneous disintegration. [377]

---

[377] CASTANEDA, The Fire From Within, Washington Square Press, The Rolling Force

EVOLUTION OF AWARENESS

"Awareness is the only avenue that human beings have for evolution,"[378] says don Juan and tells Castaneda about the hidden option of human death as follows:

- The death of human beings has a hidden option. It is something like a clause in a legal document, a clause that is written in tiny letters that you can barely see. You have to use a magnifying glass to read it, and yet it's the most important clause of the document. Death's hidden option is exclusively for sorcerers. They are the only ones who have, to my knowledge, read the fine print. For them, the option is pertinent and functional.
- For sorcerers, death is an act of unification that employs every bit of their energy. You are thinking of death as a corpse in front of you, a body on which decay has settled. For sorcerers, when the act of unification takes place, there is no corpse. There is no decay. Their bodies in their entirety have been turned into energy, energy possessing awareness that is not fragmented. The boundaries that are set up by the organism, boundaries which are broken down by death, are still functioning in the case of sorcerers, although they are no longer visible to the naked eye.

---

378 CASTANEDA, Magical Passes, HarperCollins Publishers Inc., The Fourth Series, The Separation of the Left Body and the Right Body: The Heat Sences

- I know that you are dying to ask me, if whatever I'm describing is the soul that goes to hell or heaven. No, it is not the soul. What happens to sorcerers, when they pick up that hidden option of death, is that they turn into inorganic beings, very specialized, high-speed inorganic beings, beings capable of stupendous maneuvers of perception. Sorcerers enter then into what the shamans of ancient Mexico called their definitive journey. Infinity becomes their realm of action. [379]

If you say how this happens, it is worth remembering that first proposition don Juan mentioned about the evolution of awareness:

- The first step of evolution is the acceptance of the premise that human beings are perceivers. [380]

Elsewhere he was also saying, "As long as you think that you are a solid body you cannot conceive what I am talking about."[381] So, mankind is first and foremost a perceiver and the body they possess is the bearer of this awareness. Therefore, even though the seers leave their bodies in the sense that we know by this method, they do not give up their awareness, and they turn into the "energy", just as matter turns into energy. Thus, the circle of evolution, that starts with the transformation of energy into the matter at Big Bang is closed, and turns back to the starting point. In other words, the evolution of awareness completes the biological evolution and turns back to where they have started.

<u>Entering into the third attention</u>:

- People are asleep; they wake up when they die. (Prophet Muhammad)

---

[379] CASTANEDA, The Active Side of Infinity, HarperCollins Publishers Inc., Inorganic Awareness

[380] CASTANEDA, Magical Passes, HarperCollins Publishers Inc., The Second Series, The Series for the Womb

[381] CASTANEDA, Tales of Power, Washington Square Press, The Secret of The Luminous Beings

The seers say there are three different levels of attention in a person. According to them, the first attention is the animal awareness we use in normal life, while the second attention is the level of awareness we reach when we use other emanations that we do not normally use, but which are available to us. The third attention, on the other hand, arises in a state of "total awareness" that only human beings can reach among the sentient beings.

- Seers say that there are three types of attention. When they say that, they mean it just for human beings, not for all the sentient beings in existence. But the three are not just types of attention, they are rather three levels of attainment. They are the first, second, and third attention, each of them an independent domain, complete in itself.
- The first attention in man is animal awareness, which has been developed, through the process of experience, into a complex, intricate, and extremely fragile faculty that takes care of the day-to-day world in all its innumerable aspects, in other words, everything that one can think about is part of the first attention.
- The first attention is everything we are as average men. By virtue of such an absolute rule over our lives, the first attention is the most valuable asset that the average man has. Perhaps it is even our only asset.
- The second attention, on the other hand, is a more complex and specialized state of the glow of awareness. It has to do with the unknown. It comes about when unused emanations inside man's cocoon are utilized. The reason I called the second attention specialized is that in order to utilize those unused emanations, one needs uncommon, elaborate tactics that require supreme discipline and concentration.
- The third attention is attained when the glow of awareness turns into the fire from within: a glow that kindles not one band at a time but all the Eagle's emanations inside man's cocoon.
- The supreme accomplishment of human beings is to attain that level of attention while retaining the life-force, without becoming

> a disembodied awareness moving like a flicker of light up to the Eagle's beak to be devoured. [382]

Don Juan says that at the time of death, our awareness enters into the third attention, only for a moment, before the Eagle tears through our life force. Don Juan calls it "the totality of the being that is going to die." [383]

At the time of death, the emanations that are in human potential but never used before, are fully operational. Most people remember this side of their existence that they weren't aware of until then, but it is too late.

As we said before, don Juan calls it the "revelation of total mystery during the death." So the seers ask that question, "If we're going to die with the totality of ourselves, why not, then, live with that totality?":

- The totality of ourselves is a very tacky affair. We need only a very small portion of it to fulfill the most complex tasks of life. Yet when we die, we die with the totality of ourselves. A sorcerer asks the question, "If we're going to die with the totality of ourselves, why not, then, live with that totality?" [384]

Therefore, the seers have studied the situation that every human being faces at the moment of death and have found its secret. And they try to use it to spread wings to freedom.

- I have said that the bubble of perception is sealed, closed tightly, and that it never opens until the moment of our death. Yet it could be made to open. Sorcerers have obviously learned that secret, and although not all of them arrive at the totality of themselves, they know about the possibility of it. [385]

---

[382] CASTANEDA, The Fire From Within, Washington Square Press, The First Attention

[383] CASTANEDA, Tales of Power, Washington Square Press, The Island of The Tonal

[384] CASTANEDA, Tales of Power, Washington Square Press, The Island of The Tonal

[385] CASTANEDA, Tales of Power, Washington Square Press, The Bubble of Perception

Burning with the fire from within:

- I was raw. I cooked, then I burned. (Mevlana Jalaluddin Rumi)

According to don Juan, old seers have learned to move the assemblage point beyond the limits of the known, so they were able to connect new worlds. However, despite this tremendous success, what they were doing was choosing between dying in the world of ordinary affairs or dying in the world of inorganic beings. The new seers, on the other hand, have discovered that the key is not simply to choose an alternate world in which to die, but to choose total consciousness, total freedom:

- The old seers moved their assemblage point to inconceivable dreaming positions in the incommensurable unknown; for the new seers it means refusing to be food, it means escaping the Eagle by moving their assemblage points to a particular dreaming position called total freedom.
- Adventurous men, faced with the choice of dying in the world of ordinary affairs or dying in unknown worlds, will unavoidably choose the latter, and that the new seers, realizing that their predecessors had chosen merely to change the locale of their death, came to understand the futility of it all; the futility of struggling to control their fellow men, the futility of assembling other worlds, and, above all, the futility of self-importance.
- One of the most fortunate decisions that the new seers made was never to allow their assemblage points to move permanently to any position other than heightened awareness. From that position, they actually resolved their dilemma of futility and found out that the solution is not simply to choose an alternate world in which to die, but to choose total consciousness, total freedom.
- By choosing total freedom, the new seers unwittingly continued in the tradition of their predecessors and became the quintessence of the death defiers. [386]

The new seers discovered that if the assemblage point is made to shift constantly to the confines of the unknown, but is made to return to a

386 CASTANEDA, The Fire From Within, Washington Square Press, Epilogue

position at the limit of the known, then when it is suddenly released it moves like lightning across the entire cocoon of man, aligning at once, all the emanations inside the cocoon.

- The new seers burn with the force of alignment; with the force of will, which they have turned into the force of intent through a life of impeccability. Intent is the alignment of all the amber emanations of awareness, so it is correct to say that total freedom means total awareness. [387]

According to don Juan, this was the natural end of mastery of awareness; and in one single stroke, they extended the glow of awareness beyond the bounds of the luminous cocoon:

- The third attention is attained when the glow of awareness turns into the fire from within: a glow that kindles not one band at a time but all the Eagle's emanations inside man's cocoon. [388]
- Seers who deliberately attain total awareness are a sight to behold. That is the moment when they burn from within. The fire from within consumes them. And in full awareness they fuse themselves to the emanations at large, and glide into eternity. [389]

<u>Eagle's Gift</u>:

Don Juan says that for the new seers to enter into the third attention is a gift, is more like a reward for an attainment. According to him, this reward is given to them by the "Eagle".

- The Eagle, although it is not moved by the circumstances of any living thing, has granted a gift to each of those beings. In its own way and right, any one of them, if it so desires, has the power to keep the flame of awareness, the power to disobey the summons to die and be consumed. Every living thing has been granted the power, if it so desires, to seek an opening to freedom and to go through it. It is evident to the seer who sees the opening, and to

---

387 CASTANEDA, The Fire From Within, Washington Square Press, Epilogue

388 CASTANEDA, The Fire From Within, Washington Square Press, The First Attention

389 CASTANEDA, The Fire From Within, Washington Square Press, The Assemblage Point

the creatures that go through it, that the Eagle has granted that gift in order to perpetuate awareness. [390]

- Freedom is the Eagle's gift to man. Unfortunately, very few men understand that all we need, in order to accept such a magnificent gift, is to have sufficient energy. [391]

As you can see, the highest achievement of the seers happens with the permission of the Eagle, and the Eagle offers this opportunity to the person He likes and pleases.

In other words, the seers only act within the limits set by God Almighty, whom they call the Eagle. And God Almighty, the source of life and awareness, leaves such a door open for them as a gift of their maturity besides the normal death command.

31. We will attend to you, O prominent beings.
32. So which of the favors of your Lord would you deny?
33. O company of jinn and mankind, if you are able to pass beyond the borders of the heavens and the earth, then pass. You will not pass except by authority from God. (Koran/Chapter 55)

In the Koran, God Almighty refers to this option provided for the seers as "passing beyond the borders of the heavens and the earth" and says, "You can do this only with an 'authorization' from Me." In other words, God Almighty confirms the possibility of this option, which don Juan mentioned; and the seers, with His permission, use this "freedom" option.

Also in this verse, mankind is mentioned along with the jinn, and the verse speaks to both communities. This is meaningful, because the seers enter this path with care towards the jinn, the opposite twin of mankind. And through this established relationship, they move on this path.

---

390 CASTANEDA, The Eagle's Gift, Washington Square Press, The Rule of The Nagual

391 CASTANEDA, The Fire From Within, Washington Square Press, Epilogue

Don Juan also mentions inorganic beings, saying: "They are beings whose consciousness can evolve just like ours."[392] And this verse also confirms that they also have this option.

Why does the Eagle's Gift exist?:

- The Eagle, although it is not moved by the circumstances of any living thing, has granted a gift to each of those beings. In its own way and right, any one of them, if it so desires, has the power to keep the flame of awareness, the power to disobey the summons to die and be consumed. [393]

That's what don Juan said when he explained The Eagle's gift. So why is there such a gift? Why does God Almighty, whom they call the Eagle, bestow such a gift on mankind? There is no answer to this question that the seers can give.

According to don Juan, since this phenomenon cannot possibly be explained in terms of standard logic, all that sorcerers could aspire to do was accomplish the feat of retaining their life force without knowing how it was done.[394] He says that in the act of doing, one can find liberation, and that to explain it was to dissipate our energy in fruitless efforts.[395]

So, in short, don Juan says, "Just do it, don't ask why." "We have been given a way out, and there are thousands of those who have achieved it before. So do not bother with explanations." However, God Almighty creates everything based on wisdom and does not give mankind their mind in vain. Therefore, what don Juan says does not make sense.

---

[392] CASTANEDA, Magical Passes, HarperCollins Publishers Inc., The Magical Passes For The Center For Decisions

[393] CASTANEDA, The Eagle's Gift, Washington Square Press, The Rule of The Nagual

[394] CASTANEDA, Magical Passes, HarperCollins Publishers Inc., The Magical Passes For The Center For Decisions

[395] CASTANEDA, Magical Passes, HarperCollins Publishers Inc., The Second Group: The Recapitulation

Castaneda asks:

- What I want to know is what can be the driving force to do all this for a lazy bum like myself, don Juan?
- To seek freedom is the only driving force I know. Freedom to fly off into that infinity out there. [396]

So, why does one have that driving force for freedom? Why do the seers go to all this trouble not to die? It is because of the desire for eternity that God Almighty has placed in Prophet Adam at the very first moment.

- To enter into total freedom, a human being must call on his or her sublime side, which, he said, human beings have, but which it never occurs to them to use. [397]

So why is it that only humans have that "sublime side", but not horses or flies? Why are all these devices given to human beings and not to others?

There are no answers to all these questions the seers have; they take and use. However, God Almighty creates mankind in this way, so they may possess devices that can address the revelation and use them when it is reached.

However, the seers use them out of purpose, and God Almighty still does not turn them into idle ones. He gives them a temporary exit from his mercy as a parable of the Hereafter. Nevertheless, He still gives its essence not in this world, but in the Hereafter.

---

396 CASTANEDA, The Art of Dreaming, HarperCollins Publishers Inc., The Fixation of The Assemblage Point

397 CASTANEDA, Magical Passes, HarperCollins Publishers Inc., The Second Group: The Recapitulation

THE NATURE OF IMMORTALITY

34. We did not grant to any man before you eternity; so if you die - would they be eternal?
35. Every soul will taste death. And We test you with evil and with good as trial; and to Us you will be returned. (Koran/Chapter 21)

Don Juan says the freedom that the seers intended did not mean eternal life as eternity is commonly understood, that is to say, as living forever. According to this, the seers could keep the awareness which is ordinarily relinquished at the moment of dying.[398] Don Juan explains it as "defeating death":

- Sorcerers defeat death and death acknowledges the defeat by letting the sorcerers go free, never to be challenged again.
- Does that mean that sorcerers become immortal?
- No. It doesn't mean that. Death stops challenging them, that's all.[399]

This meant to don Juan that those sorcerers did not die in the usual sense in which we understand death, but that they transcended it by

[398] CASTANEDA, The Eagle's Gift, Washington Square Press, The Rule of The Nagual

[399] CASTANEDA, The Power of Silence, Washington Square Press, The Somersault Of Thought

retaining their life force and vanishing from the face of the earth, embarked on a definitive journey of perception. [400]

- Is this state immortality, don Juan?
- This is in no way immortality. It is merely the entrance into an evolutionary process, using the only medium for evolution that man has at his disposal: awareness. The sorcerers of my lineage were convinced that man could not evolve biologically any further; therefore, they considered man's awareness to be the only medium for evolution. At the moment of dying, sorcerers are not annihilated by death, but are transformed into inorganic beings: beings that have awareness, but not an organism. To be transformed into an inorganic being was evolution for them, and it meant that a new, indescribable type of awareness was lent to them, an awareness that would last for veritably millions of years, but which would also someday have to be returned to the giver: the dark sea of awareness. [401]

Accordingly, new seers are not caught in normal death by this evolutionary process and are transformed into special inorganic beings. Don Juan explains the end of their awareness of these beings as follows:

- My sobriety as a sorcerer tells me that their awareness will terminate, the way inorganic beings' awareness terminates, but I haven't seen this happen. I have no firsthand knowledge of it. The old sorcerers believed that the awareness of this type of inorganic being would last as long as the earth is alive. The earth is their matrix. As long as it prevails, their awareness continues. To me, this is a most reasonable statement. [402]

---

400 CASTANEDA, Magical Passes, HarperCollins Publishers Inc., The Magical Passes For The Center For Decisions

401 CASTANEDA, Magical Passes, HarperCollins Publishers Inc., The Second Group: The Recapitulation

402 CASTANEDA, The Active Side of Infinity, HarperCollins Publishers Inc., Inorganic Awareness

As a result, the seers temporarily cancel the death as we know it, but still do not achieve immortality. Although they maintain their awareness for a very long time, eventually death catches up on them anyway.

Therefore, God Almighty does not give them immortality, but he puts a carrot in front of them and allows them to improve their knowledge. And what they do is again within the limits set by God and by His leave.

112. God says, "How long did you remain on earth in number of years?"
113. They say, "We remained a day or part of a day; ask those who enumerate."
114. He says, "You stayed not but a little – if only you had known.
115. Then did you think that We created you uselessly and that to Us you would not be returned?"
116. So exalted is God, the Sovereign, the Truth; there is no deity except Him, Lord of the Generous Arsh. (Koran/Chapter 23)

Don Juan says the awareness the seers kept was an "awareness that would last for veritably millions of years, but which would also someday have to be returned to the giver: the dark sea of awareness." In other words, even though they live for millions of years, they are returned to God who created the time, and that time given to them eventually ends one day.

What's more, time is relative. As stated in the above verse, people who are satisfied with this temporary life on the Day of Judgment are asked, "How long did you remain on earth?" They reply, "We remained a day or part of a day." Consequently, their whole lives seem like a day to them.

As Einstein showed that time is relative in this universe, don Juan also talks about times that flow at different speeds in different universes. And he says that while some flow much faster than us, others are much slower.

- When warriors talk about time, they are not referring to something which is measured by the movement of a clock. Time is the essence of attention; the Eagle's emanations are made out of time; and properly speaking, when a warrior enters into other aspects of the self, he is becoming acquainted with time.

In addition, a female member of don Juan's party, Florinda says: "The Eagle's emanations are made out of time." So, it means that time is relative because it is at the command of God, and it flows as He wills.

130. "O company of jinn and mankind, did there not come to you messengers from among you, relating to you My verses and warning you of the meeting of this Day of yours?" They said, "We bear witness against ourselves"; and the worldly life had deluded them, and they beared witness against themselves that they were disbelievers. (Koran/Chapter 6)

God Almighty also says that I will bring jinn together on the Day of Resurrection like mankind. So the longevity of the inorganic beings that are the inspiration of the seers does not change anything either. God will certainly hold them to account despite their long lives and will put them together with human beings.

47. Never think that God will fail in His promise to His messengers. Indeed, God is Exalted in Might and Owner of Retribution.
48. On the Day the earth is converted into another earth, and the heavens as well, and wrongdoers come out before God, the One, the Prevailing. (Koran/Chapter 14)

As mentioned above, the old seers say about the awareness that the seers try to keep: "The earth is their matrix. As long as it prevails, their awareness continues". And don Juan interprets it as an awareness that will last for millions of years.

On the other hand, God Almighty informs us that the heavens and the earth will end with the apocalypse, and then the reckoning begins. Therefore, the seers have no chance to run away from the account. Sooner or later, that account will reach them, and it's not as far away as we think it is:

77. To God belongs the unseen of the heavens and the earth. And the command for the Hour is not but as a glance of the eye or

> even nearer. Indeed, God is over all things competent. (Koran/Chapter 16)

So, one day there will be an inevitable end for both heavens and the earth. And even if this time is long for us, it is in the glance of an eye for God Almighty. As all times and places belong to Him, it is impossible to escape from this fact. And to Him we all return:

> 8. Say, "Indeed, the death from which you flee - indeed, it will meet you. Then you will be returned to the Knower of the unseen and the witnessed, and He will inform you about what you used to do. (Koran/Chapter 62)

The seers keep running away from death, and whatever they do is aimed at achieving that goal. However, it will get to them eventually. Even though God has given them an option based on wisdom, it will end one day, and they will be brought up to the Knower of the unseen and the witnessed. Then He will inform them about what they used to do.

IMMORTALITY BY DISOBEYING GOD

Liberation from being a "beser"[403]:

5. They said, "These are legends of the former peoples which he has written down, and they are dictated to him morning and afternoon."
6. Say, "It has been revealed by He who knows the secrets within the heavens and the earth. Indeed, He is ever Forgiving and Merciful."
7. And they said, "What is this messenger that eats food and walks in the markets? Why was there not sent down to him an angel so he would be with him a warner?
8. Or why is not a treasure presented to him, or does he not have a garden from which he eats?" And the wrongdoers also said, "You follow not but a man affected by magic." (Koran/Chapter 25)

"For shamans, the moment in which practitioners are transformed from beings that are socialized to reproduce into beings capable of evolving, is the moment when they become conscious of seeing energy as in flows in the universe,"[404] says don Juan. And what don Juan calls

---

403 As we told in the previous pages, the word "beser" does not have one to one translation in English and it is the name of the body based animal side of human being. So we can call it homo-sapiens.

404 CASTANEDA, Magical Passes, HarperCollins Publishers Inc., The Second Series, The Series for the Womb

"socialized being" is what the Koran calls "beser".

According to this, the Koran uses the "human" word when it is mentioned in the meaning of species, while the "beser" word is used when it is mentioned in the social and animal side of mankind (homo-sapiens). While Man is the opposite twin of Jinn as a species, he is the opposite twin of Angels as a "Beser", and it is used in the Koran in this way all the time.

When the Prophets sent by God have come to their people, the unbelievers expect them to be an "Angelic Messenger". It's strange for them to eat or to have children as a Prophet. They want a superhuman messenger walking around with angels, with a lot of treasure.

Just as the unbelievers find it unnecessary and humiliating to be a "beser" and desire an angelic Messenger, the seers try to find a way out to be free from it. And their whole purpose is to get rid of the bonds of humanity and become immortal beings.

For that, don Juan uses the phrase "freedom from being human".[405] So, just as he once called the universe a description and erased it, now he's ridding himself of being human.

However, God creates people and Prophets as "beser", so the goal is not to break it down. The seers are trying to leave humanity in this life and become "angels". However, God Almighty gives immortality not in this world, but in the hereafter.

Dart past the Eagle:

> I am already given to the power that rules my fate.
>
> And I cling to nothing, so I will have nothing to defend.
>
> I have no thoughts, so I will "see".
>
> I fear nothing, so I will remember myself.
>
> Detached and at ease,

---

405 CASTANEDA, The Art of Dreaming, HarperCollins Publishers Inc., The Fixation of The Assemblage Point

> I will dart past the Eagle to be free. [406]

Silvio Manuel[407] teaches him these strings shortly before their departure from Castaneda and asks him to use them when his task would be greater than his strength.

In these verses, it is clear that the ultimate goal of the seers is to achieve freedom, and the way to do so is to "surpass the Eagle", that is, God Almighty.

- We're warriors, and warriors have only one thing in mind - their freedom. To die and be eaten by the Eagle is no challenge. On the other hand, to sneak around the Eagle and be free is the ultimate audacity. [408]

As you can see, death is the end for them, so all they have in mind is to get rid of the Eagle and get their freedom. And they hope to do this by "sneaking around" God Almighty, whom they call the Eagle. It means that to operate the secret option of death and to keep their awareness for a very long time.

Don Juan explains this by the fact that "the way out of obeying the commands of Eagle is in obeying them". In other words, this is done with the permission of God and His knowledge. But this does not mean that God Almighty approves of their actions. Just as He gives Prophet Adam the right to do wrong, He gives them the right to do so, and they head to a dead end with a desire for eternity.

Not by disobeying God, but by submitting to Him one might be immortal:

115. We had already taken a promise from Adam before, but he forgot; and We found not in him determination.
116. And mention when We said to the angels, "Prostrate to Adam," and they prostrated, except Iblees; he refused.

---

406 CASTANEDA, Eagle's Gift, Washington Square Press, Losing The Human Form

407 A member of don Juan's party

408 CASTANEDA, The Eagle's Gift, Washington Square Press, Florinda

117. So We said, "O Adam, indeed this is an enemy to you and to your wife. Then let him not remove you from Paradise so you would suffer.
118. Indeed, it is for you not to be hungry therein or be unclothed.
119. And indeed, you will not be thirsty therein or be hot from the sun."
120. Then Satan whispered to him; he said, "O Adam, shall I direct you to the tree of eternity and possession that will not deteriorate?"
121. And they ate of it, and their private parts became apparent to them, and they began to fasten over themselves from the leaves of Paradise. And Adam disobeyed his Lord and erred.
122. Then his Lord chose him and turned to him in forgiveness and guided him.
123. God said, "Descend from it - altogether, being enemies to one another. And if there should come to you guidance from Me - then whoever follows My guidance will neither go astray nor suffer." (Koran/Chapter 20)

Don Juan referring to his benefactor says, "He was a modern nagual, involved in the pursuit of freedom". And this quest for freedom is the ultimate goal of all the things that the seers do.

God Almighty composes this desire for eternity into mankind at the very first moment and determines this situation, which the seers think is their own purpose, as the main goal of all humanity. And God Almighty narrates this in the Koran, in the story of Prophet Adam, where the main codes of all human beings are described.

According to this, Satan deceives Prophet Adam and his wife, the prototypes of mankind, over this desire for eternity, and says to them, "Your Lord did not forbid you this tree except that you become angels or become of the immortal."[409]

Prophet Adam and his wife have everything in heaven, but they still eat from that tree, which has been offered to them as a test for their desire for eternity. God Almighty says that you are not yet pure enough to

[409] Koran/Chapter 7, verse 20

stay in paradise and sends them to this world which is a house of purification. Moreover, He implicitly says, "not by defying me, but by following what I say, you can become immortal."

So the seers try to be immortal, just like Prophet Adam, but God Almighty does not give them immortality because they try to achieve it against God. They deny all His revelations and His prophets, but they use the option He has given to them and try to protect their lives.

God Almighty, on the other hand, gives them this carrot to produce the opposite twin of the science of matter. Even though they do not realize it, He uses them as a conduit and makes them a means to show the truth. And He gives eternity to his sincere chosen servants, who do not oppose Him for the sake of eternity.

IMMORTALITY BY ACHIEVEMENT

58. "Then, are we not to die?
59. Except for our first death, and we will not be punished?"
60. Indeed, this is the great triumph.
61. For the like of this let the workers work. (Koran/Chapter 37)

"Warriors aim at succeeding," says Florinda.[410] And it is nothing but trying not to die what she means by this word.

According to the Koran, the greatest achievement is also to achieve immortality. But God Almighty does not attribute this salvation to a mechanical success as the seers think, and says that the main thing is the forgiveness of God:

45. If God were to impose blame on the people for what they have earned, He would not leave upon the earth any creature. But He defers them for a specified term. And when their time comes, then indeed God has ever been, of His servants, Seeing. (Koran/ Chapter 35)

Therefore, no one can enter paradise for what they have done, and only God's forgiveness provides it. And God Almighty alone decides who is more worthy of it.

---

[410] CASTANEDA, The Eagle's Gift, Washington Square Press, Florinda

So there is no validity in the sight of God for what the seers strive for. On the Day of Resurrection, God Almighty will also hold them to account, and the first thing He will look at in this account will be their "intentions."

The need for forgiveness is not success but sincere commitment:

124. Whoever does righteous deeds, whether male or female, while being a believer - those will enter Paradise and will not be wronged, even as much as the speck on a date seed. (Koran/ Chapter 4)

According to the Koran, the first is faith, and the second is doing righteous deeds, which are the means for mankind to gain God's forgiveness and enter paradise. Rather than worshiping a lot or working hard, it is important to do these things in a sincere way.

Therefore, the main thing is not to achieve, but to be on the road. God gives success if He wants it, and He knows best what is good for us. And those who leave sincerity for the sake of success get frustrated.

The equivalent of the concept of sincere commitment in the Koran, is the concept of impeccability for the seers. They are after the impeccability and the success it will bring. However, impeccability is unique only to God Almighty, and it is only Him who gives success. The seers, on the other hand, use this feature for themselves and try to reach immortality with their own success. However, when they fail at the last point, they can't stop falling into despair.

When they fail, they despair:

87. Jacob said, "O my sons, go and find out about Joseph and his brother and despair not of relief from God. Indeed, no one despairs of relief from God except the disbelieving people." (Koran/Chapter 12)

Don Juan says that so far, thousands of seers have managed to maintain their life force. But there are also those who fail, and Castaneda is one of them:

- My life is an endless joy. But at the same time, it is an endless, merciless quest. Infinity will swallow me, and I want to be prepared for it. I don't want infinity to dissolve me into nothing because I hold human desires, warm affection, attachments, no matter how vague. [411]

Castaneda does not want to die. But after his death, God will resurrect him anyway and an eternal life will be his. Yet Castaneda despairs, because he does not believe it.

A similar despair lives on in don Juan's seer group. They search for a nagual disciple for a long time before finding Castaneda but are unable to find him. Then, one day don Juan realizes that he and his group are getting old and there seems to be no hope of ever accomplishing their task. And that is the first time they feel the sting of despair and impotence.

According to Castaneda, the same thing happened to the party of don Juan's benefactor:

- His benefactor explained to don Juan that when he was young and was first introduced to the idea of the rule as the means to freedom, he had been elated, transfixed with joy. Freedom to him was a reality around the corner. When he came to understand the nature of the rule as a map, his hopes and optimism were redoubled. Later on, sobriety took hold of his life; the older he got, the less chance he saw for his success and the success of his party. Finally he became convinced that no matter what they did, the odds were too great against their tenuous human awareness ever flying free. [412]

The response of his benefactor to this sense of failure is cold comfort. He supposedly made peace with himself and his fate, and surrendered to failure. Also, they decided to live their lives with their community impeccably, for no other reason than to be impeccable.

---

[411] CASTANEDA, The Wheel of Time, Washington Square Press, Quotations from the Power of Silence, Commentary

[412] ASTANEDA, Eagle's Gift, Washington Square Press, Nagual Woman

This is how the seers see death as an end, so they are forced to get cold comfort in the face of failure. Failure leads them to despair because they have no hope from God. However, God Almighty says in His Koran, "Do not despair of God's mercy," and He does not close the door to repentance, even for his most sinful servants:

53. Say, "O My servants who have transgressed against themselves, do not despair of the mercy of God. Indeed, God forgives all sins. Indeed, it is He who is the Forgiving, the Merciful. " (Koran/Chapter 39)

Therefore, there is no despair in the sight of God, no end, no extinction. Moreover, the door is always open, as long as mankind brings a heart towards Him that is pure, like in the prayer of Prophet Abraham:

83. "My Lord, grant me authority and join me with the righteous.
84. And grant me a mention of honour among later generations.
85. And place me among the inheritors of the Garden of Pleasure.
86. And forgive my father. Indeed, he has been of those astray.
87. And do not disgrace me on the Day they are all resurrected -
88. The Day when wealth or children do not benefit anyone
89. But only one who comes to God with a pure heart reaches salvation."
90. And Paradise is brought near to the righteous.
91. And Hellfire is brought forth for the deviators. (Koran/Chapter 26)

WORLD AND HEREAFTER

Polar Twins: World and Hereafter:

5. O People, if you should be in doubt about the Resurrection, then consider that indeed, We created you from earth, then from a sperm-drop, then from an attached embryo, and then from a lump of flesh, formed and unformed – that We may inform you. And We settle in the wombs whom We will for a specified term, then We bring you out as a child, and then We develop you that you may reach your time of maturity. And among you is he who is taken in early death, and among you is he who is returned to the most old age so that he knows, after once having knowledge, nothing. And you see the earth barren, but when We send down upon it rain, it quivers and swells and grows something of every beautiful kind.
6. That is because God is the Truth. He gives life to the dead and He is over all things competent.
7. And the Hour will come – no doubt about it – and that God will resurrect those in the graves. (Koran/Chapter 22)

God Almighty created the whole universe from twins that are opposite and complement to each other. And as a reflection of it, created humans and jinns as opposite twins. As we stated before, although the science of seers has discovered this reality, the science of matter which has discovered the polarity in the laws of physics, has failed in that "life is also polar".

As a result of the same principle of polar creation, God Almighty creates the opposite twin of the lives of humans and jinns in this world as the Hereafter. So, He makes the Hereafter the opposite twin of their world life.

And this is where the seers who try to cancel the death are led to failure. They seek immortality in this world, but God Almighty gives immortality not in this world, but in the Hereafter, which He has created as the complementary twin of this life.

The seers discover the jinns, which are the opposite twin of humans in world life, but they do not think that this world life may also have an opposite twin. They are pursuing immortality based on the desire for eternity that God Almighty has put into mankind, but they are looking for it wrongly in this life.

The words "World" and "Hereafter" are used in equal numbers in the Koran:

62. Unquestionably, for the friends of God there will be no fear concerning them, nor will they grieve -
63. Those who believed and stayed away from sins.
64. For them are good tidings in the worldly life and in the Hereafter. No change is there in the words of God. That is what is the great attainment. (Koran/Chapter 10)

God Almighty creates the Hereafter as the opposite and complementary twin of our world life and uses these two words in His Koran in equal numbers. He uses both of them 115 times in order to establish the relationship between the world life and Hereafter.

As we have explained in the previous chapters by giving many similar examples, these are not random uses, but rather seals placed in the Koran by God Almighty, based on the needs of the people of our age who are waiting for objective evidence.

Hence, the Hereafter is a reality and by this mathematical relation, God Almighty shows that this world life and the Hereafter are identical and complementary to each other. In this way, He also protects the Koran against all kinds of falsifications with hundreds of such correlations: because if you change even one word, all equality and order is broken. So, the Koran tells us the truth, and it tells us that the Hereafter is a reality the same as this world life you have.

The real life is the Hereafter:

60. Whatever thing you have been given - it is the enjoyment of worldly life and its adornment. And what is with God is better and more lasting; so will you not use your reason?
61. Then is he whom We have promised a good promise which he meets like he for whom We provided enjoyment of worldly life but then he is, on the Day of Resurrection, among those presented in front of Us? (Koran/Chapter 28)

The meaning of the worldly life, used in the Koran as the counterpart of the Hereafter, is temporary life. In other words, God Almighty shows this life to us as an example, an intro to the Hereafter, which is the main life. And He gives us the real ones of what He shows here as an example, in the Hereafter.

He introduces Himself to those who ask the wisdom of this life with these examples and the revelation He sends. Then He gives them the merits of these blessings at Hereafter.

As for those who do not question the life given to them and find satisfaction with these samples, they, unfortunately, lose the ones they already have. Therefore, the life that is essential for mankind is the life afterlife, and this place is only a little blessing compared to the Hereafter.

The "Hereafter" for the Seers:

77. Does man not consider that We created him from a sperm drop - then he became a clear adversary to Us?

78. While forgetting his own creation, he presented for Us an example and said: "Who will give life to bones while they are disintegrated?"
79. Say, "He will give them life who produced them the first time; and He is, of all creation, Knowing." (Koran/Chapter 36)

Although Castaneda had a religious education when he was young, he was not a religious person. And for the view of the afterlife of the modern world in which he is a member, he uses the definition of "the vague and idealistic state that modern man calls life after death". [413] So, modern man's attitude towards the hereafter is vague, and therefore does not do much to win it over.

The purpose of the seers is to exercise the option they have discovered and try to avoid death. Therefore, the "hereafter" of the seers becomes the "opportunity of freedom" that they chase as its equivalent. And they substitute the real Hereafter with it.

The seers see it as their only goal and stick to it, and they do not care about anything else. For example, during his own apprenticeship, don Juan says that the people in nagual Julian's house were extraordinary. And he attributes this to their pursuit of "freedom" as their abstract purpose.[414]

So, once again, the seers operate the nature created by God on the people. And their focus on their "hereafter" is admirable, even though they cannot hit the bulls-eye.

Modern men, on the other hand, do not have a "hereafter" to focus on themselves and try to take the job in "vague". "For now, I'm living somehow. And when I die, the microorganisms will eat me, and this movie will be over," he states, but that's not how it works. When he does so, he does not have the discipline that is necessary in this world, and he also makes his work in the Hereafter difficult.

---

413 CASTANEDA, The Active Side of Infinity, HarperCollins Publishers Inc., The Active Side of Infinity

414 CASTANEDA, The Power of Silence, Washington Square Press, The Ticket To Impeccability

CARROTS FOR TWO SCIENCES

God Almighty gives an outlet to both Sciences:

Evolution is one of the most important regimes that God Almighty created in this universe. The whole universe works accordingly and every moment everything turns into another thing. As a result of this, these two opposite but at the same time complementary sciences that explore the universe finally find the evolution in their respective fields of interest.

While the seers pursue the "evolution of awareness", the modern science also pursues the "evolution of matter". Essentially, God Almighty gives both sciences as much of an outlet as a pinhole, enabling them to keep their goals alive.

The seers are trying to extend their lives as long as they can. Their aim is to reach something close to immortality, and they chase after this carrot. The science of matter, on the other hand, is trying to uncover the order in which it all began. In other words, scientists are trying to move evolution backwards and reach that first moment, and the seers want to go in the opposite direction and crown the evolution with its final point.

The evolution of both Sciences is nearly impossible, but also a reality; by God's leave and Grace. The seers know that this is the case, and they are aware that every step of their evolution is through the permission and knowledge of God Almighty, whom they call the Eagle.

On the other hand, the Darwinists persistently deny this, as they are not as good as the seers in understanding the universe. They insist that chemical and biological evolution, which is impossible to happen without a guiding mind, happened randomly without this guidance. However, the existence of evolution is something that actually proves the existence of God.

Therefore, there is the evolution of matter, but there is no way this could happen on its own; the camel would have to go through the pinhole. However, God Almighty gives them that carrot and tries them what to do. Darwinists deny both reason and themselves for that carrot. Even though they have built the whole science structure with reason, when they see an exit there, even if that exit requires denial of mind, they do so for the sake of denying God without even blinking their eyes.

> 39. But those who disbelieved - their deeds are like a mirage in a lowland which a thirsty one thinks is water until, when he comes to it, he finds it is nothing but finds God next to him, and He pay him in full his due; and God is swift in account. (Koran/Chapter 24)

God Almighty tries them by giving both Sciences an outlet, but they both think that going through that hole is a real skill and are arrogant towards God. But, when they pass through the hole, the mirage ends, and they find God beside them, and He is swift in account. However, God has promised them all a true eternity, but they trusted themselves and were pleased with a simple copy of it.

<u>The two Sciences ignore each other and God</u>:

Castaneda says, "Evolution, as a theory, has enormous loopholes; it leaves tremendous room for doubt."[415] When he has the alternative of his knowledge, he underestimates it.

---

415 CASTANEDA, Magical Passes, HarperCollins Publishers Inc., The Second Series, The Series for the Womb

For the science of matter, likewise, the teachings of the seers are relative things that cannot be taken seriously. However, it is true what they both discover, but there are no intersections at first, because their methodologies are different. And the only place they meet is to deny God Almighty, who created them.

However, God Almighty does not create these two Sciences for anything other than to introduce Himself to us. He makes them cross-check each other and makes them unite in energy. But they both ignore God Almighty, just as they ignore each other.

They discover the mechanisms created by God and use them for their own benefit. Then they trust themselves and deny God Almighty, the Owner of all these mechanisms. However, what they do is only witness to what exists. And God makes them serve Himself.

Both Sciences declare their own victory:

> 72. God has promised the believing men and believing women gardens beneath which rivers flow, wherein they abide eternally, and pleasant dwellings in gardens of perpetual residence, and an approval from God is greater than all. It is that which is the great attainment. (Koran/Chapter 9)

In many parts of the narratives, don Juan speaks of the tremendous achievements that the seers have achieved over time and the triumphs of discovery they have made. And biology documentaries, accompanied by proud music, tell us about Darwin's great discoveries.

The science of seers says that with the evolution of awareness, mastery in awareness reaches its natural conclusion. The science of matter, on the other hand, claims, "It's all over, we put the last point". Hence, both Sciences have declared their own victories, and all of these victories have been declared against God Almighty.

Scientists say, "We have already explained everything, there is no need for God anymore." The seers know Him clearly, but in the same way, they say, "We have explained everything that can be explained," and look at ways to sneak away from Him.

However, God Almighty creates these two Sciences to cross-check each other and to show the truth. Moreover, while both their claims ignore and deny each other, both Sciences meet in energy as the final point. Although they are diametrically opposed to each other, their final destination is the same as a result of God's unity.

So, these two Sciences are like soul mates with different bodies. And God Almighty, who created them as opposite twins, gives them both a way out and makes them chase after it. They think that it is the true victory, but they have as much victory as He wills and within the limits set by Him.

And in the sight of God Almighty, the Creator of the Heavens and Earth, the main victory is to make good use of this world and earn the Hereafter. And God Almighty gives the Hereafter to His righteous servants who do not declare victory over Him and turn this world life into paradise.

Made in the USA
Middletown, DE
30 June 2021

43419343R00241